READING THE MODERN CHINESE SHORT STORY

Studies on Modern China

UNITED STATES ATTITUDES AND POLICIES TOWARD CHINA
THE IMPACT OF AMERICAN MISSIONARIES
Patricia Neils, editor

READING THE MODERN CHINESE SHORT STORY
Theodore Huters, editor

Studies on Modern China

READING THE MODERN CHINESE SHORT STORY

THEODORE HUTERS
editor

MARSTON ANDERSON
CYRIL BIRCH
YI-TSI MEI FEUERWERKER
ROBERT E. HEGEL
THEODORE HUTERS
LEO OU-FAN LEE

Routledge
Taylor & Francis Group
LONDON AND NEW YORK

An East Gate Book

First published 1990 by M.E. Sharpe.Inc

Published 2016 by Routledge
2 Park Square, Milton Park, Abingdon, Oxon OX14 4RN
52 Vanderbilt Avenue, New York, NY 10017

Routledge is an imprint of the Taylor & Francis Group, an informa business

Library of Congress Cataloging-in-Publication Data

Reading the modern Chinese short story / edited by Theodore Huters.
p. cm.
"An East Gate book."
Includes bibliographical references.
ISBN 0-87332-572-9—ISBN 0-87332-710-1 (pbk.)
1. Short stories, Chinese—History and criticism. 2. Chinese fiction—20th century—History and criticism. I. Huters, Theodore.
PL2443.R43 1990
895.1'30109—dc20 90-8088
CIP

ISBN 13: 978-0-87332-572-1 (hbk)

CONTENTS

Translations

PREFACE

THE PAPERS in this volume are the product of the workshop on critical approaches to modern Chinese short stories, held at the East-West Center of the University of Hawaii in December 1982. The workshop was generously supported by the American Council of Learned Societies, with funds provided by the Andrew W. Mellon Foundation. The guiding idea behind the conference was to apply various theories about narrative developed outside of China to fiction created in China after the May Fourth Movement. At first thought, twentieth-century Chinese literature may seem like sterile ground on which to apply theories about narrative originally developed for writing produced under vastly different assumptions about the role of literature in society and the status of individual creativity. In the event, however, the interaction of narrative theory and the texts we had chosen revealed numerous fruitful approaches to the modern Chinese story that had not been explored previously.

In taking account of something that happened so long ago, there are many people who helped out along the way to whom our gratitude is due. Thanks go first to John Berninghausen, who wrote the proposal that was eventually funded in the form of the workshop. In addition, he did all the organizing work in putting the program together and setting the agenda for our highly successful meetings. He was joined in this important task at a slightly later stage by Sophie Sa, then a staffer for the Social Science Research Council, who did a magical job of handling the logistics and planning that actually got us to Hawaii and keeping track of us after we dispersed.

Thanks also go to those participants whose papers are not, for one reason or another, included in this volume. These include Chang Han-liang, Milena Dolezelova-Velingerova, Michael Egan, Jeannette

Faurot, Wolfgang Kubin, and Donald Rimmington. Those invited to participate without papers included William Tay, Yue Daiyun, Susan Chen, Gilbert Fong, David Palumbo-Liu, and Wang Jing, all of whom added greatly to the quality of the discussion. Zbigniew Slupski was invited and intended to come, but the particular circumstances of Polish politics at the time prevented his departure from Warsaw. Special thanks also to our two "outside experts," Seymour Chatman and Lubomir Dolezel, who added their expertise as literary theorists, thereby contributing significantly to broadening of the intellectual horizon, which participants in the workshop were virtually unanimous in remarking upon.

We are grateful to the publishers of *Chinese Literature* for granting us permission to reprint the story "Black Li and White Li," which originally appeared on pages 87–109 of the collection of Lao She's stories entitled *Crescent Moon and Other Stories*, published by Panda Books in 1985.

Last, but by no means least, my particular thanks to Doug Merwin and the production staff at M. E. Sharpe, who made it possible to publish what the organizers of the workshop had hoped for from the beginning—a series of studies together in the same volume with translations of the stories being discussed. It is our hope that such a format will prove uniquely useful in introducing to a wider audience the still too little known world of modern Chinese literature.

CONTRIBUTORS

Marston Anderson teaches Chinese literature at Yale University. He is the author of *The Limits of Realism: Chinese Fiction in the Revolutionary Period* (1989).

Cyril Birch studied Chinese language and literature at the School of Oriental and African Studies at the University of London, where he taught until 1960. Since then he has taught at the University of California at Berkeley, where he is Agassiz Professor of Oriental Languages. His writings include a two-volume anthology of Chinese literature, several translations, and numerous critical articles on Chinese fiction and drama.

Yi-tsi Mei Feuerwerker (Mei Yici) teaches modern Chinese literature and comparative literature at the University of Michigan. She is the author of *Ding Ling's Fiction: Ideology and Narrative in Modern Chinese Literature* (1982).

Robert E. Hegel teaches Chinese literature at Washington University in St. Louis, where he is chairman of Asian and Near Eastern languages and literatures. He is the author of *The Novel in Seventeenth-Century China* (1981). He is currently working on a history of the Chinese novel.

Theodore Huters teaches in the Department of East Asian Languages and Literatures at the University of California at Irvine. His work focuses on those elements of the Chinese literary tradition that have most critically affected the transformation of that tradition in the twentieth century.

Leo Ou-fan Lee is a professor in the Department of Far Eastern Languages and Civilizations at the University of Chicago. His most recent book is *Voices from the Iron House: A Study of Lu Xun* (1987).

READING THE MODERN CHINESE SHORT STORY

1

INTRODUCTION

Theodore Huters

IT IS no secret that modern Chinese literature has yet to live up to the hopes that readers have held for it in the years since Lu Xun's "Madman's Diary" so auspiciously inaugurated a new literary scene in 1918. Numerous hypotheses—from obsession with China on the part of authors to political repression on the part of governments—have been advanced to explain this disappointment, and most of these hypotheses are at least partially valid. Yet, given the contradictions one runs up against in attempting to assign cause to such a complex phenomenon, most single explanations fail to answer the many vexing questions raised as part of the very process of their being posed. With this in mind, then, perhaps it is best when confronting this issue to settle on an approach in which the numerous contradictions are deliberately set in the foreground—the better to examine them more closely and to allow them to sustain the intractability that gave them their initial force.

Such is the goal of this introduction. In seeking to set the stage for the essays that follow, it was difficult to develop any thesis that could encompass the variety of problems posed by the stories themselves, not to mention the complexities of the discussion each of the contributors offers. It seemed more fruitful simply to set forth a series of observations and speculations on some of the factors that lay behind the difficult passage toward the creation of a modern Chinese literature. But for all the stereotyping of that literature as a flat and didactic creative arena, the one thing that emerged from careful reading of the stories we chose is their great complexity and evident concern with technique. It is true that the stories discussed here were chosen by a committee attempting to find narratives representing the fullest diversity within modern Chinese literature. The extent to which close reading, informed by a concern for methodology, revealed ambiguities and extensive involvement with craft in the works analyzed, however, is still impressive. This is particularly so when one contrasts the richness of the stories with the generally dismal critical environment in which authors had to work. Given the intolerant hectoring that most twentieth-century Chinese critics have used as their normal tone of voice, it is remarkable that anything got written at all.

This contrast between the innovation apparent in the narratives produced and the rigidity of critical comment about them suggests one of the most obvious impediments to the creation of a multifaceted new literature. This critical narrow-mindedness raises difficult questions about why contemporary reviewers went about their business as they did. The problem is significantly complicated by the realization of the overlap between those who created literature and those who evaluated it in modern China.

Before getting too far into this question, it is perhaps worth comparing the Chinese situation with the atmosphere for literary analysis in the West during the same period. In modern Western narrative theory, the distinction between story and discourse, in which the former is the basic stuff to be conveyed and the latter is the means by which it is conveyed, is a basic one on which most other avenues of critical inquiry have been built. The inclination to separate out formal elements of a literary text from the content that they present can be traced as far back as Aristotle.[1] But the real impetus for the advancement of this idea in twentieth-century literary criticism came from a series of developments in literary practice that coalesced in the modernist movement. The modernist impulse to engage in a highly self-conscious critique of traditional notions of writing fostered an atmosphere in which literature turned in on itself and in many ways became the principal object of its own inquiry.

The tendency of language and literature to engage in formal self-analysis was given particularly acute definition in the first decade of this century. The linguist Ferdinand de Saussure originated the concept that language can be divided into two elements: the signified, or the basic idea to be communicated, and the signifier, the form by which that idea is communicated. Perhaps his most important insight within this scheme is that the link between the two aspects of language is entirely arbitrary and conventional. Saussure's ideas constituted the analytical basis for the slightly later theory of story and discourse, or *fabula* (fable) and *sjuzet* (plot), as the Russian formalist critics who developed the distinction in the 1910s called the categories.

The notion of the separability of form and content that the Russian critics borrowed from Saussure represented a culmination of trends in literary criticism dating from Flaubert and Henry James in which the analysis of literary form became a study in its own right, often even eclipsing the study of surface meanings and their moral overtones, which had been the traditional focus of literary thought. The undeniable power of this new set of analytical tools gave rise to unprecedented capacity to uncover structural patterns in narrative and just as surely contributed to the atmosphere of literary modernism in which equally unprecedented experiments were being made by authors of literary texts. Over the past twenty years, poststructuralist critics have been at considerable pains to dismantle the force of the notion of binary opposition that lies behind the division of content and form. The immense effort that this project has involved, however, is perhaps the most telling indication of the enduring power of the distinction.

In looking at modern Chinese literary criticism of the period after the sweeping literary reform that began about 1917, by contrast, the almost complete absence of analysis based on these principles is striking. This is not to imply that Chinese critics were under any obligation to borrow Western ideas about literature. In a period, however, in which there was large-scale importation of Western theories—particularly ideas that had an iconoclastic thrust to them—the formalist view is noteworthy by its conspicuous absence. This is in spite of a rhetorical tradition in China within which there was considerable attention to structural analysis of textual patterns.[2] The key to this enduring determination not to separate content and form, even provisionally, lay in the attitude modern Chinese literary reformers held toward traditional literature. More than anything else, the premodern genres of writing were seen as having been composed of nothing but empty and impersonal forms that had been paralyzed as useful avenues of expression by their own punctiliousness about observing older structural models. If the best literary minds of the twentieth century were firmly of the opinion that the evil in premodern literature lay in its thrall to dead forms long severed from substance, it is understandable that disinterested argument over form had a difficult time making the critical agenda any time after 1920. The aversion either to build upon an indigenous tradition or to show any trace of what eventually became the dominant critical tendency in the West makes sense only when seen in this context.

There was, however, a serious tension beneath this disinclination to discuss questions of formal structure: The general critical insensitivity to matters of form ran completely counter to the actual practice of developing a new literature. As Bonnie McDougall has pointed out, "modern Chinese writers were *all* formal experimentalists, for undoubtedly the major concern of the Literary Revolution was after all the abolition of old literary forms and the substitution of new forms."[3] Linguistic exploration was, by virtue of the May Fourth Movement's openly espoused iconoclasm, implicit in virtually every sentence of post-1917 vernacular prose. Since the initial focus of that iconoclasm was on the nature of literary language and the transformation of traditional notions of genre, the first moves toward reform were of necessity in the realm of the mode of representation rather than on the object of representation. In other words, at its founding moment, modern Chinese literature was, despite later protestations to the contrary, more concerned with form than content, with discourse than story.

Yet later critical glosses on these efforts were overwhelmingly on the semantic value of what was represented, willfully ignoring the enormous complexity of all the attempts to develop new forms. To the extent that writers and critics regarded themselves as a single cohesive unit and that critics were most often also engaged in creative writing, the failure to devote substantial attention to matters of literary structure represents a real failure of self-awareness. This unwillingness or incapacity on the part of both writers and critics to recognize the actual course of literature's own development doomed writing to a status that was dependent on more powerful discursive formations within society. It was thereby put in a position of constantly having to react to overt ideological pressures rather than having the leeway to formulate its own creative agenda. Notwithstanding these pressures not to examine itself too closely, the demands on literature for new formal innovation remained constant (if spurred on only by the prodigious demand that semantic content find a more perfect vehicle). But each innovation was forced to present itself primarily in terms of its object of representation rather than the means of representation itself. The mentality of the age, in other words, demanded that form masquerade as content.

Much of this circumspection with regard to speculation about form resulted directly from the idea that even the traditional literary language itself (*wenyan*) had been throttled to death by its fidelity to rigid formal norms. As a consequence, faith was placed in the written vernacular language (*baihua*) that it serve as the antidote to this stifled means of expression. It was to be an avenue of direct communication. The dominant opinion among those advocating the adoption of baihua saw it as something that had to be newly fabricated out of a number of different elements. This prevailing view lent force to the utopian idea that this new language would provide the unmediated voice that an iconoclastic generation was so in need of. Baihua was therefore valued precisely to the extent that it was regarded as infinitely manipulable and not subject to formal restraint.

For all that baihua was thought of as a clear channel of expression, however, there was little consideration given to the contradictory aspects of the various purposes ascribed to this new literary voice. Most agreed that a primary function was to be the expression of a newly freed personal voice of the individual creative author. But at the same time the vernacular was also celebrated as the only way to communicate with the theretofore silent and illiterate masses. Baihua was thereby simultaneously freighted with enormous social responsibility. These two ideas—one, that literature serve as the unmediated voice of individual expression, and two, that writing serve a fairly strict definition of social utility—crop up over and over again in looking at modern Chinese criticism. At first glance the ideas are so contradictory that it is difficult to imagine how any sort of satisfactory literary environment could possibly spring up between these two apparently mutually exclusive poles.

If one assumes, however, that what the individual wishes to assert is but the expression of values that most of society holds in common, the contradiction suddenly disappears. Such were, in fact, the two poles of the Neo-Confucian theory of self-cultivation that had such an influence on traditional theories of literature.[4] That personal expression and social utility could coexist, then, is but one indication of the unconscious debt modern literary theory owed to traditional ideas of writing, for all the conscious iconoclasm of post–May Fourth writers and critics. But by the 1920s, both the institutions of the empire and the values associated with them had been thoroughly discredited, at least in the realm of the new literature. The ability to hold notions of personal expression and social utility on the same mental horizon, therefore, became intensely problematic, even if both ideas remained as core assumptions on the literary agenda. The transformed context is the crux here. If both ideas were profoundly embedded at an almost preconscious intellectual level, new definitions of the natures of both the individual writer and social utility rendered previous assumptions regarding their congruence notably unstable.

The high social and intellectual status of newly imported Western ideas contributed mightily to this instability. That some of these borrowed ideas superficially resembled certain crucial traditional Chinese concepts often made the prospect of successfully melding Western ideas into Chinese intellectual life more promising than it turned out to be in practice. The key idea of personal expression, for instance, took on a new coloration after 1918, one that stressed a romantic notion of the inevitable conflict between self and society, something quite at odds with the old idea of self-cultivation, no matter how many surface characteristics they seemed to share.

The upshot of this mixing of ideas new and old was an enormous responsibility placed upon the person of the author. For if literature viewed as social instrument and as avenue of free expression have anything in common, it is the precept both ideas share that the writer has to take personal responsibility for what he or she has written. In fact, from this perspective, the two views of literature actually complement one another. The notion of writing as personal expression validates the assumption that the author is constantly embodying his or her most closely held views. And when this assumption is projected onto the public arena, it becomes almost a matter of course to assign personal accountability for political or social opinions at odds with whatever authority has set itself up to sit in judgment. Given the fragmented nature of the relationship between new and old ideas on the Chinese literary arena in the years after 1920, then, the particular emphasis within contemporary literary criticism on authorial voluntarism, or the ability of writers to have complete command over the intellectual consequences of their creative work, becomes easier to understand.[5] Convergence between the political and personal had been long established in the tradition. The way was thus set for critical opinion to establish responsibility for gaining control over an amorphous cultural situation in the person of the author.

The tensions just described constitute a body of the most immediate problems confronting modern Chinese writers and critics as they strove to reconstruct a new environment for literature during and after the May Fourth Movement. These problems, however, are but the symptoms of a more global crisis in which a particular system of ideas about writing and literature was disordered by an elaborate combination of accumulated internal contradictions, deliberate rejection, and collision with an alien system. This, in turn, was part of the larger structure of cultural signification that was itself absorbed in precisely the same sort of all-encompassing crisis. To understand fully the magnitude of the resulting predicament, it is first necessary to look into a few general critical motifs where Chinese notions of writing intersected with broader cultural issues. And to ground these general ideas in the actualities of historical transformation, it will also be necessary to look into certain specific features of the Chinese literary history of the past 150 years. It is to be hoped that amplification of these points will make the paths of transition that modern literature eventually took more comprehensible.

In a sense, the overt political strictures imposed by various authoritarian governments are the easiest thing to understand. As recent events have only too painfully reminded us, pure political repression has been a constant feature of Chinese literary life through much of the twentieth century, reaching a maximum in the various intense campaigns of the Communist period. It needs to recognized, however, that many of the pressures that became overt with Communist literary policy have features in common with the creative and critical practice of periods even when political interference is relaxed. One need only consider remarks the dissident writer Liu Binyan made in November 1986 to realize how persistent this complex of political and moral themes has been from all sides of the ideological spectrum:

> Since 1982 I have noticed that there is a force at work which aims to transform literature into something like music or painting. Works lacking in social concern, intellectual content, and rationality are not only appearing in increasing numbers, but occupy the center pages of many periodicals and have garnered bandwagon applause from critics. . . .
>
> Moreover, there is a widespread bias that contributes [to this tendency], in which writing about social and political subject matter is regarded as less conducive to the production of works of artistic merit. This is not entirely unreasonable. Life and death, love and hate—these kinds of perennial subject matter may indeed reveal human nature more directly. But we must go deeper to excavate social and political contradictions.[6]

While it is impossible to question Liu's personal courage or commitment to questioning all sorts of repression, it would seem equally impossible to ignore the filiation between his views on the ultimate function of literature and those of the didactic majority of both party and nonparty intellectuals in modern China.

In exploring the circumstances within which modern Chinese literature has had to develop, it therefore becomes necessary to look beyond politics for factors that ultimately lead to the political pressures themselves. As I outlined above (and as Liu Binyan gives strikingly direct testimony to), perhaps the most powerful common denominator of the constraints upon literature is the disinclination to turn literature loose from a focus upon the social bases of human problems. In pursuing this issue, one comes upon a series of firm expectations and habits surrounding the practice of literature. The sum of these expectations resulted in predetermining many of the options modern Chinese literature was able to take even before the undertaking had begun. These boundaries, many and complicated as they may have been, can be broken down into two main categories—those conditioned by longstanding cultural patterns, and those conditioned by historical contingency, in particular by the post-1895 challenge the encroaching West presented to the images that traditional China had of itself.

In the realm of long-term cultural patterns, the traditional Chinese sense that writing was absolutely central to cultural continuity must be given substantial weight in considering the possibilities for literature in that country. For its part, the view of the centrality of writing was concomitant to a notion even more fundamental to the traditional Chinese world view. To simplify a still controversial idea that by its very difference will perhaps always resist conclusive formulation, the Chinese viewed the world as monistic and regarded all phenomena within it as being immanent to it. Pauline Yu has described this:

> The cosmic principle or Tao may transcend any individual phenomenon, but it is totally immanent in this world, and there is no suprasensory realm that lies beyond, is superior to, or is different in kind from the level of physical beings. True reality is not supernal but in the here and now, and this is a world, furthermore, in which fundamental correspondences exist between and among cosmic patterns (*wen*) and operations and those of human culture.[7]

It should come as no surprise that writing, which shared the same signifier (*wen*) as cosmic pattern, came to be seen as the natural expression of things and events within this world. If all human communities share an urgent need to confer meaning upon their affairs, this predilection must be particularly acute in those communities that assign relatively little emphasis to supernatural intervention in those affairs. It is perhaps inevitable that *wen* came to be vested with the immense authority due that which provided ultimate definition. At the same time, however, it was subject to strict control precisely because of this immense explanatory authority. Given such a view of the function of writing, the idea of separating it from its social responsibilities at any level becomes, to say the least, highly problematic. But the notion of social responsibility does not fully explain the complexities of the Chinese case. After all, highly didactic notions of writing are not unknown at various junctures in Western history, even if they have generally failed to dominate for any great length of time.

The historical contingencies of the past hundred years, however, dramatically altered the concern with cultural continuity that had always been part of Chinese literary thought. The coming of the West transformed perception of the issue of continuity from one of cultural constancy to one of national survival. One could argue that it was the very abruptness of the literary revolution's move to the vernacular that brought about this sense of cultural crisis. The traditional literary language, however dry and restrictive it may have been regarded as being, was the last and arguably most deeply felt of China's links to the traditional system of meaning. The move in the late 1910s to toss away this language thus rendered the whole enterprise of cultural signification problematic in an unprecedented way. Given the authority invested in the traditional system of writing, experiment with new cultural forms ran a continual risk of rapid drop-off into utter intransitivity and meaninglessness.

The drastic otherness that the new system of vernacular writing represented to Chinese intellectuals did not allow them any real confidence that the newly formulated ideas of the May Fourth period could be manipulated successfully in a way that did not threaten their sense of cultural significance or national identity. With all authority thus undercut, the only recourse was perhaps to agree that the risk of communicative breakdown that ensued could be minimized only by general agreement on a theory of writing that included as its central tenet the idea that there were no theoretical impediments to the expression and reception of clear and simple messages. If, in other words, all cultural forms had been reduced to a highly contingent status, the risk of meaninglessness that followed could be minimized by general agreement on the possibility (or perhaps it would be better to say the devoutly wished for inevitability) that every utterance could be made completely transparent. With all recourse to the past denied and the West threatening the imminent demise of the viability of the whole concept of a national culture, the only resort was tenacious faith in the possibility that all writing could be made completely clear and rational. Any ideas that language by its very nature had textures that brought on ambiguity or that the legacy of the past was inescapable in certain crucial ways simply posed too great a threat to be entertained.

But even with this theoretical agreement on the essential communicative competence of baihua, departure from the traditional aesthetic canon and the loss of the old aesthetic hierarchy created a terrible contingency in letters. What with social and political demands having always been prominent in Chinese literary thought, these emerged with renewed and overwhelming force. Pressure from the dominant aesthetic canon of the powerful West—with its stress on the autonomy of art—presented an ineluctable challenge as well. How was the Chinese literary world to deal with the claims to universality so firmly embedded in the Western aesthetic code? By simply asserting over and over again one's claims to exist as a separate entity (as Frederic Jameson would have it).[8] Or by joining in the West's dominating discourse? Or by seeking some other ground or other faction within it? None of the alternatives presented the sort of secure answer that Chinese writers needed in the face of the complete rejection of their own aesthetic tradition that was the keystone of the May Fourth movement. The general rush to didactic and highly prescriptive notions of literature's role reflected the need for some firm base on which to stand.

Add to these general theoretical issues a series of specific events within the course of modern literary history and the difficulties facing Chinese writers become even clearer. It is generally accurate to say that in the twentieth century, particularly after 1918, increasing prestige devolved upon prose fiction written in the vernacular language at the same time that the idea of a new and autonomous realm for literature came into existence. While in a sense these two developments were able to parallel each other in the West, there are certain specific features of Chinese literary history that put them at odds with one another.

While China had a long and sophisticated tradition of vernacular writing, as well as a long tradition of dialogue represented by the open-ended colloquies of the Neo-Confucian thinkers, the principal movements in late Qing dynasty literary thought opposed both of these tendencies. One only need contrast the prose purification movements represented by the Tongcheng and Wenxuan movements that came to dominate scholarly discourse by the nineteenth century with the freer attitude toward language manifest in the sixteenth and seventeenth centuries to realize that the intellectual atmosphere was becoming increasingly hostile toward linguistic openness. The school of Han learning that so dominated Chinese discourse in the century after 1750 also poured scorn upon what they regarded as the linguistic laxity of not only prose narratives, but also the vernacular tradition of Neo-Confucian colloquies. There can be little doubt that the atmosphere of political crisis that became ever more pressing in Chinese intellectual life after c. 1800 at the very least significantly contributed to the various movements for literary rectification that had the refinement of prose style as their point in common.[9]

Explosive urban growth, however, ran parallel to these nineteenth-century calls for a purified uniformity in prose. Scholars were not long to realize that some sort of cultural accommodation would have to be made with the ever-growing group of people within the cities who were, at least from the traditional academic perspective, "semi-educated." In the period after 1895, this trend was given a push by the introduction of Western literary ideas that had for some time been relatively more aware of the need to account for a larger audience than that represented by the highly educated elite.[10] At first thought, one might speculate that the elaborate scholarly focus on traditional genres that accompanied the prosodic revival in nineteenth-century China, combined with the acknowledgment that new groups would have to be made part of the literary community, would prepare the ground for the sort of literary pluralism that had been such a conspicuous feature of seventeenth-century intellectual life. And even if the new pressures toward orthodoxy occasioned by the threat to cultural continuity that the looming presence of the West represented would have made accommodation with the fact of pluralism difficult for many in the scholarly community, one would expect at least that the tension between the strong prescriptivism of late Qing theories of prose and the recognition of the need to integrate the vernacular would somehow force its acceptance.

Some of the developments in late Qing fiction in fact would seem to have been leading in this direction: satire and mockery of official voices, for instance, seem an important part of at least some of the novels produced between 1900 and 1910. In the end, however, any such potential openings were complicated by other factors. On the one hand, the threat to national autonomy represented by the West augmented in some quarters the pre-existing efforts to purify prose. Such new efforts at the renewal of old forms were undertaken with the new spirit of nationalism and thus given the new label of efforts to preserve the "national essence."[11] This entailed a need to segregate strictly any new vernacular style from older and more "pure" forms. On the other hand, a movement also developed to create a new vernacular novel that would serve as conduit of the official ideology to the masses. So instead of new literary pluralism, the last years of the Qing witnessed a new literary stratification.[12]

The lingering effects of the sort of thinking embodied by the national essence movement understandably made literary experimentation even more difficult than it otherwise would have been. In the last years of the 1910s, however, young literary radicals headed by Hu Shi and Chen Duxiu led a successful movement that called for the ostensibly complete repudiation of any notion of using old literary forms as well as a sudden turn both to Western models and to unrestricted use of the vernacular. On its face this seemed to represent the genuine potential of an opening for complete linguistic and literary freedom. The literary revolution of the period seemed to call, at least initially, for its critique of tradition to be embodied in the encouragement of the free exchange of linguistic and literary norms. While the new writers that emerged in this period certainly were intent upon social critique, however, with the notable exception of Lu Xun—and a few who closely emulated him—there is very little evidence of the use of a self-consciously radical play of discourse as a means of undermining prior literary and ideological forms. Instead, as I explained above, there was a pervasive fear that anything but the most carefully constructed and limited narrative forms would allow for the subconscious reversion to the tradition.[13] Since culture was seen as immanent in traditional literary form, a negative attitude toward that culture required the same sedulity in avoiding old literary forms as had earlier attempts to preserve them.

This situation created its own paradoxes. If the May Fourth turn to the vernacular was marked by a continuous linguistic experimentation with a new medium, it was also characterized by an equally marked unwillingness to experiment with indigenous literary forms and languages. This in turn combined with the ingrained habit of reverence toward the function of literature to create a new vernacular that was a sterile and largely foreign-oriented business. When questions arose, however, as to the appropriateness of such a limited and stilted medium to the new social situation, the dominant voices in dissent from the new baihua sought, perhaps characteristically, to limit the linguistic scope of the new language rather than to broaden it. In short, it should not confound expectation that the most powerful and enduring challenge to baihua, that issued by Qu Qiubai, should still be seeking a pure language, although it was now called the language of the proletariat rather than of an authentic "national essence." For all his protestations to revolutionary activism, Qu's assumptions about linguistic purity shared with an earlier generation a fear of foreign pollution of Chinese, as well as a disinclination to mix elements of classical, the old vernacular, and the new literary language.[14] One may even say that Qu shared with Zhang Binglin, a national-essence advocate of the prior generation, the faith that there was a pure language of the folk that formed the essential basis for Chinese culture.[15]

These factors combined to create a series of demands on literature so intense that there was almost no way to satisfy them. On the one hand, the influence of nineteenth-century initiatives to purify writing and the related notion of national essence combined with visionary aspirations sparked by May Fourth iconoclasm to create a fervently utopian concept of the new literature. On the other hand, the influence of traditional ideas about the social responsibility of writing combined with a radically broadened sense of what the potential audience for literature had become and should be in the future to impart a grindingly strict notion of the utilitarian function of letters. This juxtaposition of utopianism and utility—which has remained the dominant motif for modern Chinese literature virtually to this day—has, rather than expand literature's potential, left it open to demands from each side of this polarity that cannot possibly be reconciled with one another. The stories we have collected here all bear the marks of having been caught between conflicting pressures to attain to the loftiest of aspirations (both cognitive and aesthetic) even as they served the most mundane of political roles.

This contentious critical environment posed difficulties for our own attempts to analyze the stories we chose. While it was a relatively simple matter to forswear the didactic values that have so dominated modern Chinese criticism, it was more difficult to find the proper critical voice to replace them. In searching for this voice, however, we found it particularly important to reject an alternative approach that had considerable initial appeal. This was the inclination often so characteristic of work done in the West to impose upon Chinese literature a canon of evaluation built on "universals" that upon close examination reveal themselves to be criteria based directly on Western aesthetic practice. The insistence upon passing judgment based on these criteria has often sprung from the laudable conviction of the need to present a counter-aesthetic strong enough to oppose the explicitly political standards that have been the norm within China.

But in the rush to present a less politically fixed view of the possibilities for literature, there has been an almost equally tenacious imperative to apply an aesthetic that also has as its heart a powerful moral essence constructed on such Western ideas as individualism, tragedy, or the notion that great literature must reveal human frailty. In this sense, critics of Chinese literature in the West have often applied a literary standard that ends up being in its own way almost as didactic as the Chinese. If this does not initially seem to be the case, it is probably because critics in the West have built upon ideas familiar to our experience that are thus more able to be passed off as simple common sense. The profoundly didactic atmosphere surrounding modern Chinese literature has thus permeated even Western discussion of the field, providing a kind of mirror-image of Chinese critical practice.

Seeking to free literary analysis from a priori judgments and the application of alien standards is not, however, either to urge a reductionist relativism or to suggest that ideas about literature developed in the West have nothing to say about Chinese writing. In the first place, it is to argue instead for the idea that one should defer ultimate judgments about the moral nature of literary work until one has made an exhaustive effort either to understand the full context of the work or, even more to the point, to explore a full variety of perspectives on how the various elements in any individual piece of literature might be working with one another. In the second place, all the essays in this collection begin with the assumption that particular notions developed in Western literary theory have something in them that can at least be of some use in looking at Chinese literature. This should make it clear that no one is arguing for the idea that Chinese literature occupies a realm beyond the capacity for discussion as one facet of a general category. What makes these essays unique, however, is the effort common to each of them to keep the notion of the difference between Chinese and Western literatures as a central analytical concept.

The first essay in this collection, Leo Lee's discussion of Lao She's "Black Li and White Li," directly confronts the issue of the contrast between authorial morality and political utility. To do this, however, Lee had first to frame an analysis recognizing that certain features of the story that initially seem to be pure failures of craft in fact grow out of the complex pressures of the historical moment in which Lao She found himself. Lee in the end does not shrink from passing judgment on what he perceives to be the inadequacies of the story. But his treatment of Lao She's text gains its real force from his determination not to stop at merely pointing out the peculiar imbalance in narrative texture in the depiction of the narrator and the two Li brothers, but to show how it came into being. By dealing directly with the way in which the tale's complicated theme actually seems to force this imbalance into existence, Lee is able to bring some of the tensions affecting modern Chinese literature into particularly sharp focus.

The next three essays, Marston Anderson's discussion of Xiao Jun's "Goats," Yi-tsi Mei Feuerwerker's analysis of Mao Dun's "Algae," and my own of Shi Tuo's "A Kiss," all set the question of how to use Western critical categories in high relief. The concepts of realism, of hermeneutical code, and of dialogism, all profoundly embedded in current Western critical practice, could be made to fit Chinese stories only imperfectly. The complications raised in the three essays will provide no comfort to those who may still hope that such standards of evaluation can provide an infallible basis for interpretation. But in the course of manipulating these specific critical concepts, a more general issue constantly surfaces, and with every story in the collection: Much of the reason that Western ideas never quite fit was that the stories themselves were pulled by motives so conflicting that it was impossible finally to declare one interpretive strategy competent to encompass the full variety of any one of them.

But in coming to this conclusion, we see again the profound difference between Western and modern Chinese critical practice. Most contemporary Western theories, if used with any sensitivity, have a built-in tolerance for textual indeterminacy, even to allowing the text to be so open-ended as to throw some doubt on the capacity of the theory to explain very much about what it has under its immediate scrutiny. Good critical models should simply have no vested interest in forcing their interpretations upon the text. The comments Chinese critics have to make about Mao Dun and Shi Tuo, however, clearly demonstrate the tendency of Chinese interpreters to seek a determinate meaning to the texts they analyze. The contrast between the inability of the literary texts to square the many demands on them and come to closure and the hidebound injunctions from critics that stories present a firm ideological message can only be brought to full light by the application of a critical structure that is not caught up in this web of contradiction. It is ultimately only in this sense that Western criticism has an essential task in the analysis of modern Chinese literature. But it is important to realize that this essential task really consists of little more than breathing room and thus requires as part of its charge a light and even tentative touch.

Robert Hegel's explication of Ru Zhijuan's "Lilies" brings up the question so central to modern Chinese literature of individual isolation from society. It is striking how constant this theme, given such brilliant initial expression in Lu Xun's "Madman's Diary"—the story that can be said to have inaugurated modern Chinese literature in 1918—has been throughout the years since. From our perspective, such alienation is virtually inseparable from the concept of modernity itself. Hegel, however, elegantly demonstrates through his analysis of "Lilies" how much pressure there was on literary texts to close this gap between the individual and society. One persuasive reading of Mao's aggressively influential "Talks at the Yan'an Forum on Literature and Art," the words that delimited the literary world in Communist China for the generation after their promulgation in 1942, would be to see it as essentially an effort to banish the self-society split from the contemporary literary arena.[16] It goes without saying that an issue as highly ramified as this will only fester if repressed in this way. Hegel's comments on the continuing inability of the figure of the intellectual narrator in the story to participate fully in the events represented in "Lilies" fully captures both the sincerity of the desire to join and the anxiety involved in the awareness of the compulsion to do so.

But the particular form of the alienation of the intellectual cannot be laid exclusively at Mao's door. As Anderson makes clear, the inability of the narrator in "Goats" to make any meaningful contact with the society around him is a manifestation of the same problem. In spite of the lack of overt political control over literature when the story was written, "Goats" is similarly incapable of setting the problem of the intellectual vis-à-vis society in a fundamentally more satisfactory way than Ru Zhijuan was to do in "Lilies." If anything, the definition of the gap between the two is much less clear in "Goats" than in "Lilies." The same issue comes through in Feuerwerker's reading of "Algae" as well. Even though Mao Dun does not dramatize his narrator, the incapacity of the urban intellectual voice that is so clearly telling the story to resolve even the status of the issues he has brought up in the course of his telling represents yet another case of the paralysis sensed by the intellectuals in their twentieth-century separation from the course of ordinary life.

In his observation that "Daybreak," Zhu Xining's 1963 story from Taiwan, functions as a kind of discourse on the traditional story "Fifteen Strings of Cash," Cyril Birch illuminates the crucial difference between Zhu's story and most of the others in the collection. In his willingness to abstract himself from the moral strictures that served as guideposts for all the traditional renditions of the same material, Zhu has quite deliberately taken a decisive step away from the didactic pressures surrounding modern Chinese literature. (Not surprisingly, he has in the process horrified Hou Jian, the translator and most careful early commentator on the text.) In the process of doing this, he takes advantage of the wholesale iconoclasm toward the past so characteristic of post-1917 literature by creating a picture of a life in which the moral choices available to anyone are all unacceptable. He also uses first-person narration to introduce the main character initially as a helpless victim, but then he goes on to hint at the prospect that he will become part of the system he at first found so shockingly inhuman. With this, Zhu at once recalls Lu Xun's most powerful stories and allows his readers the freedom to decide for themselves what their reactions will be to the events represented so dispassionately in the story.

Notes

1. Seymour Chatman, *Story and Discourse: Narrative Structure in Fiction and Film* (Ithaca: Cornell University Press, 1978), pp. 19–20.

2. While it would be misleading to argue that Chinese literary thought ever

advocated separating form and content, various developments in the practical criticism of the latter half of the Qing dynasty manifest considerable sophistication in the realm of formal rhetorical analysis. Much of this developed under the influence of the late eighteenth- and nineteenth-century movement to revive archaic prose (*guwen*), which came to be known as the Tongcheng school (*pai*). The most notable exemplar of this in the formal analysis of verse is the *Zhaomei zhanyan* of Fang Dongshu (1772–1851). Structural analysis of narrative work is also notable in those critics inspired by Jin Shengtan's (d. 1661) comments on the *Shuihu zhuan.*

3. Bonnie S. McDougall, *The Introduction of Western Literary Theories into Modern China* (Tokyo: The Centre for East Asian Cultural Studies, 1971), p. 213.

4. The major statement of this is in the important Neo-Confucian text, "The Great Learning," with its clear sequences of cause and effect: "The ancients who wished to illustrate virtue throughout the kingdom, first ordered well their own States. Wishing to order well their States, they first regulated their families. Wishing to regulate their families, they first cultivated their persons. Wishing to cultivate their persons, they first rectified their hearts." Translation from James Legge, *The Chinese Classics* (reprint, Taibei: Wenxing, 1966), 1:357.

5. Paul Pickowicz's *Marxist Literary Thought in China: The Influence of Ch'ü Ch'iu-pai* (Berkeley: University of California Press, 1981) contains the most extensive discussion of the issue of authorial voluntarism.

6. Quoted in Yu-shih Chen, "Efforts and Achievements: A Profile of the 1986 Jinshan Conference on Contemporary Chinese Literature," *Modern Chinese Literature* 2.2 (Fall 1986): 238.

7. Pauline Yu, *The Reading of Imagery in the Chinese Poetic Tradition* (Princeton: Princeton University Press, 1987), p. 33.

8. In his article "Third-World Literature in the Era of Multinational Capitalism," Frederic Jameson describes the difficulties facing national survival in third-world countries. He finds that as a response to this, "third-world literature" has become dominated by a form that he calls "national allegory." See *Social Text* 15 (Fall 1986): 65–88. In his "Jameson's Rhetoric of Otherness and the National Allegory," Aijaz Ahmad vigorously protests the boundaries to literary creativity he perceives in Jameson's formulation. See *Social Text* 17 (Fall 1987): 3–25.

9. For details on these nineteenth-century literary movements, see my article, "From Writing to Literature: The Development of Late Qing Theories of Prose," *Harvard Journal of Asiatic Studies* 47.1 (June 1987): 51–96.

10. On the status of vernacular literature, see Milena Dolezelova-Velingerova, "The Origins of Modern Chinese Literature," in *Modern Chinese Literature in the May Fourth Era*, ed. Merle Goldman (Cambridge: Harvard University Press, 1977), pp. 17–35. See also Perry Link, *Mandarin Ducks and Butterflies: Popular Fiction in Early Twentieth-Century Chinese Cities* (Berkeley: University of California Press, 1981), esp. pp. 1–15.

11. The definitive essay on the "national essence" movement remains Laurence Schneider, "National Essence and the New Intelligentsia," in *The Limits of Change: Essays on Conservative Alternatives in Republican China*, ed. Charlotte Furth (Cambridge: Harvard University Press, 1976), esp. pp. 57–72.

12. For a brief overview of the literary trends in these years, see my "A New Way of Writing: The Possibilities for Literature in Late Qing China, 1895–1908," *Modern China* 14.3 (October 1988): 243–76.

13. For an excellent analysis of the strictures that literary realism was forced to work under in modern China, see Marston Anderson's *The Limits of Realism: Chinese Fiction in the Revolutionary Period* (Berkeley: University of California Press, 1990).

14. On Qu Qiubai, see Pickowicz's *Marxist Literary Thought in China.* For further discussion of some of the linguistic issues involved, see my "A Difficult Guest: May Fourth Revisits," *Chinese Literature: Essays, Articles and Reviews* 6 (1984): 135–49.

15. Wu Wenqi, *Jin bai nianlaide Zhongguo wenyi sichao* (Chinese literary currents over the past one hundred years) (Hong Kong: Longmen, 1969), pp. 58–59.

16. The complete translation with a valuable introduction is contained in Bonnie S. McDougall, *Mao Zedong's "Talks at the Yan'an Conference on Literature and Art": A Translation of the 1943 Text with Commentary* (Ann Arbor: University of Michigan Center for Chinese Studies, 1980).

2

LAO SHE'S "BLACK LI AND WHITE LI"
A Reading in Psychological Structure

Leo Ou-fan Lee

PSYCHOLOGY may not be the center of Lao She's story, "Hei-Bai Li" (Black Li and White Li), but it serves as a convenient point of departure for an attempt at uncovering its structural design and its meaning. It may also have a bearing on Lao She's intention when writing this story.[1]

On the superficial level, this is a story of two brothers, nicknamed Black Li and White Li, who look very much alike. At the same time, they are made to represent two contrasting character types. As the narrator comments at the beginning: "The brothers' characters were as different as their nicknames: Black Li was old-fashioned; White Li was very modern."[2] Thus the story is structured on the basis of a "doubling" design in characterization, to illustrate, presumably, the conflict between old and new styles of thought and behavior—one of the most common themes in modern Chinese literature, especially of the May Fourth period. But the story certainly goes beyond this clichéish bifurcation. For Lao She puts it in a category of works that are carefully wrought and in which "there is first an idea before I construct character and incident"; according to him, characters so designed move in their clearly circumscribed orbits and do not "go astray."[3] Such seriousness of purpose calls for an equally serious consideration of the author's intention as a valid factor for interpretation. Consequently, my concern in this essay is not only with Lao She's artistic design—how he portrays the interaction between the two central characters in the unfolding plot—but with his intellectual purpose, the story's alleged revolutionary message. Since the "message" is contained presumably in the author's preconceived "idea," a comparison between conception and execution is also in order. This strategy may provide a clue to the "mystery" of the story and its uniqueness in the corpus of Lao She's fictional works.

A psychological approach may well begin with the characterization of the two brothers. At the beginning of the story, we are told that "Black Li wasn't really black. He was called Black Li on account of a big black mole over his left eyebrow. His young brother had no such mark, so he became White Li" (p. 121). The symbolic implications of this "double" image are evident. One is reminded of the facial makeup in Beijing opera (a popular art form Lao She loved) in which black and white faces represent well-defined character traits—one generally positive, the other negative.[4] On the basis of such a polarity, the moral equation would seem to favor Black Li and put White Li in a bad light. On the other hand, the black mole could also be seen as a stigma. Since Lao She is said to have once been converted to Christianity,[5] hence certainly well acquainted with Biblical references, the mole on Black Li's face recalls the mark of Cain, the killer of his brother, whereas White Li may be the innocent one, without blemish, who is not accursed. Thus the double image of the two brothers contains deliberately confused symbols. If we apply these categories, derived from Chinese and Western sources, to the story itself, they do not exactly fit. Black Li is not quick-tempered or volatile, like the prototypical "black face" character in Beijing opera, but rather slow-witted and mild. Nor is White Li as conniving as a "white face" character. On the other hand, the Biblical Cain is wild and impetuous, who strikes down his gentle twin due to unbearable envy. In Lao She's story, the situation is almost the reverse: White Li is the more wild and tempestuous character, whereas Black Li, being so protective and yielding, eventually has himself killed on behalf of his brother. In the story's rather melodramatic ending, Black Li removes his mole in order to assume his brother's identity, thus changing into White Li, who survives and begins to look like his dead brother. This shifting identity underscores a basic unity of the polar opposites: one could almost imagine that the mole—and the curse—had been exchangeable between the two brothers. Herein lies the intriguing enigma of Lao She's "double" characterization.

The Western theoretical literature on the issue of the double is voluminous; the exchangeability between the two polar components of the double is one of the recurring hallmarks.[6] Lao She, however, does not employ this device to probe the inner psyche of the central protagonist (as is the case in many Western modernist novels). Rather, he seems to have a penchant for externalized action and interaction.[7] In my opinion, this story is not exclusively a psychological study of Black Li but is "set up" on an external plane so that the interactions between the two brothers are, so to speak, in full view of the narrator and the reader. Interestingly, Lao She depicts their interaction through two intermediaries—a woman (called merely "she") whom they both pursue and the first-person narrator.

The formulaic device of a triangular relationship is not unique to this story. It has been tried before in Lao She's fiction and in modern Chinese literature. The only distinction that marks the "modernity" of Lao She's stories of triangular relationship (and he has done several variations of the same formula)[8] from such semitraditional works as Su Manshu's "Suizan ji" (The broken hairpin) is that the typical roles of a male protagonist torn between two females in the "talent-meets-beauty" (*caizi jiaren*) tradition are reversed in May Fourth fiction, in which more often than not two men compete for the amorous favors of one woman.[9] Lao She and others have used this modern triangular formula to buttress a comic design or to serve as foil for gentle satire. "Black Li and White Li," however, has little of Lao She's humor, which can be found in several other stories by him with similar constructs. Part of the reason may be due to Lao She's stated claim that this work marked his first serious attempt at crafting fiction after an earlier period of writing novels in a humorous vein and "playing with" short stories for fun.[10] Thus it is not supposed to contain such levity. Yet, at the same time, Lao She, through the narrator, introduces an intriguing disclaimer: "Though love was not the central theme of the misunderstanding that arose between the two brothers, I must begin my discussion there" (p. 121). What follows in the first half of the story is a narrative, as recounted through the brothers' individual dialogues with the narrator, of their respective encounters with the woman.

The attitudes of both brothers in this regard are rather strange when viewed against the standard struggle for the possession of the love object in most triangular love stories. The comic or farcical quality of such works is derived from the fact that the object often stands beyond reach. The competition becomes, from the reader's point of view, a game of folly sometimes masterminded by the object of desire, who can be the subject of dramatic action. Such is the case of Lao She's lightweight story "Tongmeng" (Alliance). In the present work, however, something other than comic chase is implied. Their "competition" is conducted as mutually yielding (hence, strictly speaking, no competition at all), whereas the woman seems more emotionally involved. Black Li's decision to yield her to his brother triggers first a strong reaction from the woman, who feels that he has intentionally "insulted" her, that he does not understand a woman's psychology (p. 123). But her feelings are clearly misunderstood by Black Li, who surmises that she wants herself pursued "by the whole world." Such an attitude would have been more fitting for the heroine in a triangular comedy or farce. Does Black Li really like her, and does she want to reciprocate his love? Could she easily transfer her love to his brother?

In comparison, the woman's relationship with White Li is even less articulated. On his part, White Li's attitude toward her is quite "male-chauvinistic": "The only reason I got involved with her at all was to cause trouble for Number Two [Black Li]; otherwise, why would I want to waste my time with her? Aren't all relations between men and women based purely on animal desire?" (p. 124). White Li's pronouncement may be mere rhetorical facade to veil his more serious intentions. But the plot does not unveil further his true sentiments toward her. (Rather, the narrator states that on one occasion when he inquires about White Li at her house she purposefully chooses to talk about Black Li.) White Li's belittling of the woman's significance can only be seen as a mocking gesture, an almost intentional putdown of the place of romantic love in the scheme of his life's pursuits—and, one might infer, of the story's plot.

In a more realistic mode, the description would have focused on the emotional interactions between the brothers and the woman figure. Yet the reader of this story is left unfulfilled, because Lao She has left this part of the plot dangling; the tension generated by the woman's initially strong reaction is not resolved. Even worse, she is made to disappear altogether at the midpoint of the story and never mentioned again. Why does Lao She even bother to introduce such a romantic complication if love is not meant to be the central theme of the story? If it is not love, what is the matter with the story?

"When the 'nature' of the object inspiring the passion is not sufficient to account for the desire, one must turn to the impassioned subject."[11] So begins the thesis by René Girard in an intricate book, *Deceit, Desire, and the Novel*. The "triangular desire" in Girard's framework is centered on the relationship between subject and object and, on top of it, a certain model which Girard calls the "mediator" of desire. In the case of Don Quixote, the model is the Knight Amadis of Gaul in his imagination: Amadis stands as the "Other" in Don Quixote's pursuits of chivalric objects. If one attempts to position the woman as the object of Black Li's desire (leaving aside the Quixotish qualities in Black Li's personality), then the "mediator" model can be no other than White Li, who stands in the structure of the story as the "Other" and who mediates, if not chooses outright, the object of Black Li's desire by virtue of his doubling relationship with Black Li. Thus we might conceive of a somewhat different triangular relationship: the psychology of the impassioned subject (Black Li) has more to do with the "Other" than with the apparent object. Instead of the woman being the center of the triangle, it is White Li who still holds center stage. Hovering behind the foreground of the love story between Black Li and the woman remains the "other" presence of White Li. The love interest is, in other words, but another way to get back at the interlocking relationship between the two brothers.

Lao She once commented on the writing of his novel *Er Ma* (The two Mas), which may be seen as a precedent to the story of the two Lis, that he tended to relegate love interests to a subsidiary position in his fiction and "put other things on the forefront." According to him, the clear advantage of such a device is that he could rescue himself from the convention of triangular or tetra-angular romance; yet the demerit also remains: "It makes me unable to confront boldly this greatest problem in life—the problem of the sexes."[12] If we follow his line of thinking, we have reason to argue that there indeed exists in this story an unfulfilled emotional "subtext"—a potential story of love and romantic sacrifice on the model of Dickens's *Tale of Two Cities.* It may not even be too far-fetched to locate, furthermore, a possible source of inspiration for the Black Li character in Dickens's Sydney Carton, who likewise willingly assumes a mistaken identity in order to sacrifice his life as an ultimate act of noble sentiment for his love object. That Lao She has chosen not to pursue this emotional confrontation of his characters may have something to do with his habitual inability to treat the subject in a serious vein. He may also have wanted to avoid the prevalent formula of "love versus revolutionary duty" in the leftist fiction of the 1930s.[13] Accordingly, the woman figure functions in the text merely as something of a "bait," perhaps vaguely comparable to the position of Ophelia vis-à-vis Hamlet in

Shakespeare's play.[14] Black Li's action to terminate their relationship can therefore be seen as a way to "exteriorize" the woman, to dissolve her as a love object in order to move on to a new and henceforth difficult identification. Yet these possible psychological implications remain speculations because, unlike Shakespeare, Lao She does not develop the intricacies of this connection. Why, then, does he bother to set up initially a pseudo–love story?

On balance, White Li occupies less space than Black Li in the story. There is only one sustained dialogue between White Li and the narrator, whereas Black Li is engaged in conversation with the narrator no less than five times. Obviously, the older brother is on more familiar terms with the narrator, who states at the very outset: "Black Li and I were good friends" (p. 121). This relative difference in the scale of the narrator's distance with the two brothers does not, however, diminish White Li's significance. If we measure the degree of a character's significance in a narrative structure by his influence on the outcome of the plot,[15] there is no doubt that it is White Li who, with his "twenty-year plan" and his hidden plot, triggers the events that follow. In other words, White Li serves as a catalyst who "emplots" the story and provides the central source of "mystery," against which Black Li's characterization is to be measured. Black Li's efforts to find out about his younger brother's real intentions—his quest for the mystery of the "Other"—thus assume a depth of tragic meaning. We might speak of his characterization as more rounded and "developmental" in the sense in which "the character's personal traits are attenuated so as to clarify his progress along a plot line which has an ethical basis."[16]

How are Black Li's personality traits "attenuated" so as to move along a plot line whose "ethical basis" is dictated by White Li's revolutionary purpose? It is noteworthy that in the first part of the story, in which he is entangled with the woman, Black Li is viewed by the narrator more or less in a sympathetic light. As the plot progresses, however, and the love interest is dropped, he begins to receive mildly negative comments from the narrator, who now sees him as slow-witted, slow-moving, and concerned only with small things (pp. 126–28). His erstwhile generosity toward his brother and the woman, which seems to endear him to the narrator, is now considered to be a sign of mediocrity: "Thus he accepted new things quite readily, but without understanding them very thoroughly. It wasn't that he lacked the desire to understand things, but when he should have used his brain, he used his emotions'' (p. 128). His mental anguish and deliberation are seen as peculiar habits—fortune-telling and church-going. His religious conversion, exemplified by his praying and singing of hymns, does not elicit any sympathy from the narrator, who seems to adopt the stance of a nonbeliever reminiscent of the intellectual narrator in Lu Xun's famous story, ''Zhufu'' (Benediction). In the light of May Fourth scientific rationalism, these habits could be seen as superstitious and negative. Yet it is through his reading of the Christian Gospels that he learns of the genuine meaning of sacrifice. But the true dimension of his martyrdom is not understood. Strange as it may seem, the progress of Black Li's character development is depicted as a process of growing peculiarities, reaching almost a point of insanity. He looks so bizarre only against a value system to which he clearly does not belong and which, alas, provides the ''ethical'' basis of the story's plot. A sensible reader would consider this jarring juxtaposition of characterization and plot unsettling. It renders Black Li pathetic and foolish, yet neither funny nor pitiable. It betrays certain contradictions that may lie beyond the ''psychology'' of the characters themselves.

In Lao She's other stories in which the device of contrasting characterization is employed, the treatment of the older and more traditional character is different. For instance, the story ''Dabei si wai'' (Outside the Temple of Great Compassion) likewise portrays the conflict between a politically active student and his kind, generous, but strict dormitory master, who eventually dies of an accident resulting from the student agitation.[17] Most Lao She scholars would agree that it is the mild-mannered, more traditional type of characters who are closer to Lao She's own sensibility, whereas he has nothing but distaste for the young and rash political agitators. One could even argue that the characterization of White Li is villainous: he typifies the single-minded revolutionary reminiscent of the Russian nihilists who harbor few human emotions, treat sex lightly, and demand sacrifices from others.[18] In the context of this story, however, White Li remains, as demonstrated earlier, the twin image—the ''double'' or ''second self''—of Black Li: the close relationship he enjoys with his brother also entitles him to perform the function of something of an outside conscience—reminding Black Li of what is historically inevitable and what he (Black Li) should strive to become. In other words, on the basis of the story's structural design, I am prepared to argue that the portrait of the revolutionary in ''Black Li and White Li,'' together with its "revolutionary" message, is more positive than in Lao She's other works written around the same time (such as the novel *Maocheng ji* [City of cats]).

The clue to this disconcerting portraiture lies with the first-person narrator, through whose eyes the story is unfolded. In a way, we can see his position vis-à-vis the two brothers as something of a counterpart to the woman's. Like her, he must react to the two brothers' differing personalities by making his own deliberations. Whereas the woman's views are barely articulated, the narrator's are placed clearly in the foreground. The obvious question that troubles him seems to be the same as that the woman faces: which of the two brothers does he prefer? But his reactions are more complex. As mentioned earlier, the narrator has seen more of Black Li and claims to be his close friend. On the other hand, he is curiously insensitive to the emotional turmoil of his friend. Rather, he chooses to see it as a manifestation of Black Li's old-fashioned personality. We could even venture the conjecture that the narrator, while on familiar terms with Black Li emotionally (though he does not fully express his feelings because of his passivity), has seen fit not to side with his friend. On the other hand, the narrator seems also psychologically removed from White Li. Their contacts are limited; we find the narrator scarcely involved in White Li's affairs. In his only sustained dialogue with White Li in the story, the narrator voices the following impressions:

> I listened carefully to what he had to say and paid even closer attention to his facial expression. Black Li and White Li's faces were similar in every respect, except for the fact that Black Li's demeanor was so totally different from his brother's. For this reason, one moment I felt I was talking to a very close friend, and the next as if I were sitting across from a complete stranger. This was quite discomfiting; the face before me was familiar, but I was unable to find its familiar expression. (pp. 124–25)

This is one of the most revealing passages in the whole story. The narrator has clearly established the double identity of the two brothers; at the same time, he also confesses to his own discomfort. Yet in spite of it he becomes rather convinced by White Li's need to break away from Black Li. (In contrast, he is not convinced by Black Li's interpretation of his brother's intention.) It seems as if the narrator *wanted* to be impressed. As the story progresses, he becomes more and more manipulative, by withholding or giving out information to the reader concerning the two brothers. He continues to view White Li as more clever, more determined, and dedicated to a higher purpose. Albeit from a respectful distance, we are nevertheless given the impression that time is on his side. And as if this were not enough to convince us, we are provided with more information in a final episode—a long dialogue between the narrator and an added character, Wang Wu (Wang the Fifth), a rickshaw puller.

Technically, this last episode reads like a rehearsal for a forthcoming novel by Lao She, *Luotuo Xiangzi* (Camel Xiangzi), a story about another rickshaw puller. Those familiar with this novel can surely find an embryonic Mr. Cao in Black Li as described by Wang Wu: that he is a decent and generous man, a "good master," but, Wang Wu hastens to add, "no matter how good a master he is, he's still a master. There's no way we can treat each other as brothers" (pp. 131–32). White Li, expectedly, is taken by Wang Wu as his true brother. (White Li is called "Fourth Brother," leading easily to Wang the Fifth.) This claim of brotherly solidarity is evidently in line with proletarian ideology, as Wang Wu further states: "He's [White Li] talking about how unfair things are for us—I mean all the rickshaw pullers in the world" (p. 132). White Li is a collectivist, whereas Black Li remains a heart-bleeding individualist. On a realistic plane, Wang Wu's comment seems too neat to be authentic. Yet it certainly adds symbolic weight and political endorsement to White Li's character.

The other function of this episode is, of course, to reveal the plot of the rickshaw puller's riot, which in turn leads to Black Li's execution on behalf of the real instigator, White Li. Leaving aside the question whether this is, in fact, an utterly foolish act on Black Li's part, one is nevertheless struck by its symbolic significance: Black Li has not only assumed his brother's identity (by removing his mole) but also, so to speak, completed his action. It is noteworthy that at the end of the story, in the baffled eyes of the narrator, the surviving White Li begins to look like Black Li, in a sense taking on his identity. The roles are now reversed. White Li's final comment is couched in his brother's Christian language: "Number Two must have gone to heaven; that's a perfect place for him. But I'm still here smashing the gates of hell" (p. 136).

How does the narrator react to Wang Wu's revelation of the plot and with the final outcome? He seems to be more understanding with White Li than with Black Li and begins to deliberate from White Li's point of view:

> White Li was involved in something dangerous. Beyond wrecking trolley cars, he probably had something even more formidable in mind. Thus his desire to move away from his brother was to avoid implicating him. White Li was not afraid of sacrificing his own life, or the lives of others, but he was unwilling to sacrifice his brother unless there were a good reason for it. (p. 133)

What is to be done? As if to lengthen the suspense, the narrator procrastinates in his deliberations. Finally he decides to warn Black Li—alas, too late, for Black Li, already informed by Wang Wu, has made preparations for self-sacrifice. The intriguing point about their last encounter is that although the narrator is clear about White Li's plans, he is still not fully aware of Black Li's proposed action: he is surprised by the latter's cold reception and thinks that his friend wants to avoid him on purpose. At this final moment, the reader may well be impatient and even infuriated by the narrator's subjugation of sensitivity and intelligence. Why is he so slow in grasping the truth and the true meaning of Black Li's action? Even at the very end, as the narrator encounters White Li several months after the death of Black Li, despite his empathy for the dead brother he still seems to evince no apparent hatred toward White Li, who, after all, is the primary cause for his friend's death. What is the reason for his one-sidedness? What is the purpose behind this device of an inconsistent narrator?

The constant presence of the first-person narrator suggests that he in fact occupies a fulcrum position: he provides the focal consciousness from which the story unfolds. The plot is a projection of his vision. In other words, this is as much a story about the two brothers as about the narrator. Yet, as analyzed earlier, the narrator seems to be of two minds, his perspective shifting from Black Li to White Li. The source of this inconsistency may be traced to Lao She's own statements concerning the production of this text.

In his preface to a collection of his selected works published in 1951, after the establishment of the People's Republic, Lao She had the following apologetic remarks about the story:

> Upon returning to China, [I found that] the discussion of literature had progressed from literary revolution to revolutionary literature. Together with theory, there was the rise of proletarian literature in creative writing. I normally did not talk about theory, so I continued with creative writing and did not participate in the polemics. However, with

> regard to the merits and demerits of proletarian literature, I had a certain judgment. I thought that it was moving in the right direction but neither its content nor its technique was entirely satisfactory. By and by, I began to write pieces like "Black Li and White Li." That I have chosen this story for inclusion is not because it's better written but because I use it to indicate how I was influenced by theories of revolutionary literature.
>
> From today's point of view, "Black Li and White Li" is a ludicrous, even absurd, piece. But at that time it was sufficient proof that I had undergone some changes in my thinking. To be sure, in its content, I did not dare to describe how White Li joined the [Communist] organization. Rather, I used the mode of a romantic story to describe the death of Black Li. However, at least I perceived clearly that Black Li had to die, and that death was the best deal for him. . . . Besides, literary censorship at that time made me reluctant to describe it too revealingly. As I did not join the revolution, I did not want to wear a "red hat."[19]

This latter-day explanation from a postrevolutionary vantage should, of course, be qualified. Should we, then, repudiate entirely this statement of "revolutionary" intention as mere rationalization (if not outright lie), or should we consider it as containing a grain of truth? My analysis of the story's text has convinced me that it can be read as a piece of "revolutionary literature"—but in Lao She's own fashion. As a conscientious craftsman of fiction, he had, indeed, intended to write a carefully conceptualized work to point toward the need for social change and the inevitability of revolution. To this extent he was very sincere. Was Lao She, however, so politically committed to the Communist cause himself? The eminent Lao She scholar Zbigniew Slupski provides a generally negative answer, with which I agree: "The political statements to be found in his works from the twenties to the forties were not the main point of his communication, but merely the byproduct of his moralizing."[20] As a moralizer, Lao She tended to be rather conservative: for instance, he ridiculed modern-style marriage and courtship. There is no doubt that Lao She harbored a moral distaste for radicals like White Li. Thus we sense an effort to hide this distaste and to overcome a certain sentimental attachment to the Black Li character—chiefly via the stance of the narrator. That the narrator is portrayed in such a passive and inconsistent way may be due to a deliberate attempt to withhold emotional identification not only between the narrator and Black Li but also between the narrator and the author. Insofar as the real author—Lao She—and the implied author can be theoretically distinguished from each other, the difference is also an indicator of Lao She's own "divided consciousness": whereas the real Lao She was a moralist, the implied author may be more political.[21] In other words, through a preconceived fictional design, Lao She may have wished to defeat purposefully the reader's expectation to have the narrator sympathize with the Black Li character, who is the embodiment of Lao She's moral choice. On the other hand, he has made a veiled effort to make the reader understand the revolutionary viewpoint as represented by White Li, although as a human character White Li fails to come alive. In sum, I think the dissonant elements in the story's structure and their disconcerting effect on the reader are intentional. It serves to distance the reader from siding too easily with Lao She's personal morality. We can look at the artistic devices as ways to measure the distance between Lao She's moral choice, on the one hand, and his acknowledgment of the possibility of political action, on the other.

Does Lao She succeed in realizing his "idea"? Although recent critical theories allow no room for the real "historical" readership, I think the story's success or failure cannot be assessed without an attempt to reconstruct the possible receptions by Chinese readers of that historical period. Perhaps we may envisage a division of opinion. The more committed "revolutionary" audience would be dissatisfied because, as Lao She later acknowledged, the undercurrent of the story's revolutionary meaning is not brought to the forefront. On the other hand, the nonrevolutionary audience, their reading tastes nurtured by works of the realistic mode in which vividly human characterization was almost the sine qua non of fiction, would also be dissatisfied because they would like to know more about the personal relationships between the two brothers and between them and the woman. Both sides, however, would be unlikely to set apart Lao She the real author from the implied author of the story, or even from its "I" narrator. They would consider Lao She (not his narrator) to be rather passive. Ironically, this unsophisticated reader's response may be more on target: Lao She was not a revolutionary writer, and sometimes he "camouflaged" his disinterest with his "art." He may have conceived this story on the basis of an abstract "idea" of revolutionary literature. But his intention and design, however lofty, are in my judgment not fully realized by his technique—nor, for that matter, fully comprehended by his readers. We may criticize the dissonance and the distancing effect as the result of a certain discrepancy in the fictional text between intention and representation: "the implied author's attitudes towards the experience that he represents, conveyed through a variety of rhetorical devices, are not always appropriate to the novel's total body of represented life," because he is "inconsistent in his interpretations of experience that he dramatizes."[22] In view of Lao She's innate talent as a "humorist" and an unassuming "story-teller,"[23] I think he would have written a better story had he given himself more freedom, without having a preconceived idea.

But then I am by no means a "revolutionary" or unbiased reader.[24]

Notes

1. The topic and the approach of this essay were assigned to me. I am most grateful to the participants at the workshop for their comments and criticisms, which compelled me to rethink and recast my paper. During the revision process, I benefited greatly from the conversations with Professor Yu-shih Chen, who helped me to crystallize my ideas in the concluding section.

2. Lao She, "Hei-Bai Li" (Black Li and White Li), in his *Ganji* (Going to the market-fair) (Shanghai: Liangyu tushu yinshua gongsi, 1943), p. 177. The story was written sometime between 1931 and 1934. Page references hereafter refer to the appended translation, which begins on p. 121. The passage cited is on p. 121. Subsequent page references are included parenthetically in the text. There is also a somewhat abridged English translation in *Contemporary Chinese Stories*, ed. Chi-chen Wang (New York: Columbia University Press, 1944), pp. 25–39. Unless otherwise indicated, I use my own translation.

3. Lao She, *Laoniu poche* (Old ox and broken cart) (Guangzhou: Renjian shuwu, 1937), p. 62. The problem with this neat design is that, as some critics of the story have pointed out, the characterization becomes somewhat "flat," lacking in liveliness and depth. See, for instance, Ma Sen, "Lun Lao She de xiaoshuo" (On Lao She's fiction), *Mingbao yuekan* (Mingbao monthly) (Hong Kong) 6.9 (September 1971): 83. For a theoretical justification of the author's intention, see E. D. Hirsch's two books: *Validity in Interpretation* (New Haven: Yale University Press, 1967) and *The Aims of Interpretation* (Chicago: University of Chicago Press, 1976).

4. A "black face" indicates a quick-tempered, volatile, yet innocent and gullible hero (the prototype is Zhang Fei of the famous *Romance of the Three Kingdoms*), whereas a "white face" connotes such negative qualities as cunningness and machination (as personified by Cao Cao from the same novel).

5. Ranbir Vohra, *Lao She and the Chinese Revolution* (Cambridge: Harvard East Asian Monographs, 1974), pp. 12–13.

6. For a general survey, see Clifford Hallam, "The Double as Incomplete

Self: Toward a Definition of Doppelganger," in *Fearful Eymmetry: Doubles and Doubling in Literature and Film*, ed. Eugene J. Cook (University Press of Florida, 1981), pp. 1–31.

7. Huang Dongtao, *Lao She xiaoshi* (An understanding of Lao She) (Hong Kong: Shijie chubanshe, 1979), esp. this statement: "An important feature of Lao She's creative method of short story writing is depicting character through the complex relationships of two personalities and their attitudes toward the same incident" (p. 47). In his own essay on characterization, Lao She attributes the psychological bent on modern Western fiction to the influence of modern science. This he deplores, because giving too much psychological information and analysis is not tantamount to creating a vivid character. See his *Laoniu poche*, pp. 99–100.

8. At least two other variations can be found in the *Ganji* collection: "Tongmeng" (Alliance) and "Yeshi sanjiao" (Also a triangle)—one written before, and the other after, the present story.

9. Even a sophisticated *savant* like Qian Zhongshu cannot escape from this formulaic trap in his novel *Weicheng* (Fortress besieged).

10. Lao She, *Laoniu poche*, pp. 58–59.

11. René Girard, *Deceit, Desire, and the Novel: Self and Other in Literary Structure*, trans. Yvonne Freccero (Baltimore: Johns Hopkins University Press, 1965), p. 2.

12. Lao She, *Laoniu poche*, p. 22.

13. But Lao She does not entirely succeed in this case, for in artistic terms White Li's action resembles precisely such a formula.

14. Hamlet's change of attitude toward Ophelia is analyzed in this way by Jacques Lacan in an extremely intricate study, "Desire and the Interpretation of Desire in Hamlet," in *Literature and Psychoanalysis, the Question of Reading: Otherwise*, ed. Shoshana Felman (Baltimore: Johns Hopkins University Press, 1982), pp. 11–52. I was tempted to build a Lacanian case for Black Li but decided that it is not appropriate, as Lao She's story is very different from Shakespeare's play.

15. Critics of the structuralist persuasion tend to see characters as only a function of plot, "means rather than ends of the story," although a recent scholar influenced by the structuralist theories and French narratology has come to recognize and argue for a more open, afunctional notion of character. See Seymour Chatman, *Story and Discourse: Narrative Structure in Fiction and Film* (Ithaca: Cornell University Press, 1978), pp. 112–13.

16. Robert Scholes and Robert Kellogg, *The Nature of Narrative* (New York: Oxford University Press, 1968), p. 169.

17. See Michael S. Duke, "A Social and Literary Analysis of the Short Stories of Lao She" (M.A. thesis, University of California, Berkeley, 1969), pp. 71–72. Duke also considers "Black Li and White Li" to be Lao She's best story about intellectuals (pp. 73–75).

18. This is Professor Yue Daiyun's view as voiced at the workshop. I am grateful for her comments on my paper.

19. "Lao She xuanji zixu" (Preface to selections from Lao She), in *Lao She lun chuangzuo* (Lao She on creative writing), ed. Hu Jieqing [Mrs. Lao She] (Shanghai: Shanghai wenyi chubanshe, 1980), p. 142.

20. Slupski, "Lao She and His Conception of Creative Writing," paper sub-

mitted to the Dedham Conference on Modern Chinese Literature (June 1974), p. 15. See also his book, *The Evolution of a Modern Chinese Writer* (Prague: Oriental Institute in Academia, 1966).

21. The differentiation between implied and real authors is, of course, taken from Wayne Booth, *The Rhetoric of Fiction* (Chicago: University of Chicago Press, 1975). That the implied author can also be "psychoanalyzed"—a controversial point—is the argument of Bernard J. Paris. See his book, *A Psychological Approach to Fiction: Studies in Thackeray, Stendhal, George Eliot, Dostoevsky, and Conrad* (Bloomington: Indiana University Press, 1974), esp. chap. 1.

22. Paris, *A Psychological Approach to Fiction*, pp. 14–15.

23. For a sensitive portrait of Lao She in this light, see Cyril Birch, "Lao She: The Humourist in His Humour," *China Quarterly* 8 (1961): 45–62. See also an incomplete biography by Hu Jinquan, *Lao She he tade zuopin* (Lao She and his works) (Hong Kong: Wenhua shenghuo chubanshe, 1977). A more comprehensive life-and-work study of Lao She is Prudence Chou's Ph.D. dissertation at the University of California, Berkeley. Paul Bady's work in French is also worth consulting.

24. The current "reader's response" theory is rather subjective and relativistic: the meaning of the text is what I as a reader make it out to be. No consideration is taken of the historical readership, which I think is also relevant to the study of modern Chinese literature because of the close connection—and sometimes interaction—between the real author and the real audience via the literary text in the actual historical milieu.

3

THE BARRED VIEW
On the Enigmatic Narrator in Xiao Jun's "Goats"

Marston Anderson

THE FIRST mark of modernity in Xiao Jun's short story, "Goats," is its opening in the subjectivity of an unidentified narrator. The traditional Chinese story-teller invariably launched his tale with the provision of crucial identifying information about the story's protagonist: "During the Da-de reign period, there lived in Yangzhou a rich man by the name of Wu who was a district defense commandant." Such introductions situated the character in the web of familial and bureaucratic associations that made up Chinese society, and set the story against a conventionalized historical background. All such information is missing in "Goats," which opens with an essentially phenomenological description of the narrator's prison environment and the view from his window. Whereas the traditional story-teller spoke in an impersonal, classifying voice that assumed his mastery over the semiotic design of the world he described, the subjective modern narrator writes from a position inside—here even from a position of entrapment within—the world of his fiction. The absence of the expected identifying information about the narrator-protagonist in "Goats" may be said, using Roland Barthes's terminology, to "thematize" the important enigmas that will haunt the story: Who is the narrator? For what crime was he incarcerated? When, if ever, will he be released?

In *S/Z* Barthes has offered us a tool for the analysis of narrative enigmas in what he calls the "hermeneutic code." Under this code "we list the various (formal) terms by which an enigma can be distinguished, suggested, formulated, held in suspense, and finally disclosed."[1] In an elaborate analysis of Balzac's "Sarrasine," Barthes shows the development of several hermeneutic sequences, or what he calls "hermeneutic sentences." He differentiates a total of ten terms (hermeneutic morphemes or "hermeneutemes"), which may be divided into those that suggest or state an enigma (thematization, proposal, formulation, and the promise of an answer); those that delay its solution (snare, equivocation, jamming, suspended answer, and partial answer); and finally, the disclosure of the solution. A particular hermeneutic sentence may exhibit these hermeneutemes in any combination or order, although it demands the exclusion of certain combinations (for example, an enigma may not be deciphered before it is posed).

The interpretive model involved here is not that of philosophical hermeneutics,[2] but the kind of vulgar interpretive practice Susan Sontag has criticized in *Against Interpretation*.[3] Interpretation in this sense means the reduction of the complexity (or polysemeity) of the text to a few elements that are said to represent its content. With the formulation of a narrative enigma, a multiplicity of possible interpretations is set into play, and through the dilatory tactics Barthes isolates, these interpretations exert a positive presence in the story until the denouement, when all but the true one are invalidated. In a sense, narrative enigmas play with the possibility of misinterpretation though, by design, only the interpretation confirmed at closure can be the "true" one. Through this highly deliberate, even manipulative process, the author regulates the reader's understanding of the plot. Where the other codes can retain their polysemic openness to the story's conclusion, and even beyond (an ambiguous symbol, for example, may be impossible to interpret in the vulgar sense), the hermeneutic code demands closure if the story is to satisfy our most basic expectations.

Closure, as the moment when the multiplicity of possible interpretations is reduced to the single "true" one, is the point to which all the terms of the hermeneutic code ultimately refer. Any analysis of a hermeneutic sequence presupposes knowledge of its final term; only by reviewing the entire sequence with the "true" answer in mind can individual "hermeneutemes" be categorized (otherwise "partial answers" could not be distinguished from "snares," for example). Whereas the reader experiences the code as a sequential development—a gradual unfolding or unveiling of the solution—Barthes the analyst sees the formulation of the enigma and its solution as parts of a single configuration, the "hermeneutic sentence." From this perspective, the temporal element of the work is no more than a strategy of delay, made possible by the technology of "dilatory morphemes"—"jamming," "equivocation," and so forth—all employed for the express purpose of maintaining obscurity. Barthes suggests the text needs these strategies of "reticence" to ensure its own survival. It is as if, without these delaying devices, the text would shrink to the configuration that underlies it.

But what is the purpose of extending and disguising the configuration? Why should the text fear its unmasking? Barthes's answer lies in his equation of the hermeneutic code with the "Voice of Truth." By "truth," Barthes does not mean the operable truth of the material, nonfictional world, but simply "what is at the end of expectation."[4] Through the hermeneutic code the text sets up a psychology of expectation in the reader; the prolonging of this expectation through dilatory devices serves to intensify the reader's sense of relief when the "truth" is revealed at closure; in fact, to heighten the reader's susceptibility to persuasion. The code does not disclose new truths but, by manipulating the reader through a casuistic interpretive process, gives the text the illusion of meaning (truth). "The truth is thereby long desired and avoided, kept in a kind of pregnancy for its full term, a pregnancy whose end, both liberating and catastrophic, will bring about the utter end of the discourse."[5] In Barthes's metaphor, it is a stillbirth that concludes this pregnancy: without elaborate rhetorical support, the "truth" revealed by the text stands exposed as trivial or specious.

Thus deflating its truth claim, Barthes proffers the hermeneutic code as above all a formal element of narrative, and this formal bias prevents him from generalizing on the nature of the enigmas he analyzes in "Sarrasine." It is remarkable, however, that of the six enigmas he isolates in Balzac's story, five are questions of identity;[6] the only exception ("What is the source of the Lanty fortune?") might easily be subsumed under one of the five ("Who are the Lantys?"). Barthes in his less formalistic moments seems to acknowledge this, albeit indirectly: he calls the denouement a *nomination* of some kind, and he refers to the Sphinx's questioning of Oedipus as the prototype of all narrative enigmas.[7] As conveyer of questions of identity, the code would seem to be a central factor in the work's fabrication of character, and Barthes does recognize the connection when he slightingly calls character "only the enigma's passage." Yet it is equally true that the enigma is constructed to delimit character, to consign the individual subject a place in the mesh of cultural values advanced through the referential and symbolic codes. The anxiety created by the enigma's formulation is not simply a desire for formal closure, but the radical insecurity of the individual as he stands subject to the assaults of time (plotting) on his sense of self. Viewed in this light, the temporal element of the text is not simply dilatory padding, but the tractile matter that must be resisted, patterned and mastered for the subject to earn the sufficiency of self-presentation at closure. Nomination is not sufficient to create character. A character is a name with a story attached, a name provided as the answer to a protracted question. The Sphinx's question is indeed exemplary in this: it gives the whole history of a man.

In sum, the interrogative model that underlies the hermeneutic code is a fundamental form-giving element of modern Western fiction, perhaps the element most responsible for that fiction's tautness, its sense of inevitability, and its focalization on closure. The code serves as well as a kind of naturalization device, whose aim is less to guide the reader to the revelation of some substantive "truth" than to persuade the reader that the text's culminating disclosure is his own discovered truth. The anxiety/relief pattern evoked in this process is, finally, intimately linked to the work's submerged ideological concerns, specifically with the consignment of social and sexual identity to the human subject.

Since the primary enigma posed by Xiao Jun's "Goats" concerns not simply the identity of a major character, but the identity of the narrative voice itself, an analysis of the "hermeneutic code" in the story is particularly revealing of the formal and ideological contradictions that inform it. The question of the narrator's identity and several subsidiary enigmas ("For what crime was the narrator imprisoned?" "Why is he given special treatment?") are carefully formulated in sections I and II of the story in a way that benefits from an analysis using Barthes's hermeneutic code. As will be seen, however, the code is finally deflected and jammed, with important consequences to both the form and import of the story. This incompleteness of the hermeneutic sequence in "Goats"—its failure to achieve closure—makes identification of "hermeneutemes" difficult, for which reason the analysis that follows employs Barthes's terms tentatively and somewhat inexactly.

The narrator's cell has two windows, one *out* to the sea, the other *in* to the prison yard; the shifting prominence of these views in the narrative reflects an alternating focus on the narrator's identity outside the prison and within prison society. The view out is associated with questions of his *biography*, his past as the chain of events that led to his imprisonment, and his future to the extent that he entertains hopes for his release. These biographical questions are the primary ones formulated by the hermeneutic code. The view in is associated with the narrated world of prison society, where the narrator explores his alienation from the other convicts. In the radical separation of these views is reflected the formal disjunction of the story: the narration poses a set of questions to which the field of narration (the internal workings of prison society) can offer no answers. These two disconnected worlds meet only in the afflicted consciousness of the narrator as he turns between views.

The seascape as we find it at the beginning of the story is the unfettered natural world, given variety by climatic and seasonal changes, but bereft of human imprint. As evidenced by the occasional steamship, men may pass through this world, but they make no permanent alteration of it. This framed, constant view would be ideal for pictorial representation, the narrator suggests, but he is "no painter, and there are no brushes or palettes here" (p. 666/*352a*).[8] His medium, language, can offer only an impoverished copy of the imagined painting, and description soon gives way to restless speculation about what lies beyond the limits of the window frame and expressions of disgust at the waste of his time and youth. The spatial limitations of life in the cell become intolerable only with the introduction of temporal concerns that shatter the stasis of the view and force the narrator to consider his own position in relation to it. The narrator has nevertheless achieved a degree of resignation through contemplation of the ocean view: the free flight of the swallows, which once aroused his envy, now seems natural and fitting to him. In spite of certain elements of foreboding in the view (the clouds that swallow up the sea, the recent storms), the seascape is above all a source of consolation to him.

The view of the prison yard, where the prisoners work endlessly on the construction of a new prison building, is by contrast a discomfitting view of human labor applied to the perpetuation of human servitude. The narrator has no direct part in this labor, one of a number of facts that together thematize an important subsidiary enigma, "Why is the narrator accorded special treatment?" The guards treat him with unusual civility, and he is provided reading material and cigarettes, the accouterments of the intellectual. Even the ocean view, afforded by his privileged accommodation in a single room, is a prerogative of his special standing in the prison. This special standing conditions his relationship with the other prisoners: in the only apparent contact he has with them, they are reduced to beggars soliciting cigarette butts from him as they are led to the yard each day. As long as the factors of the narrator's biography that might explain his privileged standing remain undivulged, the class division within prison society it reflects remains divorced from its larger social rationalizations and appears arbitrary, enforced through autocratic decree by the prison authorities.

It is the Russian children, placed in the narrator's cell for protection from the other prisoners, who finally formulate the implied enigmas and force the narrator's reconsideration of his position within prison society. They recognize the narrator's difference from the other prisoners and ask, "Are you a *xiansheng* (a gentleman or teacher)?" The narrator equivocates: he is a lawbreaker like the others, "like a thief or robber" (p. 668b/*354*). As an ironic acknowledgment of the title "lawbreaker," which society has accorded him, the answer is true enough, but the narrator's disavowal of the distinction between himself and the other prisoners is patently false. It fools the children temporarily, however, and his pleasure at their consternation ("I don't know why I felt so amused," p. 669a/*354b*) suggests a hidden desire for identification as a thief, a desire expressed again later in the text. The children also ask, "Why are you here?" and "When will you leave?" He answers, "I like to watch the sea here" (p. 669b/*355a*), "I will leave when I've seen my fill of the sea" (p. 672b/*357b*). The narrator has indeed achieved a measure of resignation through contemplation of the sea, but in these responses, he fancifully invests that resignation with intentionality, thus transforming the imposed state of incarceration into a willed one. In Barthes's terminology, these answers are all "equivocations": they have some measure of truth value, but they evade the questioners' objective, which is to discover the narrator's biography, especially the circumstances of his imprisonment. Though the text offers sufficient "partial answers" (for example, the narrator's familiarity with the Russian scene and the fact that he has traveled abroad) to identify the narrator as a radical intellectual, and perhaps a political prisoner, the specifics of the narrator's biography are obscured by these equivocations and are, significantly, to remain obscure.

The children's questions, so neatly deflected by the narrator, nevertheless have a profound effect on him. They disturb his hard-earned serenity by reviving the concerns and ideals of his former life and by reminding him of his alienation from the world outside. The children serve, in a sense, as emissaries of his fading ideals, ideals they celebrate together in the cell with dance and recitations of Russian poetry. The children's return to Russia is coded by the text as a voyage home both to national identity and to freedom. The text's "Russia" is a land where the children can feel an absolute sense of belonging while remaining totally unrestrained (they have been imprisoned, one notices, for drunken, disorderly behavior). The historical absurdity of this equation of the Soviet Union with an anarchic utopia need not blind us to its powerful value in the text as the locus of a personal and social liberation at absolute odds with the restrictive, alienating regimentation of the prison. The children's happy anticipation of their return throws painfully into relief the narrator's confinement and his political estrangement in his own land. They tell him, unaware of the irony, "We're going to our homeland. This is your country; you don't have to go home!" (p. 672a/*357b*).

The narrator now perceives his "country" to be no larger than the prison itself. After the children's departure, the revival of the narrator's ideals manifests itself not, as might be expected, in a struggle to escape his confined environment and reestablish contact with the world outside, but in a new curiosity about his neighbors within the prison. It is as if, by jamming questions about his past, the narrator denies the relevance of such biographical information to a determination of his identity: that identity can be established only through dynamic exploration of his relationship with the other prisoners, specifically with the goat thief. Evading the expected nomination that would close the hermeneutic sequence and confirm our recognition of the narrator as a discrete character with a unique past and determinate personality traits, the text embarks instead on an open-ended attempt to *re-create* that character within the limits imposed by the prison environment. The story thus abruptly shifts direction in section III: the view out is temporarily forgotten in favor of a determined view into prison society itself, now hypostatized as the only arena wherein the narrator can actualize his reawakened ideals.

The text's deflection of hermeneutic interest onto the narrator's relationship with the goat thief has been foreshadowed early in the story, in an episode preceding the arrival of the Russian children. On seeing the goat thief for the first time, the narrator asks about him the very questions the reader has been wondering about the narrator himself: "Is he new?" "What's the charge against him?" (p. 667b/*353a*) They are given prompt answers by the guard: "Just three days"; "Petty theft." The narrator, as the object of the reader's deferred and frustrated curiosity, is presented by the story as an insufficiency that the text promises to make up; the thief shows from the start a kind of excess, a "robustness" out of place in the confined surroundings of the prison. His physical strength wins the narrator's admiration but presents a challenge to the guard, who vows to wear the goat thief down: "Robust? . . . Wait and see" (p. 668a/*353a*).

The goat thief's physical strength is a synecdoche for his moral wholeness, which the narrator similarly comes to admire and envy later in the story. The "crime" for which the goat thief is imprisoned is positively encoded by the text on several levels: it is an act of filiality ("If I didn't have a mother, I wouldn't be a thief") and of liberation (the goats would flourish in the natural surroundings of the goat thief's village, while the authorities who punish their theft allow them to suffer and die). Symbolically, the goats, important sacrificial animals in China as elsewhere, evoke the *pharmakos*, or "scapegoat," which in primitive societies is collectively murdered or expelled in order to purge the reciprocal hostilities of the community and thus preserve order. In René Girard's provocative thesis, it is just such ritualized violence that underlies all social organization.[9] Given such a symbolic context, the theft of the goats may be seen to represent not simply disregard for society's notions of property rights, but subversion of the ritualistic origins of society itself and the distinctions (of class, property, kinship, etc.) that are generated at its birth. Significantly, all the "subversive" acts for which the goat thief is disciplined are motivated not by rebellious rancor, but by a profound and spontaneous compassion (for the goats, for his mother, for the other prisoners), a compassion the narrator at one point calls "excessive." Such excessive compassion is in fact the mark of a transcendant innocence: blind to the arbitrary discriminations of society and the law, the goat thief lives in sympathetic communion with his fellows and the natural world.

At one point the narrator remarks on his own superior knowledge of the law: "I understand the law; laws always so prescribe. Maybe he was young and didn't know as much as I" (p. 675a/*359b*). But the price of the narrator's command over the semiotic sphere is his isolation. When in section III he asks permission, apparently for the first time, to take walks in the yard, the open view and the proximity of the working men feels unnatural to him, and the other prisoners' smiles unnerve him ("I wondered if when I smiled I looked like these fellows who shared my fate," p. 675b/*360a*). In a final attempt to overcome his alienation, he expresses a desire to take part in the prisoners' labor, but he is denied permission by the authorities, who are determined to give him special treatment. Fettered both internally and externally by the letter of the law, he is unable to establish a natural rapport with the other prisoners.

The narrator's frustration finally expresses itself in a full-fledged desire for identity transference with the goat thief. He imagines an exchange of social roles in which the thief somehow rises above his class: "If he had been born in the upper classes, he would have been a superb athlete" (p. 675b/*360a*); "He stood out from the crowd, tall and robust, not in the least shabby, not in the least like a thief" (p. 676/*360b*). The narrator conversely wishes to abandon his own class standing:

> How I regret I was not born a goat thief, or a thief of some kind. . . . I am steeped in a colorless syrupy poison. Will even my bones turn rickety? My skin bleached, my hair shedding like this . . . dissipating my strength, weakening my pulse . . . this exquisite punishment . . . (p. 676a/*360b*)

Spiritually depleted, the narrator imagines himself dissolving before his image of the thief's simple physical sufficiency. The narrator's language itself breaks down in disjointed phrases as he attempts to collapse the semic differences upon which the narration is constructed. In this process of self-erasure, the narrator renounces the search for identity that was formulated as a hermeneutical problem early in the story and is left willing upon himself the "exquisite punishment" of annihilation, a punishment that, unlike the arbitrary punishment of his incarceration, he believes is justly deserved.

After the failure of this attempted identity transference with the goat thief, the narrator's complicity with the penal system he abhors becomes increasingly evident. Earlier he had cooperated with the goat thief in conveying cigarette butts to the other prisoners, and, however ineffectually, defended the goat thief to the guard. Now he unthinkingly informs on the other prisoners after they request wire from him for an escape attempt, and he brings disciplinary action upon the goat thief. The narrator proves himself unable to use his privileges to assist in the liberation of his fellows; his presence in the prison, once benign, is now hazardous to the others.

When the narrator's hope for assimilation into prison society fails, the propulsive energy imparted to the narrative by the hermeneutic code also falters. A final reminder is given of the original enigma—the question of the narrator's biography—but in a phrase that again denies its significance: "Although my wife and my friends were also imprisoned in the other buildings, I had no thoughts of them" (p. 680a/*364a*). The nomination that would resolve the enigma never occurs, nor has the narrator succeeded in establishing a new identity for himself through association with the other prisoners. The narrative, its momentum arrested, now becomes absorbed with images of death: the female goat and her kid perish, and the goat thief begins his inevitable weakening under the guards' cruel treatment. Significantly, it is the goat thief who reveals to the narrator that it is death that underlies (both physically and figuratively) the prison structure when he brings the narrator to the window of the prison morgue and points out the corpse of a prisoner at whose side he had once labored. The face of the corpse comes to haunt the narrator obsessively: when he tries to read the magazines and newspapers that are his final ties with the outside world, they are obscured by the image of this face, which spreads out before his eyes "like a strange, disordered painting," the stasis of death obliterating the linearity of the written word.

Yet the text does not self-destruct with the blocking of the hermeneutic code, but finally resorts to another strategy of survival through the introduction of a subsidiary narrator, the pickpocket. For the duration of its telling, the pickpocket's story forestalls the demise of the narrator's own discourse that we now perceive to be inevitable. His story, though of some thematic relevance, offers an integral plot totally disconnected from the main plotline. The original narrator is reduced to the passive audience of this story, which "unfolds like a regular motion picture . . . blocking out the image of the corpse's face that had disturbed my sleep" (p. 681b/*365*).

In several ways, the pickpocket provides a revealing contrast to the goat thief. He is above all a survivor, a seasoned criminal whose spirit has remained resilient in spite of five previous imprisonments. He is wise to the workings of the law and has an established identity within the interrelated worlds of delinquents and police, as evidenced by his nickname, Scarface. Unlike the theft of the goats, his crime is a self-conscious act of defiance and even nationalism, directed as it is against a foreigner (curiously enough, a Russian). He could have avoided his present imprisonment if he had succumbed to the policeman's bribe; his decision not to succumb is at heart a political statement, a refusal to play the corrupt game of the law. It is this degree of political awareness that makes it possible for him to express what is clearly the didactic heart of the story: "Those who live off thieves are worse than the thieves themselves" (p. 684b/*368a*). Though his story embodies this theme, the goat thief would have been unable to voice it, portrayed as he is by the text as innocent of ideology. The narrator, though awash in the trappings of ideology, has not earned the right to voice this theme because of his failure to actualize his ideological commitments in his associations with the other prisoners. The pickpocket, as self-conscious thief, has been introduced into the text above all as a device to allow the surfacing of ideological dogma. Through this device the narrator is, as it were, tautologically reduced to the recipient of his own message.

The suppressed message voiced, the narration faces the deaths toward which it has ineluctably moved. The male goat exhausts its own dung, on which it had fed, and expires. The narrator's hope, the ideals rekindled by the Russian children, would seem to have expired as well. He turns again for consolation to his view of the ocean and goes so far as to bar the window in the rear with its view of the prison yard. In response to the Russian children, who have written to him on the eve of their departure for Russia, he repeats the equivocation with which he had earlier blocked the progression of the hermeneutic sequence: "Yes, my dear little friends, I am still watching the ocean . . . " (p. 686b/*369b*). Now, however, the narrator's contemplation of the sea is replete with new ambiguities. The robust goat thief, whose identity the narrator once craved, has been humiliated and finally exterminated by the text; the morally depleted narrator, whom we once saw willingly dissolve before the thief's sufficiency, lives on, aging but "healthy." A transference of life forces has indeed taken place: the physical vibrancy of the goat thief has been ground in the mill of the intellectual's narrative. The concluding sections of the story have offered a series of sacrificial victims—the goats as well as human substitutions like the goat thief—whose violent expulsion has ensured the perpetuation of prison society, of the narrator's privileged position within it, and indeed, of such literary efforts as the narrator produces. The narrator's smile at the conclusion is at least partially the ironic smile of the survivor, now resigned again to his meaningless incarceration. If the smile expresses some remnant of hope, it is a hope displaced to those in the outside world who have no use for him: the children in their enlightened homeland, or the politically awakened underclass (represented by the pickpocket) in his own. The white hair the narrator sheds on the children's letter is no other than the traditional mark of the disaffected Chinese literati who, self-nurtured on an intransitive discourse of moral consolation, are doomed to watch their powers decline against the backdrop of a corrupt, disregarding society.

"Goats" offers anything but the tight interrogative structure promised by its opening sections. After the jamming of direct questions about the narrator's identity and the narrator's further failure to integrate himself within prison society, the hermeneutic code ceases to operate, and the formal energies that the code would regulate in a "well-made" Western short story are dispersed. This dispersal of energies, however, is liberating in that it allows Xiao Jun to explore from several directions the modern Chinese intellectual's search for a voice. The three very different episodes that compose the story may be said to represent three possible directions for Chinese fiction in the 1930s. The episode with the Russian children offers a naive, "romantic revolutionary" story line, in which utopian possibilities of the human spirit override a restrictive social environment. The goat thief is the protagonist of a "naturalistic" drama in which an exemplary member of the lower classes is brought to ruin by society. The pickpocket is the hero of a "socialist realist" parable, as yet not too strident, in which the politically aware protagonist defies his oppressors. Since the story is not finally structured with the organic formal model that underlies the hermeneutic code, these episodes must be drawn together didactically in a manner more reminiscent of Chinese traditional fiction than of the Western model the story appeared to imitate at its opening. "Closure" as the moment of decipherment of the hermeneutic code is replaced with the pronouncement of the story's "moral," carefully situated in the subsidiary narrative of the pickpocket.

The text's revealed "truth" is finally trivial; the story's moral power arises not from its revelation, but from the drama of the narrator's perplexed identity and his search for assimilation within the prison community. The narrator and the goat thief enact a crucial encounter, staged frequently in modern Chinese literature, between the effete, self-questioning intellectual and the morally pure, socially victimized peasant. As in "Goats," these encounters typically end in the intellectual's failure to overcome the linguistic and class barriers that ensure his privileged segregation. The intellectual narrator, as master of language and proprietor of literature, survives, and with him the continued possibility of the narrative form in which he writes, but the legitimacy of that form is set in radical doubt. The formal disturbances we have analyzed in "Goats" are finally the result of the narrator's sense of parasitism and his concomitant insecurity of voice. Unable to erase the difference that separates himself from the goat thief and that defines him (an erasure that would simultaneously bring the annihilation of the narrative itself), the narrator retreats to his privileged contemplation of the sea. His participation in the social upheaval around him is reduced to passive observation of the proletarian "motion picture," flickering endlessly and vainly over his twilight consciousness. The closure of "Goats" is neither liberating nor catastrophic, but the whimpering reiteration of the unresolved—and perhaps insignificant—enigma of the narrator's identity. The narrator persists in life, but his existence is, like language itself in Maurice Blanchot's formulation, "the life that endures death and maintains itself in it."[10]

Notes

1. Roland Barthes, *S/Z* (New York: Hill and Wang, 1974), p. 19.
2. The term "hermeneutics" has a long history in Western thought: its original sense of "biblical exegesis" was broadened by the nineteenth-century philosophers Fr. Schleiermacher and Wilhelm Dilthey, who by "hermeneutics" meant the investigation of man's communication through cultural objects as a kind of intellectual activity fundamentally different from that required in the natural sciences. Contemporary "philosophical hermeneutics," best represented by Paul Ricoeur and Hans-Georg Gadamer, has further broadened the meaning of the word to refer to all systematic inquiry into the interpretive practices of man. Rejecting the earlier hermeneuticists' romantic notion of understanding as total subjective recuperation of the author's experience, Ricoeur and Gadamer have accepted the linguistic nature of human understanding asserted by the structuralists, but, unlike the structuralists, they have insisted on seeing all processes of interpretation as historically determined. Interpretation is a "fusion of horizons" or "dialogue" between historically bound text and context-bound interpreter. The philosophical hermeneuticists' sense of interpretation is thus very close to the Nietzschean one ("There are not facts, only interpretations") to which Barthes approvingly refers in *S/Z* (p. 5). Properly understood, a "hermeneutics" of the text would consider all the ways the reader finds significance in the text; in the context of *S/Z*, it would mean the reflexive investigation of the process of code decipherment itself.
3. Susan Sontag, *Against Interpretation* (New York: Delta, 1966), pp. 3–14.
4. Barthes, *S/Z*, p. 76.
5. Ibid., p. 62.

6. These five questions, in their most basic formulations, are: Who is Sarrasine? Who are the Lantys? Who is the old man? Who is the model for the Adonis? Who or what sex is La Zambinella?

7. Ibid., p. 62.

8. The first page reference given here is to the original publication of "Yang" (Goats) in the journal *Wenxue* (Literature) 5.4 (October 1, 1935). The second reference (in italics) is to Howard Goldblatt's English translation, included in *Modern Chinese Stories and Novellas 1919–1949*, ed. Joseph S. M. Lau, C. T. Hsia, and Leo Ou-fan Lee (New York: Columbia University Press, 1981), pp. 352–69. All subsequent page references will be in this format. All the translations are my own.

9. Cf. René Girard, *Violence and the Sacred* (Baltimore: Johns Hopkins University Press, 1972).

10. Maurice Blanchot, "Literature and the Right to Death," in *The Gaze of Orpheus* (New York: Station Hill, 1981), p. 54.

4

THE DIALECTICS OF STRUGGLE
Ideology and Realism in Mao Dun's "Algae"

Yi-tsi Mei Feuerwerker

I

MAO DUN's story "Shuizao xing" (Algae), which has also appeared under the title "Shengde zhengzha" (The struggle of life), opens with a bleak and oppressive wintry scene that has apparently subdued all within it:

> The northwest wind had been blowing hard for two days, and in the tiny village you could hardly hear a dog bark. (p. 137)[1]

But immediately in the next sentence the theme of opposition is introduced.

> The sky was a boundless leaden color, except where at the eastern horizon a pale yellow patch weakly, yet stubbornly, appeared to be trying slowly to melt away that leaden-colored cover of a sky.

This opposition, feeble but unmistakably asserting itself in the natural setting, is carried out on several other levels of the text and indeed constitutes one of its basic structural principles. The oppositional pattern is paralleled in the contrast between the two main characters and their relationship, in their mutual struggle against natural and social forces, and in the competition between the feelings of hostility and compassion, and it continues onto the problematic outcome at the end of the story.

Late in Mao Dun's life, he wrote in his memoirs, which began serialization in 1978, regarding "Algae" that what he "particularly took pains to depict were two peasants whose temperaments, physiques, thinking, and emotions were diametrically different (*jieran butong*)." He was referring to the two main characters in the story, Xiusheng, the weak, sickly nephew, "a peasant who had been completely crushed (*yakua*) by life," and his uncle Caixi, in which Mao Dun attempted to "portray the image of a true Chinese peasant, healthy, optimistic, honest, decent, brave. He loved labor, despised the forces of evil, nor did he feel bound by the fetters of feudal ethics in human relationships." Lu Xun had solicited the story for the Japanese periodical *Kaizo*, and it was the only work that Mao Dun had ever published first outside China. Through Caixi, a "true master of the Chinese earth," Mao Dun wished to tell foreign readers, "This is what Chinese peasants are like, not as depicted in Pearl Buck's *The Good Earth*."[2] What Mao Dun could have added was that the two representative peasant images as portrayed in "Algae," while mutually contradictory in many respects, were nevertheless both essential to the developing revolutionary ideology of Chinese communism.

When in the late 1920s the Communist Party discovered the peasant as the "rural proletariat" and the true vanguard of revolution, the idea of just who this peasant was became an important issue. On the one hand, the peasant was impoverished, downtrodden, brutalized, a victim crushed and weighed down by multiple oppressions; on the other, he possessed within himself the resources, vitality, and buoyant energy to carry out a spontaneous revolution. Such a double image meant that a revolution based on the countryside, such as the party had undertaken, could be both imperative and achievable.

Mao Dun's 1936 story does not explicitly mention the socialist revolution to come, but the temperament and fate of the two main characters are used to illustrate both the desperate situation of the countryside and its potential for heroic rebellion. In the process of portraying these two antithetical images of the peasant, however, and through them the dualism of a revolutionary ideology, the narrative—in yet another oppositional pattern of the story—shuttles the reader between two modes of literary realism: one, a realism that has been called "critical," representing the dark and negative side of reality; and two, a realism that is "socialist" or "revolutionary," representing its bright and positive side.

The emergence of realism as a self-conscious literary method was based historically on a notion of reality as conceived by nineteenth-century positivistic science, on the reality of an intelligible world of coherence and order "out there," which could be "represented objectively," through a more or less transparent text, "as it is." Such a realism, which, as a method of art, in René Wellek's words, actually has "its set conventions, devices, and exclusions,"[3] and which has been radically put to question by recent poststructuralist criticism, nonetheless remains operative in what may be called the "common-sense" and "natural" view that continues to be premised on the belief in a direct, reflecting relationship between the fictional text and the world.

In Chinese Marxist criticism, realism is everything, indeed the only correct literary mode, but while inheriting the nineteenth-century positivist concept of realism, the critics also insist that the representation of reality by realism not be regarded as ideologically neutral or value free.[4] The term realism then will always need to be "qualified" by appropriate preceding modifiers, depending on its placement in the historical time scale as marked by revolution. Realism could depict the evils and hardships of prerevolutionary society, especially through the plight of its oppressed and humiliated—including peasants—and thus be reformist and "critical." In the "common-sense" view, "critical realism" may be a tautology, since a critical stance is usually implied, but the term is required by Marxist critics in order to contrast it with "socialist" or "revolutionary realism."[5] This second kind of realism is guided by a revolutionary vision of reality that is coming into being and thus portrays a world less "as it is" than as it will be or ought to be. Defeat or tragic endings will therefore only be the prerogatives of critical realism, as they cannot be accommodated within the historical optimism of the socialist realist literary mode.

The coexistence in "Algae" of two contrasting concepts of the peasant, the multiple oppositions set up in the narrative, including the questions raised about the characters' fate as we leave the story—whether tragic consequences may still be around the corner even as the action ends with a moment of celebration—represent an uncertain transitional state between the two modes of realism. While the text reaches for a socialist realist conclusion, it opens up gaps and creates indeterminacies that are at odds with such an explicit program, and thus resists a final settled or definitive reading. Because of this less than complete transformation, Marxist critics, who are wont to perceive the history of modern Chinese literature as a linear development from naturalism and critical realism to socialist or revolutionary realism, have said little about "Algae" and its dichotomous structural pattern.[6]

II

The contention in nature between the leaden-colored sky cover and the pale yellow patch in the east with which the story opens sets the scene for the entrance of its two antagonists. Caixi, "a big tall fellow approaching forty," emerges from one of the low huts, and his first words, as he strides out and looks up at the sky, are to curse the wintry weather, "Damn it! It's going to snow." We are soon introduced to a "dark black object squirming in the corner [of the hut]; this was Xiusheng" (p. 138). Although younger by ten years or so, Xiusheng is enervated by jaundice and intimidated by the village tyrant: in fate and temperament he is the opposite of his uncle. These two antithetical peasant characters furthermore are sexual rivals; the baby about to be borne by Xiusheng's wife is in all probability Caixi's. Uncle and nephew are thus further set against each other in a triangular relationship, which, as the story suggests, is potentially violent and deadly. "One of these days for sure," Xiusheng is quoted as saying, "it'll be a white knife going in, a red knife coming out!" (p. 140).

But subsisting at the edge of existence, the two peasants must join hands to fight against hostile natural forces, brave the blinding, swirling snow and the northwest wind that continues to blow throughout the greater part of the story, in order to wrest from their harsh environment the only stuff left to them—the algae growing in the river—for fertilizing their fields. The main action of the story centers around this algae-gathering effort; next year's spring planting, the coming harvest, and their hope for continuing survival depend on the successful outcome of this expedition.

Caixi and Xiusheng must contend also with forces of social and economic oppression, personified in the story by the village head, the local "big shot" (*da renwu*) who is hounding them for the interest they owe Master Chen, and mercilessly extorting their labor or their money for a public road-building project. So the close relationship between Caixi and Xiusheng is marked simultaneously by a rivalry and interdependence that generates contrary emotions of hostility and compassion.

These are among the oppositions that will create tensions and conflicts, and that continually, as the action of the story unfolds, struggle for resolutions. The complexity of "Algae" arises from the way the conflicts are constructed to interpenetrate and complicate one another before arriving at the conclusion, a conclusion that moreover leaves open the possibility of alternative readings generated by the dual ideological formulas and codes of realism informing the narrative.

"Algae" gives the initial impression of being the least "sociological" of Mao Dun's fictional works; instead, the story seems to dwell for the most part on the strains of human existence as they manifest themselves on a more instinctive, "primitive" level. There the sexual rivalry and man's confrontation with nature are both meshed in the elemental fight to survive. On this same level, the overall movement of the story would seem to be toward hope, reconciliation, even triumph. But before we reach the end, the historico-political dimension, merely suggested at the beginning, intrudes dramatically with the confrontation between Caixi and the village head. It is most particularly when he stands up to this representative of oppressive authority and momentarily wins that Caixi assumes his "historical" function of embodying the peasant's inherent capacity for social revolution. Although up to this moment he has been shown to be a consistent winner vis-à-vis nature and his rival, the practical result of his challenge to the political establishment is left shrouded in uncertainty. By all the laws of the external historico-political world, his defiant act will have inescapable consequences. The story mentions this as a distinct possibility but glosses over it by ending with the victorious hero Caixi leading the laughing and singing villagers as they unload the collected algae from the boats.

The reader who so far may have been led by the text to "naturalize"[7] it according to the norms of "common-sense" realism, assuming it to be modeled on a world that he can identify as "things as they are," finds himself either projecting a different kind of ending—Caixi's ominous fate, as the authorities come down on him—or adjusting to the new direction the text has taken. The story's slide into the direction of socialist realism requires it to be judged by a different set of norms, under which Caixi's glorious exit can become appropriate or "natural." With such a shift in orientation, the issue is not so much whether Mao Dun has succeeded in transfiguring the struggling, oppressed peasant into an invincible revolutionary hero, but whether he has managed to integrate the various levels and elements in the story into a unified fictional structure, and in fact how much that matters.

Examples of heroic peasants in works of socialist realism fiction were not lacking in other stories of the 1930s, but it is questionable if Mao Dun himself ever "made it all the way" as an acceptable socialist realistic writer. In his later fiction he returned to his early interest of writing about the petty bourgeois and focused primarily on exposing the evil and corruption of life under the Guomindang during the years of the Sino-Japanese War, rather than on the revolutionary possibilities of the countryside. While his prestige as a writer has remained very high in the People's Republic of China, for all practical purposes he withdrew from the writing of fiction after 1948. "Algae" may be regarded as an unfinished foray of one of modern China's most successful practitioners of critical realism into the realm of socialist realism about halfway in his fiction writing career, and its dual orientation gives rise to the dialectic tensions in the text.

III

The main action of the story is simple and straightforward enough. It is restricted to two days in the life of a few peasants in the Jiangnan area (the delta region of the lower Yangtze River) during the winter season. The area is familiar to us through Mao Dun's other stories of the countryside, displaying the characteristic broad, flat landscape crisscrossed by waterways, made distinctive by the local customs, agricultural practices, and peculiar dialectical expressions he so carefully noted. Events are presented in a logical and chronological manner, their compositional sequence (the way they occur in the text) coinciding with their dispositional sequence (the way they would occur in "life"). A reference to a definite historical event locates the story specifically in time, and, as it were, in the "real," or the reader's, world. Normally the peasants in that area use soybean cakes, made out of meal compressed with the bean husks after the oil has been extracted, for the all-important second fertilization of the rice crop, but

> one year there had been a so-called incident in the region that produced bean cakes, so the price of bean cakes went up year by year. Peasants could not afford to buy them, and the soybean cake companies went bankrupt. (p. 141)

The "incident" is the Japanese occupation of the Northeast provinces on September 18, 1931, and explains why the poor peasants are reduced to only a first application (*touyong*) of fertilizer. The "best material for it was said to be the algae in the river, what was called *wencao* in Xiusheng's village."

The plight of the peasant in Mao Dun's more famous "Spring Silkworms" was caused by the near bankruptcy of China's silk factories when cheaper Japanese silk flooded the markets of New York and Lyons, and by the price fixing of the cocoon and mulberry leaf trust companies, so that the harder the peasants worked and the more they produced, the more heavily in debt and the worse off they were.[8] In comparison, although the village head comes around to dun the peasants for owed interest, less attention is paid in "Algae" to establishing a meticulously worked out economic and historical context. Here the peasants' experiences are emblematic rather of the continuing age-old struggle of man to survive against the world around him. The process of collecting algae is presented as a test of his ability to endure nature's harsh conditions and also to understand and exploit its possibilities:

> Algae could only be collected in the winter when the northwest wind had been blowing; the wind piled the algae together in one place, making it easier to scoop up. But the bitter cold in the open country was really hard to endure.
>
> Deprived of bean cakes, the peasants could do nothing but stake their lives on this struggle for life. (p. 141)

Caixi and Xiusheng go now for algae because the weather conditions, carefully set up from the opening sentences of the story, are right; but as they set out to brave the wind and cold in their small dilapidated boat, their expedition is also an incarnation of what Northrop Frye has called the romance-quest;[9] it is another enactment of man's wish-fulfillment dream to overcome the odds, survive, and win. The action of "Algae" conforms to the pattern of the three stages of the successful quest identified by Frye: the perilous journey, the crucial struggle, the exaltation of the hero. But Mao Dun's use of this "universal" theme (although Frye's examples are all Western) reverberates with echoes from Chinese literature, some of which go back to its very beginnings. The difficult journey by water, whether in search of the loved one, a distant lord, an elusive goddess, religious transcendence, or erotic ecstasy, is a frequent theme in the *Shijing* (Book of songs) and the *Chuci* (Songs of the South).[10] Such poetic and mythic resonances in this story of twentieth-century realism contribute to the possible apotheosis of the hero Caixi as he engages in his quest for the sustenance of life.

The central character Caixi, or, more strictly, the person-like abstraction we construct out of the pattern of certain elements and motifs that are dispersed throughout the text, is tailored for the success of this quest. He has the knowing eye, or rather, the discerning nose, to keep on climatic conditions—he can sniff the degree of moisture in the air—and moves quickly and decisively when he senses the weather will be changing soon, persuading the timid Xiusheng to go along. His physique, vigor, skill, and determination equip him to take on the antagonistic forces of nature and turn them adroitly to his own use. The following passage is an example of Caixi in action:

> The northwest wind played with the free end of Caixi's blue cotton sash, again and again entangling it round the bamboo punt pole. Caixi offhandedly took hold of the sash and wiped the sweat off his face, then with a loud swash, the pole hit the frozen earth of the river bank, the rim of the boat splashing up a jet of silver white spray. Oo-ah! A powerful cry came from Caixi's thick chest, as fast as flying the pole was deftly turned round, striking the water on the other side of the boat. With both hands Caixi pressed down on the top of the pole, gave a push and then with a pull, whirled the dripping four-meter-long pole once again over his head.
>
> He seemed to have found a target to vent his anger and wielded the pole with greater and greater energy, while all over him trickled the hot sweat of victory. (pp. 141–42)

The frequent use of onomatopoeia and the imitative movement of the prose capture the exhilarating rhythm of the man's efforts as he enters into a combative yet collaborative relationship with nature, simultaneously working with and overcoming the forces of wind and water. Indeed, the language of this sequence of motions suggests through analogy that Caixi, once picked out by the anthropomorphized wind, has himself become a force of nature. Under the pressure of strong animalistic emotions he emits one of the four long and loud cries that punctuate the story's action. His earthiness, physical exuberance, and acute senses, in particular the olfactory one, specially important to Mao Dun as an erotic stimulant, are repeatedly emphasized. Man and nature are further linked by the animal imagery used to describe both: "the river meandered westward like a black python" (p. 137), the "scull became a live dragon in Caixi's hand" (p. 145).

Some years earlier in an article on "China's Soviet Revolution and the Creation of a Proletarian Literature," Mao Dun had referred to the "peasant's primitive tendency to resist" (*nongminde yuanshi fankangxing*) as material for the proletarian literature of the future.[11] Certain notions about "primitive man" had become popular during the 1930s, evinced in the interest in works by Zola, O'Neill, and particularly in such plays by Cao Yu as *Wilderness* (published the same year as "Algae") and *Peking Man*.[12] The glorification of "primitivism" plays a part in the conception of Caixi as a heroic figure. His sexual entanglement with his niece-in-law, a woman "overflowing with youthful vitality," is a "natural" extension of his animal energy and exuberance; it is also a source of life for the next generation that is apparently not available from her "sick ghost of a husband." "Food and sex are [demanded by] human nature" (*shi se xing ye*), as the ancient philosopher put it,[13] and both of these instinctive drives are emphasized in Caixi's makeup as well as in the action of the story.

Toward the end, Caixi's physical power lifts him to the status of a superman. He is the only one, the villagers say in chorus, who will be able to loosen the hard, frozen mixture of algae and mud. And as Caixi comes on in the last scene, wielding his big iron-toothed rake, the image is reminiscent of the heroic warriors or *haohan* in traditional fiction. He is compared to the "*wuding* cutting away mountains," the five legendary strong men in that sixth-century compilation of geography, history, folklore, and myths, the *Shuijing zhu* (Commentary on the classic of waterways).[14] Thus, in the story's closing moments we have the "exaltation of the hero," the final stage of the successful romance-quest. That the character of Caixi harks back to the mythical figures of the popular imagination is also suggested in the title of the story, which literally translates as "the ballad (*xing*) of algae," *xing* being an ancient narrative or lyrical poem or song of folk origin, usually concerning the life of the common people or addressed to social themes.[15]

"Algae" tells us nothing about Caixi's origins or his early history, nothing more than that at almost forty, he had arrived about a year ago to live under the roof of his nephew. This has been time enough for him to become a hero, for he is both a disrupter of the status quo through his involvement with his niece-in-law, and an established leader in the village, outperforming everyone in the community. His nephew, the pathetic Xiusheng, has not only lost out in the sexual competition, he functions as a foil to enhance Caixi's heroic image. During the algae expedition, a testing ground for the two characters, the performances of the two peasants in the physical struggle against nature are constantly placed in contrast, Xiusheng's anemic ineffectiveness everywhere setting off Caixi's prowess and determination.

Xiusheng can only exercise what power he has by abusing someone weaker, by kicking or attempting to throttle his pregnant wife. He is utterly helpless when, as head of the household, he is enjoined to pay up the interest on his loan or pressured to work on the road-building project. Giving in or giving up is his only response to multiple oppressions:

> "I'm tired of living. From one year's end to the next they're after me for grain, for taxes, for debts, hounding me to death! If I eat today there'll be nothing tomorrow, I pawn my summer clothes, but can't get my winter ones back, I'm sick all over. . . . I'm tired of living! Living is nothing but misery!" (p. 146)

In contrast to Caixi, the peasant as superhero, Xiusheng is the peasant as victim; brutality, despair, and sheer wretchedness constitute his total existence. He is the favored target of rapacious landlords and bullying local tyrants. When the village head arrives to demand that he either put in three days of corvée or pay three dollars to hire a substitute laborer, Xiusheng can only yell in misery again about giving up his life: "I'll go! I don't have any money, but I do have a life! If I die on the road, they'll at least have to give me a coffin to lie in!" (p. 151)

These very same powers of oppression seem miraculously to circumvent Caixi until this same moment in the next to last section of the story, when he has his one confrontation with the village head. Up to this point we have been observing this giant of a man operating in the open air, triumphing confidently over a series of natural and familial adversaries. But as he returns from town and enters the dark hut, his eyes at first unable to discern the lurking figure of the village head inside, he finds himself face to face with a less predictable sinister power: a small-time representative of the political system that wields life and death power over the peasants, and that even more than the harsh winter, the blowing snow, and the recalcitrant algae has contributed to their sufferings. Is Caixi's pattern of victory to be sustained? Initially, and in contrast to Xiusheng, he appears able to dispose of the village head easily enough:

> "We don't have a cent for you!" Caixi threw down the packet of medicine, and his arms, like a pair of steel tongs, grabbed hold of the village head's chest. "Get out, you dog!" (p. 151)

While Caixi seems for the moment to have gained the upper hand, the story indicates there are unavoidable consequences for such insubordination. "Outside the door, the village head let loose a torrent of abuse, threatening to report to the 'bureau.' " Xiusheng may be too easily terrorized by the system, but his anxious question does raise a practical issue, which is hardly addressed by the answer of bravado he gets:

> "Oh, Caixi, what'll we do when he reports to the bureau and they come to get you?"
>
> Xiusheng was gasping as he spoke, his face as hot as if it were on fire.
>
> "Let them. The sky can fall; Caixi will be here." It was a calm and resolute answer. (p. 151)

Through the use of rhetoric, imagery, and mythical references, to say nothing of his almost supernatural prowess in contending with the elements of nature, Caixi has often been lifted to the status of a near mythical folk hero, whereas Xiusheng remains the creature and victim of specific social and economic conditions. In this scene within the murky hut, Caixi the superhero has been thrust back into a concrete historico-political situation—and, one might add, onto the level on which Xiusheng exists. Their contrasting responses to the local tyrant and the political establishment behind him reflect not only their different characters, but also the fact that through much of the story the two peasants are presented as functioning on two different levels of (fictional) reality.

IV

Along with the rivalry between the two peasants and their mutual struggle against natural and social forces, there is a more subtle inward moral drama that takes place in "Algae." This is the one going on mainly within Caixi, the sentient center of the story. When the story begins, the third-person omniscient narrator is located far above, taking a bird's-eye view of the geographical setting, the agricultural background, the historical context of the events. The story then closes in on Caixi as he emerges from the small hut and initiates the action. With few exceptions, his is the consciousness we enter into, or the "focalizer"[16] we are made to follow; we are given his visual impressions of the landscape, his view of the other characters, his assessment of the situation. The emotions of triumph, resentment, remorse, and self-doubt, which give the external happenings their psychological depth, are experienced only by him. He is forced to come face to face with the repercussions of his behavior; torn between the opposing emotions of hostility, remorse, and compassion, he must at one point decide what course he will take.

This is the other major "action" that occurs during the algae-gathering expedition, and it reaches a climax in section 4, the longest one in the story. Caixi and Xiusheng have been quite successful in their efforts and have already harvested the best part of the algae. Caixi gives out to the villagers in other boats that they are going home but in fact decides to go farther north into another tributary of the river, where he expects they will gather an even greater harvest. Exuberant and confident as the boat enters into new waters, he begins to sing a humorous and bawdy song about marital infidelity. To Xiusheng, every word seems directed toward his own painful situation. He suddenly stands up to protest:

> "Cai . . . xi! . . . Do you have to go on with that singing? —I'm good for nothing, sick, I can't work, but as long as there's a breath left in me, I'd rather starve to death than be a turtle [cuckold] with my eyes open!" (p. 146)

This outburst brings their conflict over the woman directly and fully out into the open for the first time, an unprecedented state of affairs that leads to the story's most extended dramatized scene.[17] Caixi has toiled his utmost to keep the family going, and what he takes now to be marching orders at first anger him.

> "All right, so I'll go then!" said Caixi coldly, unconsciously slowing down on his sculling.
>
> Xiusheng seemed not to have expected such a reaction, and at loss how to answer, dispiritedly squatted down again.
>
> "But," continued Caixi coldly and sternly, "you're not allowed to beat your wife anymore. A woman like that, and still you're not satisfied? There's a child in her belly, a shoot off our family . . . "
>
> "It's none of your business!" Xiusheng jumped up in a wild frenzy, his voice so shrill that it died away. "She's my wife, if I kill her, I'll pay for it!"

> "You dare, dare you?" Caixi sharply turned around, his fists tightly clenched, his eyes threatening Xiusheng's face. (p. 146)

What saves them from the physical violence that could have sent them over the brink at this critical moment is Xiusheng's "I'm tired of living" speech; it reminds them of their common overall plight.

> Slowly Caixi's head went down, his fists became unclenched; grief and anger filled his heart; it felt like it was on fire. With no one in charge of the pole, the boat swung sideways; instinctively Caixi took hold of the pole and gave it a push, but without taking his eyes away from his pitiful nephew. (pp. 146–47)

This is the turning point in the moral drama of the story, for at this moment Caixi realizes that just as it is up to him to take charge of the wayward boat, he must continue to bear the responsibility toward his nephew's family. This change in Caixi, as his hostility turns into compassion, pivots on the idea of life. According to traditional notions of justice, Xiusheng has the right to forfeit his life in payment for taking his wife's, since, as he claims, he has ownership over both. He is then led to observe that his life is not worth living anyway: thus, the sexual rivalry between the two men is subsumed under the broader issue of survival under adversity.

The turn in their relationship is paralleled by the sudden shift in the weather. Just when Caixi's anger flares up again—for the quarrel is soon resumed—the snow, which had been predicted with Caixi's very first words in the story, begins to fall. The situation changes dramatically—it now becomes an urgent matter for them to find their way home in the blinding snow. Xiusheng is too exhausted to do his share even if he is given the easy task of pulling and pushing the rope on which the long oar is hung. Not only is Caixi compelled to take over the whole job of poling the boat and getting them home, but when he sees Xiusheng "huddled in a heap and covered with snow," he takes his own tattered cotton jacket and covers him. He is filled with pity but also smitten with remorse for having "had that kind of thing with Xiusheng's wife."

> "Had I better not go then?" he asked himself. But he immediately reconsidered and answered himself: No! Once he left, would Xiusheng be able to do the work in the fields all by himself? . . .

> "The child is a flower! Xiusheng and Xiusheng's wife all must go on and live! What the hell would I be leaving for?" he cried out in his heart. (p. 149)

Caixi gives his chin a vigorous thrust, and his eyes shine as he makes this decision. In the oppositional drama of this extended section, compassion would seem to have won out.

But in "Algae," a story so rich in analogues between man and nature, the theme of compassion had actually been "planted" very early on with the tallow trees, which,

> stripped of their leaves reared their newly snapped branches, nobly combating the northwest wind. Those tallow trees were kindly mothers to the peasants; generally they required no special tending, but in winter when their black seed capsules burst into white tips, they sacrificed their slender fingers, endured thousands of knife wounds, and offered their tallow-rich capsules to supplement the peasants' livelihood. (p. 137)

Compassion is also shared in a brief scene between Caixi and Xiusheng's wife; he is solicitous of her heavily pregnant condition, and both feel guilt and sympathy toward the wronged Xiusheng. It is in the next to last section of "Algae," however, that the compassion theme reaches its culmination.

Caixi stands up to the village head to protect Xiusheng; the wife likewise makes a decision in favor of saving her sick husband. This happens when she places the various medicines Caixi has bought in town, medicines that "neither cured nor killed," as the narrator informs us, into the crock to brew. At the last moment she picks up the plaster, an important ingredient for bringing down fever, "gave it a few pinches with her fingers, as if unable to decide what to do, but finally added it to the pot also." Xiusheng had once bitterly accused them, "If I'm dead, you'll all be happy," yet these two lovers, not without some hesitation on the part of the wife, and with untold risks on the part of Caixi, each make the decision to help him live.

The story leaves uncertain what the end result of their compassion actually will be. Since both the efficacy of the medicine and the effectiveness of Caixi's defiance are put in question, we do not know whether these sacrificial acts will prove sufficient to cure or protect the possibly already dying Xiusheng. Nor does the story make explicit whether the strong peasant Caixi has undone himself in defying the authorities to save the husband of his mistress, whether he has carried his compassion toward the weak peasant Xiusheng, like the nurturing tallow trees yielding their limbs, to the point of self-sacrifice.

V

As we reach the end of "Algae," other gaps of indeterminacy are opened up, and how the various oppositions ultimately come out will depend on the approach the reader takes in his interpretation of the story. We are not dealing here with one of those texts that clearly "works towards an end that confers unity on the parts and permits the interpretation of a stable meaning,"[18] particularly since the end itself raises some new questions and can be subject to alternative readings.

The brief section that ends the text is festive in mood; the oppressive atmosphere with which the story opened has been lifted, and the action has moved into the bright sunshine. That feeble yellow patch in the first paragraph struggling to melt away the leaden-colored sky has now expanded into the golden sunlight enveloping and warming the tiny village and its people. They are busily moving the algae from the boats into the field reservoirs where it will be composted with garbage in readiness for spring planting. The stark branches of the beneficent tallow trees are enlivened with chirping sparrows.

The perilous journey-quest is over, the algae at last successfully gathered, the obstacles of nature overcome, human antagonisms put aside, and the forces of social oppression at least in momentary retreat. Thus, the multiple oppositions set up in the story can be said to be resolved, and thus would be one reading of the end of the story.

With this ending, which we may call the "utopian" or socialist realist ending, the narrated events reach the point where visionary expectations, the "happily ever after," can take over: in the stillness of the future that lies beyond the close of the narrative, changes or turns of fortune need not be considered. In conclusion is the socialist realist vision of the morrow:

> People stepped up their efforts, hoping to get all the algae in place before sundown, and hoping also that tomorrow would be another fine day, so that they could take their boats even farther to where there might be more. (p. 152)

The collective, the people, have leapt into sudden prominence in these closing paragraphs; ahead of them lie new possibilities and the bright hopes of a better future.

But this ending can be entertained only "at the expense" of leaving in suspension other issues raised by the text, more specifically, the individual fates of the two peasants who up to now have been the actual focus of the reader's attention. The sickly Xiusheng is left out of this conclusion, since he can have no place in a sunny celebration scene. He is presumably still lying inside the dark hut, his recovery, due to the dubious efficacy of the medicine, a far from certain thing.[19] And the sky could still fall on Caixi; nothing suggests that the threat of arrest hanging over his head has been removed. Both of these eventualities, which are pointed to in the next to last section, continue to be likely, and they would be more consistent with the political and social conditions of the period that the story takes pains to establish as its own historical context. Thus, it is possible to project another ending, what we may call the "historical" or "critical realist" ending, in which the pattern of oppression, struggle, suffering, and impending defeat, set in motion earlier by the story and powerfully arousing the reader's sympathetic response, is sustained. In this case, the answer to the argument that it is the socialist realist vision that has the last word (it has the last scene), and that therefore on the whole the "utopian" ending could be regarded as the true ending, would be that there is no clear indication as to how the utopian vision has displaced, or "taken care of," the view of historical reality the text itself offers.

Certain new oppositions are generated within the closing scene itself, heightening further its ambiguities. The central character seems to be simultaneously one of the villagers, joining them in their cheerful bustle and song, but also one who is set apart, his own "tragic and powerful cry" in opposition to their extemporaneous, happy, "meaningless ditties." While through his superhuman strength Caixi epitomizes the powerful revolutionary potential of the masses, he is also separated from them by his assuming of the lonely fate of the sacrificial hero; his alone is the individual consciousness that penetrates into and perceives the bitterness of collective struggle:

> They were laughing, shouting, working, and improvising meaningless ditties, and in the midst of all these voices, Caixi's long cry kept soaring up into the air, tragic and powerful. It seemed at once to be appeal and defiant protest. (p. 152)

In these final words of the story, the counterpoising of contrary adjectives and nouns in the split second before the narrative winds up harks back to Xiusheng's worried and unanswered question, and to the ominous fate that possibly awaits Caixi. His portentous and ambiguous cry, once again suggesting opposing alternatives, remains suspended in the air as the story fades out.

One reason why it is difficult to evaluate the meaning of Caixi's final action is the change in narrative distance in the last two scenes. Throughout the story, events have been selected and arranged to bring out the character's heroic qualities. Sometimes the narrator makes his presence known by means of an "overt judgmental voice,"[20] through the conspicuous use of admiring words and phrases to portray a heroic character. Caixi's "strong voice at once invigorated the atmosphere" (p. 138), "all over him trickled the hot sweat of victory" (p. 142). The mythical and folk-hero resonances of the account further reinforce his greatness. We are taken to follow him quite closely and at times penetrate into his inner life for his motivations, clearly directed as to what to think about this hero and his actions. But both when Caixi defiantly confronts the village tyrant and when he celebrates with the villagers in the final scene, the narrator withdraws to a distance and limits the narrative to an external presentation of events, thus cutting us off from insight into what might be going on in the hero's mind, from his own understanding of what is going on. We are left in the dark, for example, as to whether Caixi's sacrifice is a fully conscious one, or indeed, if self-sacrifice is what it is. The shift in narrative perspective removes the guidance of the narrator, overt up to this point, and the reader is left on his own.

Such are the indeterminacies[21] that invite the reader to make a choice between interpretive strategies as to how to read the story. The approach will determine whether the multiple dichotomies set up in the text—and emphasized in this essay—are seen as finally reconciled in a summarizing conclusion, or as setting up a "dialectical" process that lays bare the unresolved ambiguities of having things both ways. The reader can choose to see the text as a unique and unified structure with an ending that pulls together its various parts —theme, character, incident, imagery—and that confers a fixed shape and meaning retrospectively onto the whole. Or the reader can decide that "Algae" does not reach a clear definitive closure, because on its way there it has transgressed its own laws and does not finally make intelligible the relationships between its various parts. Even when contradictions seem reconciled, as in the long scene between the two peasants on the boat, residual obstacles remain or new uncertainties are put forward. This second approach opens the story to a pluralistic, deconstructive reading by dwelling on the gaps that are opened up in the text and are not completely bridged by the conclusion.

I am less interested in making the argument in favor of one approach or the other than in suggesting how this text, through the intricacy of its particular oppositional processes, enacts issues about the relationship among narrative structure, realism, and ideology. The challenge to reading the story as a coherent and unified text arises to a large degree from the story's problematic shift from the formal requirements of one mode of realism to another, a shift that in turn reflects the struggle to reconcile the duality of its ideological project.

VI

As a result of attacks by members of the Creation Society and others in the early 1930s, Mao Dun had been put on the defensive about his failure to produce characters who were "brave and worthy of worship . . . or flawless characters who could be models for everyone."[22] At first glance Caixi might appear to be Mao Dun's answer to his leftist critics. But with all his superiority, Caixi lacks the proper qualifications to be a model revolutionary peasant: his sexual entanglement with his niece-in-law transgresses the bounds of morality, and indeed seems to be a carry over from Mao Dun's earlier "naturalism" period. Moreover, as his uncertain fate in the story implies, Caixi is not proletariat hero enough to take charge of his own destiny after all; in the end, it is possible he may have not done better than sacrifice himself in a brave gesture of resistance.

The 1930s were a time when writers increasingly turned their attention to the new subject of the prerevolutionary peasant—the peasant as he was, so to speak, before the advent of the Communist Party. While works of critical realism stressed the sheer misery of the humiliated and the oppressed, works with socialist realist tendencies highlighted their capacity for revolutionary action. In his trilogy (published 1932–33) on the countryside, more particularly and more clearly in the first two stories, "Spring Silkworms" and "Autumn Harvest," Mao Dun had presented the two sides of the image of the peasant through two contrasting generations. Weighed down by a lifetime of toil and hardship, the fatalistic Old Tongbao dies to give way to his younger son Ah Duo, the heroic leader of raids on rice granaries, a harbinger of the revolutionary wave to come. What is unique and might be regarded as "retrogressive" in "Algae," because of its less clear-cut ideological orientation (*fangxiang*), is that the dual images of the peasant as victim and peasant as revolutionary hero are interlocked in contemporaneous opposition and interdependence and further bonded by their relationship with one woman, and their joint quest for the life-sustaining algae. The alternative perspectives offered in the story are not just a matter of Xiusheng the victim versus Caixi the hero, but become strikingly intertwined in the paradoxical fate of Caixi himself, the ever-victorious hero who could also be fated to lose out to the powerful forces arrayed against him.

Five years later, Mao Zedong, in his "Talks at the Yan'an Forum on Literature and Art," was to put an end to such moral and political ambiguities by setting clear standards for depicting the peasant heros of socialist realism, standards that Caixi, in spite of his great energy and strength and his spontaneous will to rebel, would not be able to meet. Moreover, the oppositional patterns of "Algae," which simultaneously exemplify the complex interrelations of its parts while opening it up to diverse meanings, make it into much too complex a literary work to be reduced to the illustration of any one particular ideological formula. The story does not unequivocally refer to a single preconception or view of the outside world that can then be found to be verified and reflected in the text.

One might argue that the story transcends narrow ideological bounds because it reflects a more complex world of reality. Mao Dun has been labeled a realist because of his consistent concern to place his fictional works in a verified historical context. The references to the Manchurian incident of 1931, and to the *baojia* system administered by the Guomindang in 1934, locate "Algae" quite precisely in historical time. As in his other fiction, references to contemporary political conditions, economic circumstances, and actual historical happenings are interwoven into the action. In his book on the representation of reality in Western literature, Erich Auerbach discusses the depicting of man "as embedded in a total reality, political, social, and economic, which is concrete and constantly evolving" to be an essential characteristic of the "serious realism of modern times."[23] Even if this should be the case with "Algae," it does not mean that the story need be evaluated by the criterion of historical accuracy, on whether it truly represents the situation in the countryside "as it really was" during the time of its production.

A critical commonplace is that the aim of realistic fiction is to "create the illusion of an objective outside reality."[24] Its creation of a "coherent and internally consistent fictive world"[25] in the text is based on the premise that an ordered and knowable reality exists externally and prior to the fictional construct that is offering itself as a realistic representation of that reality. From that point of view, "Algae" does not conform to the expectations of a realist text. In fact, its indeterminacies and possible alternative readings are an instructive reminder that the illusionistic presentation of reality is also shaped and determined by ways of looking at reality, by political ideologies that may contain their own internal contradictions. But if Mao Dun's story represents an exemplification of revolutionary ideological formula, what it primarily exemplifies is the underlying ambiguity of the formula, and perhaps even more, the "higher and more complex truth" that such ambiguity may be necessary to the revolutionary process.

Rather than two portraits of Chinese peasants "as they were" in the 1930s, what we see in "Algae" is a dramatization of the complexities of their oppositional yet mutually interdependent relationship in the emerging ideology of the Chinese revolution. The peasant as victim/hero would still require the vision and guidance of the Communist Party before being transformed into effective fighting revolutionary material. Conversely, his double-edged character could also be applied to explain somehow one of the great paradoxes in the Communist view of Chinese history: how it was that the peasant, so preeminently qualified to be the prime mover in history, had not succeeded in overthrowing feudalism and changing the world for the better in spite of thousands of years of repeated uprisings.

The dichotomized images of the peasant in "Algae," contradictory as they may be according to the logic of "reality," are both essential to the ideology and strategy of the revolution. Any revolutionary program requires the simultaneous entertaining of two opposites: an "impossible" utopian vision forever realizable only in the future, requiring superhuman heroes and a determined optimism; and a hard-headed recognition of the debilitating limitations of history, with its inevitable victims and irredeemable defeats. The suspension of definitive closure in "Algae," its multiple oppositions, its interpretive alternatives, as well as the equivocal fate of its two characters, look to both. Could not these together provide a sufficient base for forward movement? As Caixi says, whoever the actual peasant-father of the unborn child, it will come crawling out of the woman's belly, a seed of their family, ensuring its continuation into the future. As has been observed, with specific application to the Chinese revolution, had those who undertook to carry out the revolution ever known what it was they were trying to do, they would never have tried to do it. This may be true of any revolution. Might we not even conclude that the ambiguity created by the dialectical structure of Mao Dun's "Algae" is a reflection, on more than one level, of the indeterminate experience of those who have undertaken to revolutionize a refractory world?

Notes

1. Page references in parentheses are to my appended translation, found on pp. 137–52 of this volume. The text translated is "Shuizao xing" (Algae), in Mao Dun, *Yanyunji* (Smoke and mist) (Shanghai: Liangyou Printing Company, 1937), pp. 181–216. The story has also been translated by Simon Johnstone in *Chinese Literature* (Winter 1986): 14–27.

2. Mao Dun, "Kangzhan qianxide wenxue huodong—huiyilu (ershi)" (Literary activities on the eve of the War of Resistance—Reminiscences, no. 20), *Xinwenxue shiliao* (Historical materials of the new literature) 1983.3: 4–5.

3. René Wellek, "The Concept of Realism in Literary Scholarship," in Wellek, *Concepts of Criticism*, ed. Stephen G. Nichols, Jr. (New Haven: Yale University Press, 1971), p. 254.

4. Outside Chinese Marxist criticism, classic realism has also been described as an "ideological practice," which "roughly coincides with the epoch of industrial capitalism" but "effaces its own status as discourse." "Structuralist" or "poststructuralist" Marxists in the West have analyzed the complicity between realism and capitalist ideology. See Catherine Belsey, *Critical Practice* (London: Methuen, 1980), pp. 67–69, 72, and passim.

5. Socialist realism was accepted as the guiding principle in literature at the First Soviet Writers' Congress, 1934. For a discussion of the orthodox position, see Georg Lukács, "Critical Realism and Socialist Realism," in *Realism in Our Time: Literature and the Class Struggle*, trans. John and Necke Mander (New York: Harper & Row, 1971), pp. 93–135. In 1958, Chinese critics replaced the term with the phrase "the combination of revolutionary realism and revolutionary romanticism." An example of the assumed rough equation of realism with critical realism among non-Marxist critics can be seen in Michael S. Duke, "Chinese Literature in the Post-Mao Era: The Return of 'Critical Realism,' " in *Contemporary Chinese Literature: An Anthology of Post-Mao Fiction and Poetry*, ed. Michael S. Duke (Armonk, NY: M. E. Sharpe, 1985), pp. 3–6.

6. It receives half a page in Zhuang Zhongqing's comprehensive 400-page

study, *Mao Dun de chuangzuo licheng* (The development of Mao Dun's creative writing) (Beijing: Renmin wenxue chubanshe, 1982), p. 216. I am grateful to Professor Zhuang of Xiamen University for supplying a photocopy of one of the earliest versions of the story in *Yuebao* (Monthly) 1.6 (June 1937): 1321–26.

7. To "naturalize" a text is to make it readable by bringing "it into relation with a type of discourse or model which is already, in some sense, natural and legible." Jonathan Culler, *Structuralist Poetics: Structuralism, Linguistics, and the Study of Literature* (Ithaca: Cornell University Press, 1975), p. 138.

8. Mao Dun, "Wo zenyang xie 'Chuncan' " (How I wrote "Spring Silkworms"), in *Mao Dun lun chuangzuo* (Mao Dun on creative writing) (Shanghai: Shanghai wenyi chubanshe, 1980), pp. 68–69. The article was first published in *Qingnian zhishi* (Knowledge for youth) 1.3 (1945).

9. Northrop Frye, *Anatomy of Criticism, Four Essays* (Princeton: Princeton University Press, 1957), pp. 186–87.

10. One of the most beautiful examples in the *Shijing* is the fourth ode from the "Qin feng," "Jianjia cangcang/ bailu wei shuang/ suowei yiren/ zai shui yifang," in Waley's translation, "Thick grow the rush leaves; Their white dew turns to frost./ He whom I love/ Must be somewhere along this stream." See Arthur Waley, *The Book of Songs* (London: George Allen & Unwin, 1954), p. 42. The quest theme runs through the *Chuci*. Famous examples of the search along water include the "Xiang jun" (The Princess of Xiang) and "Xiang furen" (The Lady of the Xiang). See David Hawkes, *Ch'u Tz'u, the Songs of the South, an Ancient Chinese Anthology* (London: Oxford University Press, 1959), pp. 37–39.

11. Shi Hualuo [Mao Dun], "Zhongguo suweiai geming yu puluo wenxue zhi jianshe" (China's Soviet revolution and the creation of a proletarian literature), *Wenxue daobao* (Report on literature) 1.8 (1931): 15; reprinted in *Zhongguo xiandai wenxueshi ziliao* (Materials on modern Chinese literature) (Tokyo: Daian, 1968), 1:145.

12. I am grateful to Professor Yue Daiyun of Beijing University for bringing up these other literary examples of "primitive men."

13. *Mencius*, Book VI, part A, chap. 4. The remark is attributed to Gaozi.

14. Li Daoyuan, *Shuijing zhu* (Commentary on the classic of waterways) (Shijie shuju), 27:351.

15. *Xing* is found in the titles of many *yuefu* (Music Bureau) ballads, and of later poems written in imitation of the ballad style.

16. "Focalization" does away with much of the confusion surrounding the more common term "point of view." See Shlomith Rimmon-Kenan, *Narrative Fiction: Contemporary Poetics* (London: Methuen, 1983), pp. 71–74.

17. Mao Dun includes a long quotation from this scene in his "Reminiscences: no. 20," pp. 4–5. See note 2 above.

18. Alistair M. Duckworth, "*Little Dorrit* and the Question of Closure," in *Narrative Endings*, a special issue of *Nineteenth Century Fiction* 33.1 (June 1978): 117. Duckworth discusses the application of two kinds of critical reading to Dickens's long and complex novel: whether the reading "should seek 'protectively' to close a work or to open it through 'deconstructive' methods." He "closes" it in the end, having demonstrated his willingness to experiment with the deconstructive mode, pp. 114, 130.

19. This is not quite the same as the tendency to speculate on the life of

characters outside the fictional text, a tendency that has been attacked by L. C. Knights in "How Many Children had Lady Macbeth?" in *Explorations* (New York: New York University Press, 1964), pp. 15–54. The problem of Xiusheng's medicine is raised quite explicitly in the story.

20. Seymour Chatman, *Story and Discourse: Narrative Structure in Fiction and Film* (Ithaca: Cornell University Press, 1980), p. 241.

21. Indeterminacy and the dialectic relationship between text and reader in the reading process provide the base for Wolfgang Iser's theory of the aesthetic response. See Wolfgang Iser, "Indeterminacy and the Reader's Response in Prose Fiction," in *Aspects of Narrative*, ed. J. Hillis Miller (New York: Columbia University Press, 1971), pp. 1–45. The problem becomes much more acute in a text containing shifting norms.

22. Mao Dun, "Xie zai 'Ye qiangwei' de qianmian" (A preface to "Wild Roses"), in *Mao Dun yanjiu ziliao (zhong)* (Materials for the study of Mao Dun), ed. Sun Zhongtian and Cha Guohua (Beijing: Zhongguo shehui kexue chubanshe, 1983), 2:13. The preface was originally published in the 1929 edition of *Ye qiangwei.*

23. Erich Auerbach, *Mimesis: the Representation of Reality in Western Literature*, tran. Willard R. Trask (Princeton: Princeton University Press, 1953), p. 463.

24. Wolfgang Iser, *The Implied Reader: Patterns of Communication in Prose Fiction from Bunyan to Beckett* (Baltimore: Johns Hopkins University Press, 1980), pp. 102–103, 119–20, and passim.

25. Belsey, *Critical Practice*, p. 107.

5

THE TELLING OF SHI TUO'S "A KISS"
Few Words and Several Voices

Theodore Huters

SHI TUO (Wang Changjian) rose to prominence as a writer of short stories in the mid-1930s under the tutelage of Shen Congwen, during the latter's tenure as editor of the literary supplement to the liberal Tianjin newspaper *Dagongbao.* Perhaps as a result of the older writer's influence, Shi Tuo's early stories are largely set in the countryside, a countryside transfixed by a paralyzing combination of entropy and stagnation that, as C. T. Hsia has noted, is in certain respects similar to the rural decline envisioned in Lu Xun's seminal vision of village inertia.[1] Shi Tuo's wartime fiction continued in the same mood, although he extended his scope to include depictions of urban life. Of the wartime writing, *Guoyuan cheng ji* (Records of Orchard City) continues his preoccupation with life in backward rural areas. It is a varied collection of pieces unified only by a common setting, a persistently melancholic tone, and its publication between two covers in 1946. It contains eighteen mostly short tales that were written and published separately over the eight-year period from 1938 to 1946, a period, as Shi Tuo notes in his preface, almost identical in extent to the Chinese War of Resistance Against Japan.[2] Aside from a shadowy dramatized narrator who drops out toward the end of the collection, almost no characters appear in more than one story; the conventional unities of plot and time-sequence are dispensed with as well. The individual stories partake of this amorphousness, each having little in the way of character or plot development or even temporal unity.

"Yi wen" (A kiss), written sometime in 1944, is the penultimate story in the collection and was originally published in Japanese-occupied Shanghai in the magazine *Wanxiang* (Phenomena), edited by Ke Ling.[3] The tale is a deceptively simple piece of narrative told in two halves. The first half takes place just after the 1911 Revolution, but before its effects have reached such backwaters as Orchard City. Shi Tuo convincingly renders the sights and particularly the sounds of a small county city. Its bustle, its easy self-satisfaction, its petty fears, and its pervasive corruption are all given equal play. The pivotal events of the story are set in motion when, in an excessively boisterous moment, the adolescent apprentice Tigerfish kisses his childhood playmate Sister Liu. This event awakens Sister Liu's mother to the fact of her daughter's incipient maturity, and she quickly sells the young one off as a concubine to a rich old man while her virginity is still intact and at full market value. The drastic lack of proportion between the transgression and its consequences recalls the traditional "folly and consequences" stories[4] of the late Ming dynasty.

The short sentence, "time then passed by,"[5] connects the two parts of the tale; the second half consists of Sister Liu's return to a much declined city after a substantial number of years that the narrator cannot quite seem to specify. Arriving at the station, she takes a rickshaw into the city, pulled by none other than Tigerfish, whose apprenticeship at the tinsmith's came to naught when the shop in which he was employed failed. Tigerfish does not recognize Sister Liu, and most of the second half consists of dialogue between the two in which Sister Liu asks after the people and places she had known and is told by Tigerfish of their almost universally sorry fates. Upon reaching the intersection where she had once run a small food stall, she sees the devastation visited upon it by the intervening years and hastily orders Tigerfish to return to the station. In the last scene, she presents Tigerfish with a large tip, which provides the first definite indication that she has recognized him, and the author breaks in to announce his hopes that her children, should she have any, will be able to escape the sort of life that she has led.

The sketchiness of the plot, the distance the narrator keeps from his characters, and, in particular, the predominance of static description over narrative movement lend "A Kiss" many of the characteristics of a prose essay. The tale, in fact, falls into a nebulous area somewhere between story and essay. The generic imprecision of the piece extends to its thematic properties as well: the story's subject matter conforms neither to contemporary notions of rural decline nor to a more traditional idea of the powerful determinacy of fate. Zbigniew Slupski, in his perceptive remarks on Shi Tuo's novel *Ma Lan*, elegantly captures the writer's recusancy with the comment that "He starts from the assumption that every theme, plot, or motif in the story contains the germ of a certain conventional solution, which he is careful to avoid."[6] Shi Tuo was himself well aware of his tendency to depart from conventional expectation, for as he wrote in the preface to an earlier collection, *Limen shiji* (Records gleaned from the village home), of the "things" in the collection, "some resemble fiction, some resemble essays and some resemble nothing at all, but that cannot be helped."[7]

Contemporary Chinese critics were also well aware of Shi Tuo's characteristic departures from the norm. Wang Yao, for instance, although writing during the ideologically constrained 1950s, was very much in the mainstream of twentieth-century Chinese critical thought when he insisted upon treating the work more as an unmediated reflection of reality than as a literary artifact. He criticizes Shi Tuo for his inability to write up documentary accounts of the rural scene: "The work shows that even if a writer has a well-intentioned sense of what is right and relatively good technique, the significance of his work will be greatly diminished if he is removed from actual life, even should he be able to write up his recollections or things he has experienced."[8] For his part, Shi Tuo had long been inured to this propensity of critics to misunderstand him, as can be seen from his 1937 response to remarks that Li Jianwu—a critic of a very different persuasion from Wang Yao—had made about him the year before: "I am not sure what Chinese critics are up to; their tastes are decidedly narrow and they become uncomfortable whenever they see something that disturbs them." Shi Tuo goes on to add that "because of these barbs [of mine], admonition [from them] soon follows."[9]

Given the didactic bent of modern Chinese critics, it is perhaps understandable that most should either object to or thoroughly misconstrue Shi Tuo's literary iconoclasm. The coupling of political sanction to this literary judgment, however, significantly raised the stakes of this discourse. Wang Yao, for instance, does profess admiration for Shi Tuo's style. But he draws the predictable conclusion that in Shi Tuo's bleak 1930s' depictions of rural China, "we are able to see . . . scenes of the bankruptcy of [the country's] interior, but we cannot sense the underlying unrest."[10] The calmer but even glummer sketches that comprise the *Orchard City* collection inspire in Wang both respect for the writer's advances in craftsmanship and a palpable unease about the collection's theme: "The style is graceful and somewhat more crisp than before, but he only describes certain aspects of the city in its process of decline, and [there] is a pervading mood of sentimental dejection. It is as if the feudal order of the past is actually taken for a golden age worthy of fond memory.''[11] In passing this judgment, the critic admits of no possibility that Shi Tuo's focus might be on ways of remembering the past rather than on the simple representation of it. But even beyond this, he lays the text open to the charge of being an apology for political reaction.

In assessing a text that seems to bear such an adversarial relationship to its original context, the Western critic is left in something of quandary. One possibility would be to ignore the context and simply to apply a variety of critical methods that proclaim their universal applicability but that in fact are unavoidably and inextricably based on Western literary practice. Or the critic can attempt the difficult—if not impossible—task of deracinating himself or herself and trying to appreciate the story as its contemporaries would have understood it. The former course risks doing real violence to the horizon of meaning that gave the story whatever resonance it originally had, while the latter risks trivializing the text in a morass of arcane fact about original situation and audience that could end up almost defiantly ignoring any consideration of universal interest.

The problem in taking the former course of insisting upon finding some way to link Chinese and Western ways of looking at literature is rendered more acute by the fact that the most influential theories of literature developed in the West between the late 1920s and the 1970s were working in a field where, it was insisted, the issues of history and specific rhetorical traditions were essentially irrelevant. This denial of context also applies to the literary methodologies that coalesced more recently to form the field of "narratology," a discipline that must ultimately be traced back to a structuralist perspective that sought and generally found universal patterns of grammar and rhetoric within narrative work.

Since the early 1970s, however, literary theories have come to the fore that tend to focus both on the seams within what were once taken as smooth narrative textures and on the influences of context on the generation and reception of fictional work (i.e., deconstruction and reception theory). From the point of view of the analysis of Chinese literature, all of these approaches have the disadvantage of being based upon narratives produced within the Western tradition. From the structuralist perspective, with its insistence upon universality, this had never been seen as a problem. But the later theories, in insisting upon the significance of either textual lapses, on the one hand, or genetic factors, on the other, at least allow the critic room to question whether the specifics of Chinese culture may render attempts at analyzing Chinese literature through the glass of Western theory as unjust and distorting to the texts under examination.

It is interesting that structuralism has its roots in Russia, a country in which there has always been an ambiguous relationship with the West (and which was ultimately to serve an important function in mediating the West to China). Some have seen Russian formalism at least partly as a radical formulation reacting to a stale and fruitlessly eclectic late-nineteenth-century Russian disposition to borrow from Western models. In this view, formalism is something uniquely Russian rather than something growing out of the mainstream of the Western European tradition itself.[12] The response of M. M. Bakhtin and his circle to the formalists can be seen, in turn, as an effort at an equally radical counterassertion of historical relativism and the relevance of history to literature. According to Gary Saul Morson, the two movements share the spirit of "ritual inversion of European form" that Russian writers and critics "have celebrated [as] characteristically Russian."[13]

The upshot of this reaction to formalism was that, instead of obscuring historical and cultural particulars, Bakhtin in many ways anticipates some of the movements that developed as responses to structuralism in the West by insisting upon both the necessity of context and the uncertainties of the text. The most radical aspect of his thinking on this subject is that literary language, far from constituting a closed, self-referential circle, is so open that it can only be understood as a process of interaction between speaker and listener, and that all speaking profoundly anticipates an interlocutor's response. As he said, "every literary work *faces outward away from itself*, toward the listener-reader, and to a certain extent thus anticipates possible reaction to itself."[14] For the purposes of looking at literary communication across cultures, Bakhtin's view of textual flexibility not only demands maximum sensitivity to the particulars of each culture, but the very model of communication he sets forth virtually obliges the critic to take into account the nuances of reception and response that occur when literary ideas cross cultural boundaries. When applied to the enterprise of cross-cultural comparison, in other words, Bakhtin problematizes the very act of literary transmission itself.

Bakhtin believed the novel to be the literary form that best embodies the literary diversity he so prizes, since the form not only involves a relationship between text and reader, but also contains different "languages" that carry on dialogues among themselves within the individual work. The resulting mixture of these languages, which Bakhtin calls "heteroglossia," creates "images" of the modes of discourse available to a culture. It is through these images that languages reveal their basic relativity through various sorts of parody or "hybridization," "the mixing, within a single concrete utterance of two or more different linguistic consciousnesses, often widely separated in time and social space" (p. 429).

Like the linguistic structures from which it is built, the novel as a form must be seen as a kind of antigenre, in which the monologues of which other forms are constructed are forced into dialogue and robbed of their authority. Bakhtin thus saw the novel not only as central to modern literature, but also as a distinctly subversive form. Indeed, as Michael Holquist sums up the critic's concept of the novel, any positive view of the genre is thrown into question:

> "Novel" is the name Bakhtin gives to whatever force is at work within a given literary system to reveal the limits, the artificial constraints of that system. Literary systems are comprised of canons, and "novelization" is fundamentally anticanonical. It will not permit generic monologue. Always it will insist on the dialogue between what a given system will admit as literature and those texts that are otherwise excluded from such a definition of literature. (p. xxxi)

Bakhtin's theory would thus seem to provide one of the best explanations of why the novel has achieved near universality in the contemporary world. In an environment in which traditional cultural formations are under constant bombardment from a variety of alien voices, only the novel as Bakhtin conceived it can hope to represent the multiplicity of discourses that have come to echo against one another in the twentieth century.

While his theory is uniquely positioned to allow the celebration of the potential for multiplicity in the modern world, however, it fails—no doubt for very good reason, given the sordid political environment pertaining in the Soviet Union when Bakhtin was working—to deal explicitly with the sort of political barriers to multivocality applied to such nonconformists as Shi Tuo. In approaching this issue, one immediately runs up against the problem that Bakhtin regards "dialogism" in two analytically distinct ways—one, that it is the natural state of language and, two, that all language *ought* to be that way, even if restraints have been placed in the way of its natural development.[15] As a result, discussion of the political ramifications of Bakhtin's ideas often conflates the two assumptions into the militant notion that any resistance to a view of language as a protean and subversive entity is both politically repressive *and* contrary to nature.

As I have tried to demonstrate in the introduction to this collection, however, the situation in China ultimately resists any such simple formulation: most intellectuals concerned with language and literature regarded these pursuits as uniquely privileged avenues of national identity. This created an environment in which virtually all writers in the twentieth century admitted of at least some claim on them by a nationalism that most often included a highly dogmatic sense of language's function in maintaining cultural distinctiveness. While this view of language hardly put an end to literary controversy, it did tend to limit dispute to matters of linguistic application and to discourage speculation on the nature of literary language itself. In other words, while questions such as the sociology of audience and the degree of political overtness in writing were constant topics of debate, there was an equally constant pressure to avoid questions about the ultimate efficacy of literary language itself.

Given the reigning positivism about the nature of language and literature and the highly political cast to discussion on the subjects, it is hard to imagine how serious demurral to prevailing views could avoid falling into the dominant polemical patterns of the day. If, in other words, Shi Tuo, as he implies more than once in his comments about his own writing, had fundamental reservations about the determinism of the contemporary Chinese literary scene, how could he state them without setting forth an oppositional discourse that was likely to be (or at least perceived to be) just as dogmatic as the dominant discourse to which he was opposed? Shi Tuo's remote and even somewhat mysterious narrative voice is perhaps the only possible way out of this impasse. Rather than intensify the polemical atmosphere, he instead seems to stand on the sidelines with an ironic detachment that calls into question the categories of contemporary debate rather than disputing any specified discursive position. The result is a singular narrative style that Slupski sums up astutely with the observation that it embodies "the intense feeling that the world is unknowable and human behavior senseless, which leaves the reader with the impression that behind all that happens is a fourth dimension, as it were, unknown, unseizable, but ubiquitous."[16]

At least in the *Orchard City* collection, this feeling of uncertainty is most powerfully represented by the peculiar narrative voice Shi Tuo employs. While the narrator marks his presence throughout the collection (even after he has ceased to dramatize himself within the individual stories), he does so more with a singular equivocality and casualness rather than by any positive manifestation of personality. It is as if he were addressing us orally rather than demonstrating the sense of control over his material that is ordinarily expected of a narrator in conventional realism. Phrases such as "do not know in complete detail," "or maybe it was," "we don't know how," and "or perhaps we should say" abound and leave the reader with a peculiar uneasiness as to whether the speaker recalls or even really cares about what he is telling us. This narrator breaks with the self-confident authority of the story-teller manner in traditional fiction even as he separates himself from the routine omniscience of 1920s' realism or the obsessive confessionalism of the first-person stories of such modern writers as Yu Dafu.

While this type of narrative stance is not particularly common in Western literature (indeed, it would be anathema to the careful disposition of point of view so vital to Henry James and the large group of critics who follow him), it was identified and named *skaz* by the Russian formalist critics working in the period before and after the Russian Revolution. First extensively discussed (without, however, first being extensively defined) by Boris Eichenbaum in his 1919 essay "How Gogol's 'Overcoat' Is Made,"[17] it has come to mean that a story is told in such a manner as to emulate the phonetic, grammatical, and lexical patterns of actual speech and produce "the illusion of oral narration."[18]

A more rigorous definition has been set forth by Martin P. Rice in his 1975 article "On 'Skaz,' " in which he adduces some of the specific elements that render skaz a unique form rather than simply a loose agglomeration of stylistic features. Most important in creating the illusion of an oral tale is that the narrative avoid "the characteristics of most specifically literary genres, traditionally recognized as written."[19] There must also be no framing device that would call attention to the gap between the narration and the literary form in which it is contained. A third important point that separates skaz from traditional first-person form is that "the 'I' of a 'skaz' narration cannot be a central figure in the plot" (p. 418). The reader gains his or her impression of the narrator strictly through the way the story is told rather than through any direct information presented. Ironically, the obtrusive style through which the narrator presents himself serves to deflect attention away from the often insignificant details of the plot and onto himself and his purposes.

While the filiation of Shi Tuo's style to that of the traditional essay would seem to be at odds with at least part of this definition, one of the most important features that Eichenbaum identifies with Gogol's narrator in "The Overcoat" is plainly evident in "A Kiss":

> This skaz style is especially marked in one sentence: "Just where the clerk who had invited him lived, we can't say, unfortunately; our memory has begun to play real tricks with us, and everything in Petersburg, all the houses and streets have gotten so muddled and mixed up in our head that it's extremely difficult to get anything out of it in proper order." If we add to this all the numerous expressions like some . . . or other, "unfortunately, little is known," "nothing is known," "I don't remember," etc., then we get, as a result, the impression of a device which creates the illusion that the work as a whole is a real story, related as a fact but not known to the narrator in every small detail.[20]

What is noteworthy here is not the illusion of oral narration as such, but the uncertainty of the narrator, the deliberate manipulation of information so as to raise questions in the reader's mind about the teller's reliability.

This contrasts sharply with rural stories created in response to Mao Zedong's "Talks at the Yan'an Forum on Literature and Art" in 1942. In stories such as Zhao Shuli's "Rhymes of Li Youcai," its author scrupulously mimics the manner of oral story-telling. The difference between Zhao's mode of narration and that of Shi Tuo in "A Kiss," however, is that Zhao always has his story-teller maintain strict command over his material. Indeed, in many post-Yan'an stories, the narrator revels in his knowledge of every small detail. The distinction in world views between Shi Tuo and later users of the oral manner is not only sharp but extremely instructive: whereas the latter narrators give one the feeling of an ordered universe in which everything is predictable and justly fated, Shi Tuo leaves one with a sense of the utter caprice of fate and the complete lack of any measure between action and its ultimate consequences. Even more than this, the uncertainty of the narrator leaves the reader with profound questions about the possibility of accurate perception.

Of all the uncertainties that array themselves before the reader of "A Kiss," the notion of time is the most insistent. It is so strong an entity that it almost encapsulates the full force of the elusive yet fatally determining "fourth dimensional" quality that Slupski describes. For all its capacity to effect change, however, those it acts upon remain steadfastly insensitive to the nature, or even the fact, of its power. The most telling instance of this is in the ultimate disposition of the tale's main "character"—the town itself. At the end of the twenty or so years (actually "ten, fifteen, or even close to twenty years" [p. 161]—at this point the narrator suggests the full impenetrability of time with his own inability to be much more certain about it than the characters he is describing) through which the story passes, the city is transformed. In the beginning a busy center of country life, it is by the end merely a shell wholly superseded by the collection of "odd buildings" that had grown up around the station. Those who remained suffered similar fates.

Yet, upon her return to Orchard City, no one that Sister Liu encounters seems aware of the contrast between the past and the present. In fact, time here is merely asserting its constant unknowability, something the narrator signals with his remark that "*as usual*, no one had paid any attention to when [the shift from old to new city] had started" (p. 156, emphasis added). Only Sister Liu, having been away for the whole period, is in a position to perceive what has happened. Even she, however, can only realize the omnipotence of time up to a point. When confronted with the depressing collection of images that signifies the cruel passage of time, she can only sigh; it is left to the narrator pointedly to break into the narrative with the comment that

> to tell the truth, it really is worth sighing over: people give no concern to fighting, shouting, crying, laughing, and are full of mechanical calculation; but then they suddenly open their eyes and discover that, when confronted with iron-faced and impersonal time, they are so insignificant, hollow, pitiful, and that they are so powerless! (p. 159)

After Orchard City itself, Sister Liu is the story's most important character. Significantly, she is the only major player in "A Kiss" to be in a circumstantially better position in the second half of the story than in the first. She becomes rich and mistress of her own fate—at least to the extent of being able to indulge in the great luxury of traveling for what appears to be her own amusement. The major potential sources of restraint on her, her mother and her husband, are both "probably long since dead" (p. 161). She has lost her youth, but there is no particular indication that that is any source of discomfort. Yet Shi Tuo[21] feels obliged to end the story with the strongest possible hint that there is much to be regretted over the course her life has taken: "If she had a son and a daughter—if you will allow the person who wrote this piece a word—she would want them only to grow up, have good fortune, and not copy their mother's example" (p. 161).

On the face of it, the most obvious source of regret would seem to be Sister Liu's lack of say in how her life was decided, her failure ever to have been in the position of making a meaningful choice. For in spite of her having "accepted whatever was arranged for her" in the matter of her marriage, it is also true that it had "never occurred to anyone to consider whether Sister Liu had been willing or not" (p. 156). But if the reader is tempted to assume that the story is making a case for the nobility of human choice, he or she immediately runs up against the counterexample of Mother Liu, who had taken such pains to arrange things on her daughter's behalf in large part out of a sense of regret over the consequences of a willful determination to decide her own fate when she was young: "She had sowed her wild oats, but having sowed them, she had eventually tasted their bitter, medicinal flavor" (p. 156). This careful balancing of the two sides of the question of free will, combined with the narrator's propensity to draw conclusions beyond what the characters seem capable of on their own, would appear to lead the search for the story's theme in the direction of some fundamental and chronic discontent with the human condition itself.

If Shi Tuo were merely giving expression to a negative sense of life's possibilities, however, he would simply be falling into the trap of presenting the trite and equally romantic antithesis to the romantic idea of the infinite potential of the self. Instead, I think what gives "A Kiss" its special poignancy is its relentless forcing of attention on the individual inability to *perceive* the full dreariness of life as it passes by and its highlighting of the mind's paradoxical habit of playing tricks on itself even as it believes it is groping toward the truth. Time and its mental adjunct, memory, are the agents of this confusion. The question of free will, then, is in itself less important than the way in which mother and daughter conceive (or misconceive) it, and the actual nature of past experiences is less relevant than their belief that the pursuit of alternative courses of action would have meant happier lives for them. Shi Tuo delineates this unmistakably in the case of Mother Liu, with her terror "that the daughter had the mother's blood flowing in her veins" (pp. 155–56). For the daughter, however, the pain of regret is heightened by the subtlety of its depiction, a subtlety so fine, in fact, that we are never told explicitly whether or not it is really there.

If the circumstances leading to Sister Liu's marriage are ambiguous as to the quality of her assent to it, what she encounters upon her return to Orchard City should at least convince her that her alliance and subsequent departure were the lesser of two evils. The place she remembered is largely gone, replaced with nothing but decay. Tigerfish, the most likely vehicle to a different life, is so reduced in condition that he would "not have [had] the leisure to recall her" (p. 157), even if he had not completely forgotten her. The long sequence of questions, answers and encounters on her rickshaw ride into the city and back again should at every step disabuse her of any fantasies she might wish to entertain. Indeed, her abrupt return to the station demonstrates that she consciously realizes the impossibility of any alternative. Nevertheless, the final comment of the "specified" author implies strongly that she would prefer integration into the collapsing city to her current exalted alienation. The reader cannot help wondering at a perceptual resiliency evident in this wish that exceeds even those who have lived in the city all along. Their failure to see anything amiss can be reckoned as gradual accommodation to a long decline; her failure to take any comfort in the vast contrast between what she could have been and what she has become, however, must be counted as a special and particularly moving sort of delusion.

In his discussion of Faulkner's *The Sound and the Fury*, Wolfgang Iser comments perspicuously on the power of time to foster delusion:

> The present actualizes particular impulses in the past, which appear strange and fragmentary because they are not remembered as they were, but as they are now under the influence and in the context of the present. This breaking up of the past is a sign of the inevitable change which it must undergo in the course of its re-enactment, for now something is added which did not exist at the time, imposing an order which

> discounts the conditions and demolishes the context which originally prevailed.[22]

In Sister Liu's case, it is the very dreariness of her present, much reinforced by her return to Orchard City, that seems to render the past so alive with possibilities. The bitter irony beneath this, however, is that it was sequences of events beyond the ability of anyone to see, ineluctably at work in the past, that brought about the dismal and alienating present. Once in that present, the mind must take refuge in fondly romantic visions about roads not taken in the past. What Shi Tuo has thus created is a cycle of incapacity to see in which the hopelessness of the present is so painful that it cannot be faced, and people must build illusions based upon a past that never was. In taking the path of least resistance, the mind thereby forecloses any realistic attempt to cope with the present on its own terms.

This cycle exists independently of specific personalities or as a simple function of the particular viciousness of modern times. Mother Liu's distaste for *her* circumstances at the beginning of the story had caused her to reach back retrospectively to create for her daughter the sort of future that the older woman had come to imagine had always existed. The narrator's intervention in the story's final paragraph plays a key role in drawing attention to this process of self-delusion. Instead of ending with Sister Liu's revelry of what might have been, the narrator takes it upon himself to summarize the point of the story and thereby to reinforce the notion that no one within the story itself would be capable of this perception. But in making the wish that her children have better lives, he paradoxically joins in the story's ruling delusion: that things can somehow be better if only we undertake them in a different fashion.

The narrator's professed uncertainty about time and memory ("It was 1913 or 1914 or 1915, I do not know in complete detail," p. 153) is the essential mediator of the doubt about whether positive knowledge of the past is at all possible. But the narrative voice in "A Kiss" is complicated by a countervailing tendency from time to time to enter into a sententious and declamatory mode. The previously quoted intrusion about "iron-faced and impersonal time" is only the most marked of a series of comments the narrator interjects on behalf of a capricious and omnipotent fate. As Eichenbaum pointed out in the case of a similar layering of narratorial voices in "The Overcoat," the mixture must be seen as adding decisively to the story's theme.[23] The narratorial oscillation between fatal earnestness and cavalier indifference is the ultimate emblem of the finality of human uncertainty: If the narrator must yaw between these two extremes, how can the reader of the story possibly gain a firm footing concerning the meaning of his text? The terrible unknowableness of the world is most forcefully brought home by the narrator's conscious inability to recount his story other than from a position of profound ambiguity.

The structural device that brings this deliberate thematic uncertainty into being, however, has profound implications for the world of Chinese fiction and of Chinese writing in general. Bakhtin has noted the characteristic phenomenon of the novel in which the narrator is used to represent the nature of the refraction of language upon reality rather than reality itself. The implied author makes the narrator speak in a particular language of literary convention that invariably stands at some distance from the author himself. The resulting dialogue sets "one point of view opposed to another, one evaluation opposed to another, one accent opposed to another." Through this,

> the author utilizes now one language, now another, in order to avoid giving himself up wholly to either of them; he makes use of this verbal give-and-take, dialogue of languages at every point in his work, in order that he himself might remain as it were neutral with regard to language, a third party in a quarrel between two people. (p. 314)

In the resulting possibilities for parody, Bakhtin sees "the ground being prepared . . . for a radical skepticism toward any unmediated discourse and any straightforward seriousness, a skepticism bordering on rejection of the very possibility of having a straightforward discourse at all that would not be false" (p. 401).

The uncertain voice alone, therefore, lacks the ability to point beyond its own tenuous existence to comment upon the nature of literary language itself. It is the mixing of two completely antithetical voices that ultimately provides the text with its most subversive moment. By juxtaposing a portentously omniscient and thus quite orthodox narrative voice with one that at every moment confesses to its own uncertainty, Shi Tuo effectively undermines the Chinese tradition of authoritative narration. When the combination that I discussed previously of the traditionally sacrosanct essay genre with the storytelling mode is added to this mix, the result is a thorough upsetting of both stylistic and generic norms, norms that had for the most part been strictly observed within Chinese literary history. And in the twentieth century, for all their professed iconoclasm, most Chinese writers were moved by a new sense of nationalism to be even more observant of careful taxonomies of styles and genres.

The extent to which less mixed, "univocal" narratives could not avoid being infused with traditional notions of social responsibility can be demonstrated even in the case of Lu Xun. This is true in spite of the fact that he was one of the few writers in modern China almost obsessively intent upon questioning not only the content of the intellectual heritage, but also the forms in which it was expressed.[24] The self-undermining first-person narrator who appears in many of Lu Xun's most significant stories is, among other things, emblematic of the author's awareness of the danger of falling into the old ways of doing things.[25] On a more basic level, however, Lu Xun's incessant flirtation with the possibility of hope bespeaks an at least partial commitment to that profoundest of Confucian tropes: that the universe is ultimately rational and amenable to disposition by intelligent and morally upright people. His eventual turn to Marxism (if not to its particular representatives in China) bears out this view, as the most conspicuous point in common between Marxism and the old Chinese world view is a faith in the utopian prospects of human society.

Lu Xun's *Guxiang* (My old home) shares with "A Kiss" a concern with the effects of the passage of time and thus provides an ideal vantage point from which to compare the authors of the two stories. At the very beginning of *Guxiang*, the dramatized narrator sets forth the issue of time's passage with great clarity:

> The old home that I remember was not like this at all. My old home was much better. But if I were to recall its beauty or to describe its charms, I would have neither images nor words with which to do it. Yet, it seems now as if it were always just like this. I thus explain it to myself: the old home was like this all along, and although it has not progressed, neither is it as bleak as I sensed; it is merely a change of disposition on my part, because in coming back home this time I have not been in a particularly good mood.[26]

What Lu Xun does here is to present the possibility of self-delusion—represented by the idea that things must have been better in the past—only to close it off immediately by forcing himself to come to grips with the probability that things were always as bad as they seem to him in the present.

This introductory passage prefigures the message of the body of the story, an account of an urban intellectual's fruitless search for the remembered pristine innocence of his boyhood. The story differs significantly from "A Kiss" in at all times representing the protagonist/narrator as being aware of the sad chain of events which both brought about the disillusioning circumstances of the present that in all likelihood had made the actual past just as bad. Every attempt Lu Xun's narrator makes to conjure up possibilities out of the past is met by an icy wall of present impossibility, each of which he becomes starkly conscious of. The paradigmatic example is the salutation "Master!" uttered by his childhood "friend" (and representative of the hope that things might have been better than they actually were), the peasant Runtu, a greeting that makes all too clear the gap between peasant and intellectual, fantasy and reality.

For all the stolidity of the walls that Lu Xun erects around himself in this reminiscence, he will not, or perhaps it is better to say cannot, consciously make self-delusion one of them. The message that the protagonist/narrator finally imparts, therefore, for all its guardedness, is one of opening new ground for clear sight, no matter how tenuously this sight is linked to any possibility of decisive action. When the final words of the story tell of roads not *yet* created and what people must do to open them, we are at least being presented with the possibility of escape from the cycle of history. "A Kiss," however, directed as it is by a narrator so remote as barely to remember the facts that he is presenting, contains no such guarantees against the powers of memory to lead itself astray. Its effect is quite the opposite: it shows the inevitability and even necessity of self-delusion. If we can thus say that Lu Xun, for all his iconoclasm, in the final analysis sought to reassure his audience about a continuation of the potential for clear perception, no matter how painful, that had always been one of the basic ideas in Chinese thought, Shi Tuo bears the still more unsettling message that even this cannot be counted on. The latter's cynicism can perhaps be thought of as the ultimate revolt against the Chinese tradition: a willingness to countenance the lack of meaning in the posttraditional age.

The application of a particular Western view of literature to this text, while suggestive, serves to point out the ultimate incommensurability of the two narrative traditions more than anything else. Looking at Chinese literature through the eyes of Bakhtin does highlight one particularly illustrative difference between Western practice and modern Chinese literature. For the Russian critic, the mixing of genres and styles so characteristic of the novel creates an exuberant and "carnivalesque" form of writing with virtually unlimited powers of cultural introspection. In twentieth-century China, by contrast, the very gravity of the tasks that literature set for itself largely precluded the notion that writing could seek its truth through the celebration of its own infinite and playful variety. Perhaps this is the ultimate penalty a literature that asks too much of itself must come to pay.

Notes

1. C. T. Hsia, *A History of Modern Chinese Fiction*, 2d ed. (New Haven: Yale University Press, 1971), p. 463.
2. Shi Tuo, *Guoyuan chengji* (Shanghai: Shanghai chuban gongsi, 1946), "xu" (preface), p. 4.
3. On *Wanxiang*, see Edward M. Gunn, *Unwelcome Muse: Chinese Literature in Shanghai and Peking, 1937–45* (New York: Columbia University Press, 1980), pp. 53–54.
4. On this concept, see Patrick Hanan, "The Early Chinese Short Story: A Critical Theory in Outline," in *Studies in Chinese Literary Genres*, ed. Cyril Birch (Berkeley: University of California Press, 1974), pp. 325–28.
5. "Yi wen" can be found in *Guoyuan chengji*, pp. 191–204. This and all future citations to the story are from my appended translation. This sentence is found on p. 156. Further references are given parenthetically in the text.
6. Zbigniew Slupski, "The World of Shih T'o," *Asian and African Studies* (Bratislava) 9 (1973): 25.
7. Shi Tuo, *Limen shiji* (Shanghai: Wenhua shenghuo, 1948), v.
8. Wang Yao, *Zhongguo xin wenxue shi gao* (Draft history of the new Chinese literature) (Hong Kong, Bowen, 1972) 2:138.
9. Shi Tuo, *Ye niao ji* (Wild bird collection) (Shanghai: Wenhua shenghuo, 1948), ii. Shi Tuo was responding to a review of his *Limen shiji* by Li Jianwu [Liu Xiwei] collected in the latter's *Ju hua er ji* (The second tasting flowers collection) (Shanghai: Wenhua shenghuo, 1947), pp. 13–22.
10. Wang Yao, *Zhongguo xin wenxue*, 1:246.
11. Ibid., 2:138.
12. See P. N. Medvedev and M. M. Bakhtin, *The Formal Method in Literary Scholarship: A Critical Introduction to Sociological Poetics*, trans. Albert J. Werle (Baltimore: Johns Hopkins University Press, 1978), pp. 55–56.
13. Gary Saul Morson, "The Heresiarch of *Meta*," *PTL* 3 (1978): 424.
14. M. M. Bakhtin, *The Dialogical Imagination: Four Essays*, ed. Michael Holquist, trans. Caryl Emerson and Michael Holquist (Austin: University of Texas Press, 1981), p. 257. Emphasis in the original. Subsequent references to this work are given parenthetically in the text.
15. Ken Hirschkop, "A Response to the Forum on Mikhail Bakhtin," in

Bakhtin: Essays and Dialogues on His Work, ed. Gary Saul Morson (Chicago: University of Chicago Press, 1986), p. 75.

16. Slupski, "The World of Shih T'o," p. 15.

17. Boris Eichenbaum, "How Gogol's 'Overcoat' Is Made," in *Gogol from the Twentieth Century: Eleven Essays*, ed. and trans. Robert A. Maguire (Princeton: Princeton University Press, 1974), pp. 269–91.

18. Victor Erlich, *Russian Formalism: History, Doctrine* (The Hague: Mouton, 1969), p. 238.

19. Martin P. Rice, "On 'Skaz,' " *Russian Literature Triquarterly* 12 (1975): 419.

20. Eichenbaum, "Gogol's 'Overcoat,' " p. 284.

21. The widespread use of pseudonyms by modern Chinese writers probably was meant in many cases as an attempt to signify something like Wayne Booth's concept of "implied author." My use of "Shi Tuo" at this point takes advantage of this phenomenon. That readers and critics have persistently identified these pseudonyms and the characters they have created with their historical authors is another facet of the problem this paper is trying to address.

22. Wolfgang Iser, *The Implied Reader: Patterns of Communication in Prose Fiction from Bunyan to Beckett* (Baltimore: Johns Hopkins University Press, 1974), p. 144.

23. Eichenbaum, "Gogol's 'Overcoat,' " p. 282.

24. See Lin Yü-sheng, *The Crisis of Chinese Consciousness: Radical Anti-traditionalism in the May Fourth Era* (Madison: University of Wisconsin Press, 1979), pp. 104–51.

25. For discussion of Lu Xun's first-person narratives, see my "Blossoms in the Snow: Lu Xun and the Dilemma of Modern Chinese Literature," *Modern China* 10.1 (1984): 49–77.

26. Lu Xun, "Guxiang," in *Nahan* (Outcry), in *Lu Xun quanji* (Complete works of Lu Xun) (Beijing: Remin wenxue, 1981), 1:476. For a different English rendition, see *Selected Works of Lu Hsun*, trans. Yang Hsien-yi and Gladys Yang (Beijing: Foreign Languages Press, 1964), 1:63.

6

POLITICAL INTEGRATION IN RU ZHIJUAN'S "LILIES"

Robert E. Hegel

CRITICS all remark on the emotional power and the restrained didacticism of Ru Zhijuan's "Baihehua" (Lilies, 1958).[1] The story is rather brief, has only two (according to most Chinese readers) main characters, neither of which has any extraordinary characteristics or talents, and consists of just a few events, all of them common enough in wartime. Yet through those events ordinary characters become heroic, overcoming strictures imposed by culture, gender, physical limitations—even by death itself. It is ostensibly a story of ideological integration, of transcendence of political marginality, of freeing the self from isolation, from the past, even from concern for self altogether. The story is carefully wrought in structure and dense with symbols having highly emotional associations. These features, together with the subtle manipulation of its first-person narrator, produce a seemingly artless work that engaged—and eased—some of the deepest political anxieties of its original audience. Since the political climate has changed dramatically over the last thirty years, making some of its original message irrelevant to its readers in other political periods, I will deal with this characteristic briefly at the end of the essay, as a historical artifact. First, we should observe how the Maoist theory of contradictions informs the structure of this brief tale.

At least in his philosophical writings, Mao Zedong (1893–1976) advocated utilization of the dialectical approach to understanding reality. Like Lenin, Stalin, and other Marxist writers, Mao saw change as the product of contradictions within an entity or phenomenon, specifically in the alternation of relative dominance of those aspects or elements that define any contradiction. Even though the existence of each aspect is a condition of the existence of the other and identified by its difference from its opposite, shifts in the relative prominence of these aspects can effect fundamental, qualitative change. According to the dialectical materialism espoused by Chinese Marxists, change is necessarily the result of internal, not external, causes; external pressure may at most serve as catalyst to accelerate or to impede change from within. Despite the existence of numerous contradictions in complex human societies—differences in education and wealth, division of mental from manual workers, great gaps in experience of the world—the primary contradiction in a time of armed struggle is that between "ourselves" and the enemy, Mao insisted. Struggle between the two sides of the political contradiction must produce a resolution before which society's other contradictions cannot be addressed effectively. To Mao, this theory served primarily as a problem-solving approach: it allowed the production of a political agenda, mechanically forcing the political struggle to the position of highest urgency and allowing all social questions to be swept aside and ignored during wartime. Its insistence that one side of a contradiction is dominant and the other must be subordinant—and that the two sides can shift in strength—underlies the guerrilla warfare strategy for which Mao is rightly famous. To facilitate solving problems, one must focus on the differences of importance among the contradictions and between the sides of the essential one, amplifying these differences for the sake of clarity and to make one's analysis more immediately convincing.[2] While one might argue that searching for contradictions in complex human phenomena may lead to self-evident or simplistic conclusions, Mao used and endorsed this approach throughout his period of dominance, forcing interpretations of reality to fit this scheme, making it sufficiently influential to become part of the mindset of millions of his followers. Probably those who were (and are) most conversant in the dialectical materialist method of approaching problems are those who joined the Communist cause as young people during the 1930s, 1940s, and early 1950s.

Although she may not have self-consciously utilized Mao's version of the Marxist dialectic to structure her story, undoubtedly Ru Zhijuan was strongly influenced by it. She was born in 1925 in Shanghai, the youngest of five children and the only girl among them. During her third year her mother died, and before long her father abandoned the children to the care of various relatives. Ru was raised by her grandmother, who made match boxes and worked as a menial to support them. When the old woman died, Ru, then thirteen, was sent to an orphanage. Her education proceeded sporadically through her childhood, at the orphanage, and later at a girls' school; finally she became a primary school teacher. Soon afterward she published her first story in a local newspaper and joined the New Fourth Army, an anti-Japanese resistance force led by the Communist Party.

In the army, Ru became a "cultural worker." She gave performances, wrote skits, poems, and songs, and served as nurse for the wounded and guard for prisoners. She even played the leading role in an early operatic version of *Baimao nü* (The white-haired girl, a story of a landlord's cruel exploitation of a young peasant woman). Soon after one of her patriotic songs became popular, she joined the Communist Party in 1947. She became the civilian editor of a Shanghai literary periodical after victories on the battlefield brought the establishment of the People's Republic. Her creative efforts were devoted to the short story form, to little avail until Mao Dun, as minister of culture, the senior member of the literary establishment—himself a sensitive and capable writer—noticed "Lilies." By pronouncing the story "the most satisfactory and most moving among the tens of short stories I have read recently,"[3] Mao Dun immediately catapulted Ru Zhijuan to the front rank of writers. Her story came to be widely heralded as a model for emulation, and consequently she became the leading woman author of her generation.

Yet in 1958 Ru's husband was in serious political trouble: he had been targeted during the anti-Rightist campaign subsequent to the short-lived, ostensible liberalization campaign of 1956 called the "Baihua qifang" (Hundred flowers) movement. Ru's support from on high kept her safe until 1966 when Mao Dun himself was toppled from power by Mao Zedong's leftists, and Ru was sent to redeem herself through labor for her "bourgeois thinking."[4]

The story's frame presents the dominant contradiction of the time, which overwhelms its protagonists: the life-and-death struggle between Chiang Kai-shek's well-equipped Nationalist Army and the largely peasant forces led by the Chinese Communist Party. As the story begins, there is a lull in the fighting; it is a period of temporary rest for both sides. Yet the Communist army has been ordered to attack—they must seize the initiative to become the dominant aspect of that crucial contradiction. While the characters are introduced and developed, the war forms only the background, to which regular references are made; the frame reasserts its dominance when, at nightfall, the battle commences. At the beginning of the story the characters know that bloody conflict is inevitable; the tension produced by preparation for this inevitability grows through the narrated day. Once the fighting begins, toward the story's end, its impact becomes ever more intense: first the narrator hears the roar of artillery and sees the bright glare of flares, then the lightly wounded arrive, and later the most grave casualties are carried in as the battle proceeds ultimately to hand-to-hand combat. Paralleling this movement is the increase of intimacy involved in the treatment of the wounded: first the narrator and other medical aides question those wounded soldiers who are still coherent, later they give this up, merely bathing those gravely injured men covered in dirt and blood, and finally they confront the emotional devastation of seeing a familiar face among the heroic dead. This shock evokes the intense calm of transcendence of personal feelings and of integration with the common cause, heralding the ending of the story.

The story is thus framed by the dominant contradiction of the time: the political conflict between the Communists and the Nationalists. This confrontation of forces, in the context of this story as during the historical period narrated, could only be resolved by military struggle. The preparations on the part of the Red Army and its partisans, described here in minute detail, constitute the small quantitative changes that lead, by Marxist logic, inevitably to the ultimate *qualitative* change in political power, "by leaps, catastrophes, and revolutions," as Lenin phrased it.[5] By analogy with Mao's Marxist notion of revolutionary change, the actions of these characters, minor as they may be in the entire campaign or in the civil war as a whole, are charged with generalized political significance; their steadfast refusal to be swayed, deterred, or unnerved by the enemy—their psychological and ideological victory—becomes reified as the successful resolution of the conflict, with the Red forces inevitably gaining final domination over the reactionaries. The structure of the story carries the fundamental contradiction of the historical period from relative rest through a period of fierce intensification to a symbolic resolution of at least a temporary nature.

Yet, the frame story serves only as the basis that imparts significance to the subordinate dialectical alternations that create the story's sentimental power. The narrator herself announces the first contradiction of secondary importance, a product of the dominant one: the contradiction between the People's Army and the narrator ("I"). Because of the campaign against the reactionaries, there is the battle; because of the attack, even cultural workers inexperienced in war—writers included—are sent to help tend the wounded. The signalman represents, personifies, the People's Army as he escorts the narrator to her new post, a first-aid station on the front line. Significantly, in this people's war she as intellectual cannot keep up the pace set by this young peasant soldier. Although physically she is not his match, other, less essential, contradictions between the two characters soon surface: those of sex, age (she is older), experience with the world at large, and political sophistication.

Once "I" takes the initiative, she becomes the dominant side of these contradictions. She sits the signalman down, questions him about himself ("it was more like an interrogation"), teases him about his innocence, then retreats into her own reverie, drawing the reader away from any objective view of this character, to create with the reader a bond of sentimentality on the basis of her subjective reflections. The primary contradiction of the story is set aside while the narrator is personalized, individualized through a monologue on her memories and speculations. The narrator retains "command" of the narrative discourse until she is delivered to the first-aid station, becoming then directly involved in the primary political contradiction. The resolution of her contradiction with the army is suggested by a growing bond of sympathy and affection extending from the narrator to the signalman, making concrete the ideal unity of intellectuals (or at least cultural workers) and the People's Army.

The operative contradiction in this new scene at the first-aid station is that between the army's needs and the support of the local people. The narrator and others are ordered to requisition quilts from the villagers; this scene is again personalized through the actions of the narrator and the signalman, whose assistance she enlists. Again minor (in the political sense) contradictions appear: first the signalman quails before a testy bride who refuses to give up her quilt, then the narrator likewise fails to win her cooperation. The narrator once more takes the initiative and wins the opposition over by appeal to higher authority: the political significance of this people's war of liberation. Consequently, the bride hands over her quilt, and the signalman takes it from her despite acute embarrassment on both parts. The narrator teases the signalman to confirm her dominance (and to increase the sense of familiarity for the reader). Only then does the narrator—hence the reader—learn of the complex ideological factors involved in the confrontation. The quilt is the bride's only dowry; it confirms the newness of her marriage and her adult status in the community. It confounds the signalman's inexperience with women, given its sexual connotations, and it perplexes him with its intensely personal significance and value in the sexlessness and impersonality of battle. This segment of the narrative ends with the signalman released by the narrator to return to his normal duties, carrying messages in battle. Happily he shares rations with her, leaving her two cold buns; she notices the twigs stuck into his rifle barrel ostensibly as camouflage have been joined by a chrysanthemum blossom. The section thus concludes with two enigmatic images of life, food and beauty (in the form of a flower), subverted by their association with cold and death.

The story's final segment is the battle itself; its dominant contradiction overpowers all personal contradictions and values as its resolution, the outcome of the fighting, hangs in the balance. The narrator resolutely dominates the local women, cajoling, commanding, and leading them to bathe and dress wounds for the casualties as they are brought in from the front. The new bride resists most strongly, a consequence of her girlish modesty and squeamishness. And then the dying—probably already dead—body of the signalman is carried in. This young woman resolutely bathes his body and then sews up the tear in his uniform occasioned by her teasing over the quilt. The contradiction of values between "the masses" and "their army" is thus mended; personal hesitations have been overcome by the larger ideological necessity of the political struggle. The signalman had died saving a group of stretcher bearers from a grenade; his success and the personal victory won by the young woman over her traditional reserve close the story with the predictable—but unspecified—dominance of the People's Army over the reactionary forces: the bride wraps the corpse in her bridal quilt, burying death in her only tangible symbol of chastity, of fecundity, of new life in a new world.

While the structure of the story involves the identification and resolution of contradictions that are essentially political in nature, "Lilies" is also studded with contradictory elements of less public significance. It is this use of contrastive pairs of rather more personally relevant images and emotions that enhances the story's meaning. A few examples: the time is autumn, and yet the fields give the promise of verdant life to the narrator's observation; the narrator is on her way into battle, and yet she feels as if she were going to a fair. The signalman irritates her and attracts her at the same time. His rifle, a weapon of destruction, is nominally camouflaged but actually decorated by an autumn flower. Despite the location of the first-aid station in a school—a place that should be bustling with children—the place is desolate, decrepit. The peasants who ought to be "progressive" by Maoist logic are actually quite backward in their thinking. The signalman shares food (buns) with the narrator; these symbols of life are as cold and hard as death. Appropriately, the narrator rediscovers them as she views his corpse. The day narrated is of a joyous family festival, but a dreadful battle will occur; even the young woman's groom is absent despite the family reunions normal on this Mid-Autumn Festival. The quilt is for love; it is used in war. It has intense personal value and yet it serves a public need; the quilt was intended for the privacy of the bedroom; instead it is utilized outside in public view in the first-aid station. It was meant to be shared with the new, vital husband; it enshrouds a lifeless stranger instead. The battle takes place at night, a night that has effectively been transformed to day by the bright autumn moon and the enemy's incessant aerial flares. The signalman is a virtual noncombatant; he dies saving other noncombatants (stretcher bearers) from a grenade flung by an enemy soldier at the height of the conflict. If we read the flower in his rifle barrel right, he who would not kill others—who has rendered his weapon unusable—has died fighting; the bride who could only ridicule this awkward young soldier ultimately humbles herself before him in wifely servitude, washing his body, mending his clothes, wrapping him in her bedding. The bride has become more than mere physical lover to this dead signalman—she has become his comrade, to achieve total integration in the revolutionary struggle for which he has made the ultimate sacrifice.

It goes without saying that the intended readers of this story, the subscribers to the limited-circulation literary periodicals to which it was first submitted, their friends, and coworkers—in other words, relatively well educated, largely urban, primarily professional people—would have been to some degree familiar with the world view of dialectical materialism. Study of the writings of Mao, Liu Shaoqi, and major foreign Marxist thinkers would have made them conversant with the idea that change is generated by differences within a phenomenon, and with the notion of contradictions. All would have remembered with perfect clarity the resolution of the contradiction on which this story is based, the success of the Communist forces in various battles and then in the civil war that established the People's Republic. Large numbers of them had participated in one way or another; for the rest, scores of war stories had recorded that conflict. Yet most such stories repeated standard formulas: the soldiers, workers, and peasants on "our" side are heroic; the enemy is despicable, even ugly to look at, and is doomed to failure.[6] Ru Zhijuan's short piece is remarkable for the finesse with which it circumvents these clichés to present a topic worn trite by repetition, the unity of the masses and their army, in an emotionally powerful manner.

Ru's success lies in the story's ability to place in the foreground the particular effects of the civil war on three individuals. She does this through implicit reference both to the historical political situation in 1946, the story's temporal setting, and to her contemporary situation, the events of 1958 confronting her intended readers. By embedding current references in her fictional past, Ru Zhijuan engaged her original readers in a vital emotional discourse concerning the meaning of both their past and their future.

Let us examine again the story's protagonists. In 1942 at the famous—and fateful—Yan'an Forum on Literature and Art, Mao Zedong had called for characters that were easy to comprehend by the unsophisticated masses, characters that were "typical, closer to the ideal" to meet the current political needs. That proposition was discussed, debated, and always officially endorsed for the ensuing thirty-five years. Viewed in isolation, certainly the signalman fits this prescription very well. He is physically and politically pure, guileless and honest, hard working and selfless. Initially he appears slow-witted (although this characteristic fits reasonably well with urban conceptions of country people) and unheroic, a far better follower than leader. His unhesitating self-sacrifice demonstrates, however, the quiet strength, the resourcefulness, the unflinching heroism of the common man, the iron will of the masses. The signalman's final conscious act transforms the character from comic bumpkin to ideal hero.

The signalman's final action effects such a dramatic change in his character that the story's other protagonists are fundamentally altered thereby. The young bride might, in isolation, be considered a potential "middle character" (*zhongjian renwu*) because her initial traditional thinking is transformed to wholehearted devotion to the revolutionary cause through the action of the story. The signalman's death provokes her to cast off all maidenly reserve, all concern for gossip about her physical intimacy with this strange man, all revulsion over the sight of blood and death. She simultaneously and openly acknowledges her indebtedness to the young man, atones for the embarrassment she caused him, and proclaims her new-found political faith: through her attentions, her skill in needlework, and her most precious material possession, symbol of conjugal harmony and fecundity, she gives everything she has to give to the young signalman and, through him, to the revolutionary cause. Her development from "typical" peasant girl to ardent patriot is at least as profound in effect as the elevation in stature of the signalman: both approach the revolutionary ideal of 1946, still inspiring in 1958. And yet other stories are replete with such characters; the success of "Lilies" hinges on its discursive format and on the narrator, the most essential—and most frequently misunderstood—character.

While Chinese critics have praised the story for its realistic bride and signalman characters, it is the narrator who is similar in essential ways to its implied reader and probably to its real readers as well. The narrator presents the story in first-person voice; the discourse assumes a "reader" who is essentially in agreement with the narrator on all political and social issues and who at least can sympathize with—if not share—her personal experience. This sentimental closeness is effected by a technique already very familiar to modern Chinese readers. Like the more famous woman writer Ding Ling (1905–1986) before her, Ru Zhijuan in "Lilies" created a first-person narrator sharing certain biographical details with the author.[7] In the opening lines of the story, the narrator identifies herself as a member of the army, assigned to the cultural work corps, specifically a writer, and a woman. In every autobiographical statement Ru Zhijuan confirms these details of her own past. Given the assumption common among China's readers that all first-person narrators (females in particular) relate the real experiences of their authors, on several occasions Ru has had to explain that her protagonists are not real individuals, that they are purely fictitious. Assuming otherwise has contributed to the general critical acceptance of the veracity of the story's details. This habit of reading has created a sentimental closeness between reader and author exaggerated even beyond what is intrinsic to the story itself, and that has contributed greatly to the story's perceived emotional power.

In this tale of people's war of liberation, the narrator starts as a marginal character, distanced from the other characters by values and experience, as well as by sex and age. She *interacts* with the others and serves as the dominant aspect of the contradictions she forms with them. But ultimately she is merely the external catalyst that hastens change; the real changes in the story occur among and within the "masses." That is, the masses and their army win the battle (presumably); the signalman saves his fellows in response to his own devotion to the common cause; the bride's inherent faith in and love for the People's Army are awakened by his death. The narrator has delivered speeches on political morality to both (reported but not recorded in the story), thus contributing to the maturation of their "correct" values. But ultimately her function as mediator between masses and army is obviated by their unity in the fateful struggle. The narrator's initial role in the essential events of the story is thus rendered marginal to the behavioral models the other protagonists become.

The sentimentality of the narrator is effected by the particularity of the discourse: it is individual and subjective. From the story's first page, all narrated events are mediated by the narrator's emotional response to them. Not only is the discourse shaped negatively by failure to mention certain facts in order to foreground others; each image is ascribed specific significance. Fact: during the military campaign along the coast, even cultural workers (including writers), normally noncombatant members of the army, were enlisted to help. Interpretation: "probably all because I was a woman," the narrator is sent to a first-aid station. Concerning the signalman, the reader is told directly about his broad shoulders, although it is through the narrator's probing that we learn about his marital status. The reader is informed about the signalman's background largely through the narrator's daydreams, combinations of her own childhood memories and her current *speculations* about him, which may or may not be accurate about the character himself. And yet such details simultaneously affirm the signalman's "typicality" and make the narrator's feelings clearer and more familiar to the reader. Later the narrator relates what she *heard* and thinks about the bride's motivations. In these and in many other instances throughout the story, the narrator's rationalizations and emotional responses are presented in discursive form to the reader; paradoxically, they serve as a barrier between the reader and the "real" world of the action. The distancing serves to indicate the ideological isolation of the intellectual narrator—despite her rural background—from the masses she is to join, to work with, to serve as a conscientious Communist leader. The level of unity she achieves with her comrades is purely subjective: she shares experience with the signalman in reverie; memories of childhood put her in emotional contact with the women who give her mooncakes to celebrate the Autumn Moon Festival on the day of the battle.

Embedded in this detail is another figurative distancing, another significant paradox: the Mid-Autumn Festival is a time for family reunions, for young people to nurture romantic feelings, for aesthetic appreciation of the brightness of the harvest moon—itself a symbol of completeness, of closure in human affairs. Yet in each of these senses, the moon appears ironically: no family described here is complete, the bride cannot be together with her new mate, and death prevents her from developing even platonic tender feelings for the signalman; the campaign is not over, in fact the moon's light makes the Communist forces all the more visible—and vulnerable. Finally, and most essentially, while the full moon may symbolize a unity between the masses and their army, it decidedly does *not* predict a unity of intellectuals and masses. The narrator stands separate even at the end of the tale, isolated, observing, marginal, her act of mediation providing the "objective" perspective that creates, for Chinese readers, the story's remarkable verisimilitude.

Now, to return to the particular significance of the story for its original readers. The "lilies" on the bride's quilt are "hundred harmonies flowers," *baihe hua*. Without the "harmony," the title suggests the "Hundred Flowers" campaign of 1957–58, the political movement ostensibly begun in the spirit of openness to solicit new ideas from intellectuals on how to solve the state's economic and social problems. By the time this story was written, however, in March 1958, it had turned into an antirightist witch hunt that sent scores of intellectuals to factories, to the countryside, to labor camps to work—as it turned out—for the twenty years remaining of Maoist rule in order that they might "reform themselves through labor." As she wrote, Ru Zhijuan's husband was in deep political trouble. At that time her days were spent earning a living, caring for her children, endeavoring ignominiously and unsuccessfully to help her husband. Her nights were her only occasions for mental escape, retreat into the vivid memories of her relatively glorious wartime experiences, of people she met, and of the brief, intense relationships those meetings produced. Unlike the narrator in this story, Ru was a city girl working among China's farmers. This story was a product of her memories of the past and her current concerns, "and yet [the story] has no direct relation to my worries," Ru once commented.[8] This disclaimer was made in 1980, a safe remove in time and political climate from 1958 when intellectuals like herself were under suspicion for harboring backward ideas, a time when they desperately needed recognition for their positive role in the revolution, in victory, for their success in working with China's working people even if never able "to become one with the masses" as Mao had enjoined intellectuals to do. The bride overcomes the barriers of sex, age, tradition; in the final lines of its discourse the marginalized "Lilies" narrator also disappears by giving up her personalized, subjective perspective for direct, "objective" narrative. By ceasing to mediate the heroic/tragic events of the battle, by submerging her subjectivity, the story's intellectual narrator may have provided the politically similarly marginal readers with the hope for escape from their state of enforced otherness to a new political level, to a new time of acceptance, unity, and harmony with China's masses. At the story's appearance in 1958, the emotional power of such a message among real intellectuals could hardly be overestimated. Ru Zhijuan's 1980 comment is unconvincing; consciously or unconsciously, she crafted a story that confirms the political understanding of the implied (and intended) reader and rewards that understanding with the victory of personal integration in united political action with China's masses. The joy, the harmony, the life implicit in the "lilies" of its title project meaning that extends well beyond the story's surface narrative; its technique suggests that this sense of integration may be generalizable to China's intellectuals as well.

Notes

1. A major source for critical readings of Ru Zhijuan's stories as well as biographical and bibliographical detail is Sun Luxi and Wang Fengbo, eds., *Ru Zhijuan yanjiu zhuanji* (A collection of studies on Ru Zhijuan) (Hangzhou: Zhejiang renmin, 1982). The most influential reading of "Lilies," the encouragement that gave Ru a great sendoff on a glorious writing career, was by Mao Dun, in "Tan zuijinde duanpian xiaoshuo" (Discussing recent short stories), *Renmin wenxue* 1958.6; reprinted in Sun and Wang, *Ru Zhijuan*, pp. 247–51. See also Gong Zhong, Xu Runrun, and Wang Yisheng, eds., *Zhongguo dangdai wenxue shi gangyao* (An outline history of contemporary Chinese literature) (Shangrao shizhuan Zhongwenke, 1980; a limited circulation textbook), p. 97; Gong Zhong, *Zhongguo dangdai wenxue shi xinbian* (New edition of an outline history of contemporary Chinese literature) (Nanchang: Jiangxi jiaoyu, 1985), pp. 255–58; Ma Fengzao, "Suzao renwu xingxiang yao xunqiu dianxing xijie" (In portraying

character images, one must seek representative detail), *Duanpian xiaoshuo* (Jilin renmin, 1980), pp. 152–55.

2. Mao's major philosophical essays are "Shijian lun" (On practice) (1937); "Maodun lun" (On contradiction) (1937); and "Guanyu zhengque chuli renmin neibu maodun de wenti" (On the correct handling of contradictions among the people) (1957); see Mao Tsetung, *Five Essays on Philosophy* (Beijing: Foreign Languages Press, 1977), and *Selected Works* (Beijing: Foreign Languages Press, 1965–1977), 1:295–309, 311–47; 5:384–421. The last of these three formed the rationale for the "Hundred Flowers" movement of which this story is a product. For background on Marxist dialectics, see Joseph Stalin, *Dialectical and Historical Materialism* (New York: International Publishers, 1940; frequently reprinted). For studies of these ideas and their effect on modern China, see Maurice Meisner, "Harmony and Conflict in the Maoist Utopian Vision," *Journal of Chinese Philosophy* 4 (1977): 247–59; Meisner, "Marxism and Chinese Values," *The China Difference*, ed. Ross Terrill (New York: Harper & Row, 1979), pp. 99–116; Donald J. Munro, "The Malleability of Man in Chinese Marxism," *China Quarterly* 48 (1971): 609–40.

3. Sun and Wang, *Ru Zhijuan*, p. 251.

4. For biographical detail, see ibid., pp. 3–5, and Ru's autobiographical comments reprinted there, pp. 6–108, in *Ru Zhijuan xiaoshuo xuan* (Selected fiction of Ru Zhijuan) (Chengdu: Sichuan renmin, 1983), pp. 375–83; Ru Zhijuan, *Lilies and Other Stories* (Beijing: Panda Books, 1985), pp. 203–205; see also Zhang Wei, "Ru Zhijuan: From Orphan to Author," *Beijing Review* 29.9 (March 3, 1986): 20–23, and Suzanne Bernard, "An Interview with Ru Zhijuan," *Chinese Literature* 1980.3: 92–98; an older view is Fang Wen-jen, "A Woman Writer of Distinction," *Chinese Literature* 1963.7: 104–13.

5. Vladimir I. Lenin, *Karl Marx* (1913) (Beijing: Foreign Languages Press, n.d.).

6. See Li Chi, "Communist War Stories," *Chinese Communist Literature*, ed. Cyril Birch (New York: Praeger, 1963), pp. 139–57; cf. Joe C. Huang, *Heroes and Villains in Communist China* (London: C. Hurst, 1973), esp. chap. 6. See also Bonnie S. McDougall, "Writers and Performers, Their Works, and Their Audiences in the First Three Decades," in *Popular Chinese Literature and Performing Arts in the People's Republic of China 1949–1979*, ed. Bonnie S. McDougall (Berkeley: University of California Press, 1984), pp. 269–304.

7. I refer to such stories as the famous "Shafei nüshi de riji" (The diary of Miss Sophie) (1928) and her wartime stories "Wo zai Xiacun de shihou" (When I was in Xia Village) and "Zai yiyuan zhong" (In the hospital) (1941). For texts, see *Ding Ling duanpian xiaoshuo xuan* (Selected stories of Ding Ling) (Beijing: Renmin wenxue, 1981), pp. 43–82, 541–60, 569–89. Translations appear in *Masterpieces of Modern Chinese Fiction 1919–1949* (Beijing: Foreign Languages Press, 1983), pp. 240–79; and Joseph S. M. Lau, C. T. Hsia, and Leo O. Lee, eds., *Modern Chinese Stories and Novellas 1919–1949* (New York: Columbia University Press, 1981), pp. 266–91.

8. See "Wo xie 'Baihehua' de jingguo" (My experience in writing "Lilies"), in *Ru Zhijuan xiaoshuo xuan*, p. 344.

Chen Ju notes the essential role of the narrator in his " 'Baihehua' fenxi" (Analysis of "Lilies"), in *Zhongguo dangdai wenxue zuopin xuanjiang* (Selected lectures on contemporary Chinese literary works), ed. Shiliaosuo gaodeng yuanxiao (Nanning: Guangxi renmin, 1980), pp. 478–83, but he stops short of calling her a central character; see p. 482.

7

THE FUNCTION OF INTERTEXTUAL REFERENCE IN ZHU XINING'S "DAYBREAK"

Cyril Birch

IT IS a truism that a literary text, any text, is generated from earlier texts. In illustration of this principle, Robert Scholes cites a poem by W. S. Merwin:

> Elegy
> Who would I show it to

As Scholes says, this is "one of the shortest poetic texts in the English language," yet it exerts a powerful effect on the reader *provided* the latter is properly equipped.[1] Without title the poem would of course be meaningless. Via the title, the poet prescribes the qualifications the reader needs: a knowledge of the generic tradition of the elegy, a recollection however vague of "Lycidas," "Adonais," and other monuments, to reveal the immensity of the awful gap that Merwin's self-doubt opens up. "Now *you* are dead" (or "should *you* die") "who would be left to share my grief, and what would be the point of my setting it down on paper?" Read against the background of traditional eloquence in the expression of bereavement, Merwin's "Elegy" develops a great power of irony.

An important part of the modernity of Chinese writers in this century has been the precise nature—often, but not always, ironic—of the dialogue they have conducted with older texts, the texts of the tradition. This dialogue emerges most clearly in certain works that draw material from traditional sources, which have, in other words, particularly strong intertextual references. One thinks of works like Guo Moruo's historical plays, as early as *Zhuo Wenjun* (1923), which borrows a positive romantic symbol from an old tradition in order to promote the new message of feminine emancipation. Or there are more subtle and involved reworkings of earlier material. One such is Feng Zhi's *Wu Zixu* (1943), in which the Rilke-inspired poet uses a classic revenge narrative as vehicle for an extraordinary prose meditation on fate, duty, and the stern complexities of the patriotic wartime stance. Or the modern work may be not so much a retelling of a traditional tale as a variation on it, as is the case with Bai Xianyong's "Wandering in a Garden, Waking from a Dream" (1967).[2] Here a classic dramatic romance sets up a world of glamor and innocence combined, against which a totally modern nostalgia develops extraordinary depth.

What we are speaking of here is much more than merely allusion, even systematic allusion on a large scale. It is the overt development of a text from earlier sources, sources which serve as a necessary commentary, as it were, to the new work. Hans Robert Jauss speaks of the work of art as presenting the answer to an implied question. Discussing interpretation and reinterpretation, he says:

> The question, which enables the past work of art to affect us still or anew, has to be implicit because it presupposes the active mind's testing the conventional answer, finding it convincing or otherwise, discarding it or putting it in a new light so that the question now implied for us may be revealed. In the historical tradition of art, a past work survives not through eternal questions, nor through permanent answers, but through the more or less dynamic relationship between question and answer, between problem and solution, which can stimulate a new understanding and can allow the resumption of the dialogue between present and past.[3]

Zhu Xining's story "Daybreak" (1963) is a modern fable that gains in moral impact from antecedent treatments of its subject matter in a late medieval story and a seventeenth-century play.[4] The text of "Daybreak" makes no explicit reference to either, but few Chinese readers could fail to pick up the echo of the celebrated "fifteen strings of cash" theme. Zhu Xining, in Jauss's terms, puts new questions to the "fifteen strings" motif, and the answer which his "Daybreak" constitutes puts the reader in turn in the position of participant in the ongoing "dialogue between present and past." Bai Xianyong played skillfully, in "Wandering in a Garden," with the irony inherent in the situation of an aging socialite trapped in the memories of her great operatic role as cloistered young maiden. Zhu Xining may be said almost to have reversed the direction of the innocence-experience axis, but he derives comparable ironies from the shocking impact on his first-person narrator, the "green" Young Three, of the world devoid of justice and decency to which he is exposed, the world of the old-time magistrate's court.[5]

"Daybreak" is about twenty thousand Chinese characters in length, about sixteen thousand words in Hou Jian's fine English translation.[6] The text is undivided but can be described in four roughly equal segments. The narrator of the first quarter, which functions as an unmarked prologue, describes the predawn chill and gloom of the magistrate's court where he is putting in his first day of duty as an attendant. The second quarter consists of the deposition of a young woman defendant. Apart from an early paragraph of direct speech and a question or two from the examining magistrates, her story is presented in indirect third-person narrative with herself as center of vision. She is the seventeen-year-old concubine of an unsuccessful businessman three times her age. This man comes home late at New Year's, drunk, and throws five hundred taels (ounces) of silver on the table, telling her he has sold her to another man who will be coming to collect her in the morning. While he sleeps she hides the silver and runs away. On the road she accepts a ride on a merchant's donkey. Pursuing constables find 480 taels of silver under the saddle and arrest the two. They are taken back to the woman's house where her husband lies murdered, the silver gone.

The young attendant feels the woman has "stated her case fair and square" and is "dumbfounded" when her recital leads only to the application of severe torture. As the torture proceeds through the third quarter of the story he begins to "doubt his aptitude for this new trade."

But in the last segment of the story the narrator is assigned, first to beat the male defendant who perseveres in protesting his innocence, then to impersonate a witness and give false testimony to refute the merchant's alibi. In the customary traditional fashion, as a witness he is himself beaten, but only in a make-believe show before he is released and congratulated by his seniors. He ends the story musing on his fitness for the job.

If Zhu Xining's story is a whodunit it is a very poor one. We must surely believe in the innocence of the young concubine, whose own account of her adventures is filtered through the sympathy of the listening narrator. But what of the male defendant, the merchant with the donkey? No doubt innocent of the adultery he is charged with, he could still be guilty of the murder. He overtook the woman and so was coming from the direction of her home, and he had silver under his saddle—only 480 taels, true, but the husband could have been talking in round numbers with his "500." The defendant claims to have been collecting year-end accounts, but we are given no particular reason to believe him.

Perhaps it doesn't matter one way or the other. The magistrate has been bribed, the case is decided before it is heard, and truth or falsehood, guilt or innocence, are irrelevant. As the senior attendant says, "Are you so sure the keeper of the Welcome Inn hasn't been bribed beforehand by the defendant to bear false witness?" Zhu Xining's story is not a whodunit, but a moral indictment of an amoral world via the revelation of the corruption, in a single morning, of the green young attendant, the narrator himself.

The merchant with the donkey is in fact as innocent as the young concubine. Zhu Xining is relying on our foreknowledge of the facts of the case, on our familiarity with the theme of the "fifteen strings of cash." The first inkling of this reference comes at the beginning of the young woman's deposition, when the husband returns home drunk and flings the silver on the table, telling her it represents the recovery of her bride-price. The mind of the Western reader might well travel to Hardy's *Mayor of Casterbridge* at this point, to Michael Henchard's sale of his wife at the fair. But to the Chinese reader the allusion is inescapable. It is to the prompt-book story "The Wrongful Execution of Cui Ning"[7] and the Ming play made from this, *Fifteen Strings of Cash.*[8]

In Patrick Hanan's dating, "Wrongful Execution" is an "early story," most probably within a few decades either side of the year 1400.[9] It is set in Hangzhou and is the product of a Hangzhou realist school: witness the account of how the husband, Liu, was actually murdered:

> At that moment a certain burglar, made desperate by losses at gambling during the day and out to see what he could pick up that night, came by chance upon Liu's door. Since the concubine had pulled the door shut without locking it when she went out, with only a light shove from the thief it swung open. He stole his way into the bedroom without being discovered. When he reached the head of the bed and took a look about him in the still-bright light of the lamp, he could see nothing worth taking. Groping around on the bed, he noticed a man sleeping there with his face toward the wall. At his feet was a pile of copper

coins. He picked up a few strings but in the process woke Liu, who rose up shouting, "Hey, you've no right to take that! I borrowed those few strings from my father-in-law to support myself. If you steal them, what will I do?"

Instead of replying, the man struck at Liu's face with his fist. Liu dodged to one side and then got to his feet, ready to fight with him. When the robber saw how nimble Liu was, he fled from the room. Liu raced after him out the door and straight into the kitchen where he was about to cry for the neighbors to come seize the thief.

Becoming frantic and seeing no way out, the burglar suddenly caught sight of a gleaming axe for chopping firewood, near at hand. In desperation, he picked it up and swung it at Liu, striking him squarely in the head and knocking him to the ground. Again he swung, chopping him on the side. Liu clearly was dead. Alas! May his soul be blessed![10]

This passage comes from the main body of the story, which Hanan classifies as a "folly and consequences" tale, prototype of a subgenre that was to gain in popularity through the Ming dynasty.[11] Through his drunken teasing of his concubine, telling her the money was her bride-price, Liu forges a chain of events that result in the deaths of two innocent people after his own murder. But Feng Menglong, the seventeenth-century editor of the story, adds a sequel that converts the whole into a conventional "court-case" (*gongan*) story. After the mistrial and wrongful execution of the concubine and her merchant companion, the following homily appears:

Now listen, dear audience, if the concubine and Cui Ning had in fact murdered for money, they would certainly have fled on that same night. Is it likely that she would have gone and spent the night at a neighbor's house? Would she have gone to her parents' place the following morning only to be seized on the way? This injustice could have been brought to light with a close examination of the facts. But who expected the judge to be so muddled, intent only on concluding the case without ever realizing that under pain of torture, one would confess to anything? In the netherworld, accounts are kept of one's misdeeds. Whether retribution be as far removed as his descendants or as near as his own life-time, the spirits of the two who were wronged will not let him go. Thus, an official must never pass judgments according to whim nor mete out punishment as he pleases. Rather, he must strive to make just and proper decisions. It is all too true that the dead can never be brought back to life nor the broken be made whole. Alas, the pity of it! But no more idle talk.[12]

The editor follows this homily with a "distinctly inferior" sequel (Hanan's evaluation), an account of the murderer's subsequent turn to brigandage, his marriage to the widow of the murdered Liu, and her discovery of his identity and success in handing him over to justice. In this way the late-Ming editor satisfies what he judges to be the popular taste for retribution. He underscores also the "folly and consequences" message by adding a prologue in the form of a simple tale of a man who jokes in a letter to his wife about taking a secondary wife in her absence. She jokes back that she has taken a secondary husband, her letter falls into the hands of an inquisitive colleague, and when the scandalous tale spreads, the man's bureaucratic future is ruined.

Murder will out, the tongue is the source of disaster: "Wrongful Execution" bristles with moral messages, all of which are studiously avoided by the modern author Zhu Xining. Even the basic coincidence of the two identical sums of money is paid little heed, left ambiguous, in "Daybreak," its impact reduced by the slight discrepancy in the amounts.

Zhu Que, the early Qing author of the *chuanqi* play *Fifteen Strings of Cash*, picks up precisely on this basic coincidence and further elaborates the plot to suit the needs of an action-packed form of drama. If two identical sums could give rise to a story, how much more fun to try three. Of the three piles of cash in the *Fifteen Strings* scenario, each pile of exactly fifteen strings, the first is stolen by rats (onstage) from a merchant's house and deposited on the shelves of the poor student next door, who is thus implicated in a theft of which he is innocent. The second pile is loaned by another merchant to the student's brother to help clear the student's name. The two brothers are surnamed Xiong, "Bear," and the play goes by the alternative title of *Shuang xiong meng* (Dream of two bears). The third pile of cash is loaned by his sister to You Er, who fulfills the function of the husband Liu of "Wrongful Execution." You Er teases his stepdaughter (not concubine in this case) by telling her this is the price he has been paid for selling her off. She runs away, and on the road she falls in with the student's brother, who of course has the borrowed "second" fifteen strings of cash in his possession. Meanwhile, her fatally facetious stepfather You Er is murdered by a gambler named Lou the Rat. Halfway through the play, in scene 13, Prefect Kuang Zhong is introduced to the audience as the reincarnation of the legendary, incorruptible Judge Bao. Kuang Zhong's brilliant unraveling of the crimes, both the original theft (by the rats) and the murder, occupies most of the remaining thirteen scenes of the play and provides some of the best moments. The gods send him a dream (onstage, again) in which two bears enter carrying rats in their mouths and knock his hat off. He muses on the phrase *mian guan*, "removing the hat": if you put a "hat" (*guan*) or topmost element on the graph of "remove" (*mian*) you get the graph for "injustice" (*yuan*). Clearly he must look carefully into the cases coming up for his review![13] Scene 18 presents splendid dramatic irony and much witty double entendre when Prefect Kuang, conducting his own investigations disguised as a fortune-teller, covertly "interrogates" Lou the Rat and, convinced of his guilt, interprets his name as predicting disaster and advises him to flee—on Kuang's own prefectural barge, straight into the arms of the waiting constabulary.

"The Wrongful Execution of Cui Ning" was already an amalgam of elements from popular traditions of story-telling, and the play *Fifteen Strings of Cash* incorporates still more strands from a range of oral and performing literature. A modest collection of research materials published in 1957 includes a Shansi drama version (*Qinqiang*), a Peking Opera version (Lao She revised this about that time), a drumsong (*guci*) from the mid-eighteenth century and a slightly later Suzhou ballad (*tanci*), a Cantonese "wooden fish" (*muyu*), and a "precious scroll" (*baojuan*) version from Suzhou in the late nineteenth century.[14]

All of these materials without fail pay great attention both to entertainment value and to the didactic function, concerned on both accounts to round out the patterns of action, bring malefactors to justice, unite marital partners, and generally leave the world of fiction, when the action ends, in a state of restored order and harmony. Zhu Xining, by doing nothing of the kind, breaks radically with the tradition. Why does he bother to borrow at all from this hoary mishmash of melodrama?

What he borrows, first of all, is severely limited. To make any reference at all to the "fifteen strings" motif he must, of course, use the basic situation of the two similar sums, one flung on the table by a drunken husband, the other found in the saddlebag of the runaway woman's companion. But even here Zhu Xining plays an intriguing twist: the plaintiff (the murdered man's widow) sues at first only for two hundred taels, which suggests that that was the actual sum borrowed, and stolen—the "five hundred" was mere boasting on the husband's part, the concubine never counted it anyway, and the wife upped her demand to five hundred when she learned that almost that sum was found in the young merchant's saddlebag. Is this what we are to believe?[15] Or is it better simply to leave everything vague, ambiguous, to add to the sense of confusion, corruption, and absurdity?

"Daybreak" follows the course of events as far as the mistrial and no further. The time-scale is precisely indicated by the title, an early-morning court scene that incorporates the background events culminating in the arrest. What will follow the trial is only too obvious: there is talk of flaying or of the "standing cage" as a convenient though unauthorized alternative form of execution, but the executions themselves do not take place in Zhu's story.

In addition to personages and a partial pattern of action, Zhu Xining borrows, or re-creates, much of the mindset of the past. The trappings of popular religion are reflected in Young Three's imaginings, which turn the court (very plausibly) into a fair imitation of a Buddhist hell. The shadows of men above him on a flight of steps point downward, so that "they looked like men trussed upside down and swinging to and fro." The magistrate "needed but a flowing red beard to look like the hellish judge so often seen in a temple," and (since the macabre interweaves closely with the devout in this psychology) at close quarters his face "resembled that of a corpse, recovered days after the drowning." Specifically, toward the end of the story the court is likened to Yama's infernal halls, and its kitchens to "hell's torture chamber, complete with mountains of swords and cauldrons of boiling oil." Such indices set Young Three before us as a commoner of his time (which is presumably nearer the end of the Qing dynasty since muskets and the ticking of a clock are mentioned).

What Zhu Xining eliminates is the executions and all that follows these in the traditional versions of the tale: the detective work, the bringing to book of the real murderer, all reference to the complications caused by the third "fifteen strings" of the *chuanqi* play, and in fact all elements tending toward the composition of a pattern of experience, the achievement of justice, the working out of destiny, and the restoration of harmony in a rationally ordered world.

In place of a pattern of experience, Zhu brings the reader a conviction of intensity. Young Three feels what is happening around him to a degree unknown in the earlier versions. Contrasting images of existential comfort and discomfort abound in the introductory section. Bitter cold, frost, steaming breath are countered by padded uniforms, three poached eggs for breakfast, peddlers selling "chili soup, tarts, cakes, and steaming gruel." The slovenly magistrate with his urine-spattered boots lolls over his pipe while the defendants' chains crush them to the frozen floor.

All of this is much more than just "atmosphere"; it lays down the essential conditions under which the protagonist, Young Three, must make his moral decision, which is the heart of the story just as the restoration of order is the heart of the earlier didactic versions of the theme. All else is secondary to the central concern, Young Three's decision on this first day at his new job: will he recoil in revulsion from the evil of the world, or will he assume his humble place within its well-established system?

In terms of the basic structuralist concepts of "story" and "discourse," Zhu Xining has borrowed an old story, a pattern of events, and set it in the framework of a discourse, a mode of narration, which dominates the first quarter of "Daybreak," is held almost in suspension through the second quarter (the woman's court deposition), then fuses with the "story" in the second half of the piece, as Young Three becomes involved in the trial, first as torturer and then as false witness.[16] The ending of "Daybreak" is dominated by the conclusion of the discourse as Young Three's desire to conform slowly gains the upper hand over his impulse toward justice and mercy. As he kneels in court by the side of the accused, so close to the end of the story, we do indeed see this narrator himself as one of the victims of the tale he tells. Young Three is the sole narrator of "Daybreak," though in the second segment he is filtering the woman's deposition for us and often assumes the authority to present her point of view. He is sensitive, observant, imaginative in his presentation of scene, and he is reliable; we are never given any reason to doubt his account of the facts. He is a decent young man whose humane impulse, at the very beginning of the woman's self-history, is to compare her with his own wife:

> It was pitiful, of course, to become a widow at seventeen. My wife married me when she was eighteen, and a very naive girl she had been, too. But here was one who had a lover at such a tender age, and could murder her husband for money to give to another man. Either her mistress had framed her or she must be a real monster.

Since he cannot stand outside his own text, Young Three cannot benefit from knowledge of the "fifteen strings of cash" motif and the events connected with it. The intertextual reference works only for the reader, not for the narrator. It is at some point during the woman's deposition that the pleasant shock of recognition strikes us, perhaps not until the drunken husband announces the "bargain" he has struck in the sale of his wife, certainly not later than the appearance of the man Dai on his donkey. This is a story we know—how cleverly the modern author has disguised it thus far, by his radical shifting of point of view to the insignificant yamen attendant! We know of the husband's foolish and fateful joking, the sheer coincidence of the identical strings of cash, the innocence of the accused. So many clues that Zhu Xining's narrator has been giving us now fall into place with a click: the cynicism of the older bailiffs, the slovenliness of the magistrate.

Our knowledge of the woman's innocence and the corruption of the court shapes our relationship with Young Three. We find ourselves pushing him toward sympathy with the victims and away from acceptance of—let alone participation in—this mockery of a trial. Young Three is representing the reader's feelings, then, and all is in harmony, when he resonates in sympathy with the story of the accused, "so young and so helplessly mired in ice and hunger." Soon he begins to wonder why she is forced to kneel during the questioning. Toward the end of her narration he thinks of her and her ostensible lover as "poor wretches" and is convinced she has "stated her case fair and square." He is astounded and appalled when a beating is ordered and closes his eyes as it begins: "Somehow, I felt it was not the woman who was going to be thrashed, but myself." By the time two huge guards are crushing her legs beneath their own weight transmitted through a heavy, rolling cedar pole, the narrator is convulsed with pity for her. He relates her terrible shrieks to the cries of his own wife in a long, hard childbirth, and he feels them in his own head "like a dentist's file when it moves back and forth across the teeth." By this point his readers may well be feeling their own teeth ache in sympathy.

But Young Three's next comment pulls us up with a shock: "I began to doubt my aptitude for this new trade." It is all very well for us as readers to merge our sympathies with Young Three's, to shudder in rhythm with him and hear the woman's shrieks with his sensitive ears. We can afford such humane responses. It is not our rice bowl. It is not our first day on a job that has cost our father five stone of wheat just for an introduction.

All of the sympathetic responses cited above occur around the midpoint of the text. Before and after come numerous reflections that reveal a more calculating side to the narrator. He is a decent enough young man, but he has to eat. He has to please his superiors, to be "friendly, even deferential" to colleagues of his own low rank. And more than the prospect of economic security, the job itself attracts him with its arcane rituals and codes, its esoteric skills, the fellowship of "friendly and jolly elders." He longs to shed the feeling of being "left out" of their fraternity. He makes a preliminary commitment when he joins in the chorus of low growling intended to intimidate the accused upon entrance into the court, and he not only joins in but finds himself "soon cowed by it." The torturing of the woman after her statement shakes him, as we have seen, but when subsequently the "lover" is brought in, Young Three is "not at all sure (he) succeeded in making the proper kind of growl." But he is still trying to conform, and he puts up only token resistance when ordered to participate in the beating of the accused man ("a timid man like me—how could I beat anyone?"). By the time the beating is over, Young Three is "good and mad" but has no idea with whom or what. It is up to us, as readers, to help him sort out his feelings. They are complicated enough by this stage to enrage a saint, compounded as they are of pity, fear of humiliation, ambition, shame, anger at his elders who have got him into this predicament, even a hint of sexual lustfulness or sadism as the victim's bulging bare flesh reminds him of love-play with his wife.

This daze of feelings persists until Black Eight orders him to take off his uniform in preparation—though this is not yet clear to him—for the impersonation he is to give of the innkeeper as witness. Young Three's reaction to the command may be seen as a major turning-point of the story: "I turned cold: so the job bought with five stone of wheat is lost, and lost in such a casual manner!"

The process of Young Three's initiation is not yet over—even at the very end of the story the sun has still not risen. Though more and more feebly, he still struggles against the forces dragging him into participation in these hellish rites. He searches for excuses: the onlookers will see through his impersonation, it is wrong to frame a man whose guilt is uncertain. When his protests have failed and he kneels, posing as witness, beside the accused, he doesn't "have the heart to look him square in the face." But at the moment of his own greatest peril a stroke of mother-wit impels him to save his skin with a wise-cracking retort to the magistrate's question: " 'Please, your Worship, if I'm not the keeper of the Welcome Inn, could it be this lunatic?' "

Young Three has passed his test, his "unaccustomed and outrageous lie" qualifies him for a lifetime of service in this court of injustice. He will have more to learn, and indeed immediately following the above false testimony he is admiring the skill with which the old-timers, "real pros," are administering a phony beating upon his own person.

The reader of the traditional "fifteen strings" story, or the audience for the ballad or dramatic versions, could complacently reflect when all was over on the marvelous ways of providence by which justice was brought to prevail. Zhu Xining's text, as we have seen, downplays the story in favor of the discourse, and the discourse is open-ended. So vividly are the narrator's thought processes set before us that we have no choice, as readers, but to follow him through his valley of decision. We pity the unfortunate young widow and her alleged lover, we pity Young Three for the shock of his discovery of the wickedness of this world. But most of all we feel the horror of involvement in his plight. More and more we find the text urging us to accept Young Three's self-justification, to excuse his failure to strike out against the injustice he faces. He will "wait and see"—in other words, he will surely continue in this job and in the process of corruption commenced this day. Day will fully break and the sun will rise, but it will bring no real enlightenment, it will shine only on scenes of quotidian cruelty and corruption. This is certainly the interpretation of Song Chengshou, who directed the excellent film version of the story.[17] No clear light of truth floods his final frames, but only a murky half-dawn as Young Three walks pensively, broodingly away from the camera.

In his detailed analysis of "Daybreak," Hou Jian identifies the central importance of the initiation theme and sees the use of the point of view of the young yamen attendant as a uniquely modern device. I believe, however, that he is placing too much emphasis on story as against discourse (to return to our narratologist's dichotomy) when he describes the "tragic status" of the concubine and the fearless honesty of the peddler under torture and comments, "But the author does not allow Young Three to perceive, from their demonstration [of integrity], the conduct that is proper to humanity, the road it is proper to follow."[18] Hou Jian finds the moral lesson of "Daybreak," in consequence, "unacceptable." But the very incompleteness of the intertextual reference shows that Zhu Xining is in no way engaged in retelling the "fifteen strings" story. He lays little stress on the character of either of the victims. He eliminates all reference to the righting of the wrong done to them. He uses them, as he uses the "fifteen strings" motif altogether, as ciphers in a code, the code of reference to the world of corruption and cruelty we associate with the archetypal magistrate's court of former times.[19] Not through "story" but "discourse," the presentation of all data by the naive initiate, this is how Zhu Xining answers the central question we ask of his text: how will Young Three commit himself to this world, through what processes of rationalization and self-deception? This is quite different, of course, from the question to which "The Wrongful Execution of Cui Ning" is an answer. That question, however—something like "How does providence work to overcome the evil of this world?"—ironically underlies "Daybreak" as part of the "dialogue between present and past." And much of the irony lies precisely in the silence of Zhu's text in those areas of the "fifteen strings" story dedicated to the correction of injustice.

The question we put to Zhu's text is "How does the process of corruption begin, in Young Three, in any of us?" It is as solemn a theme as a literary text can bear.

Notes

1. Robert Scholes, *Semiotics and Interpretation* (New Haven: Yale University Press, 1982), pp. 37 ff.

2. *You yuan jing meng*. The title of Bai Xianyong's story is identical to that of the most popular piece on the Kunqu stage, which in turn derives from two scenes of the late-Ming play (*Mudanting*) (Peony Pavilion), by Tang Xianzu.

3. Hans Robert Jauss, *Towards an Aesthetic of Reception* (Minneapolis: University of Minnesota Press, 1982), pp. 69–70.

4. Zhu Xining, *Poxiao shifen* (Taipei, n.d., actually 1967). The title story of the collection, pp. 275–316, is dated 1963.

5. Since *lao* is merely a prefix indicating familiarity, "Young Three" is more appropriate than "Old Three" for Lao-san.

6. Hou Jian's translation handles late-Qing yamen slang with great skill. It is appended on pp. 173–208 of this volume. The story appears under the title "Dawn" in Chi Pang-yuan and others, *An Anthology of Contemporary Chinese Literature, Taiwan, 1949–1974* (Taipei, 1975), 2:115–57.

7. *Cuo zhan Cui Ning, Jingben tongsu xiaoshuo*, identical with the story "The Disastrous Coincidence from the Joke about Fifteen Strings of Cash," *Shiwuguan xiyan cheng qiao huo*, *juan* 33 of the late-Ming collection *Xing shi heng yan*, ed. Feng Menglong (1574–1646). An English translation, "The Jest that Leads to Disaster," by Jeanne Kelly, appears in *Traditional Chinese Stories*, ed. Y. W. Ma and Joseph Lau (New York: Columbia University Press, 1978), pp. 467–78.

8. *Shiwu guan*, by Zhu Que, text (based on a pre-Qianlong edition) in *Shiwu guan xiqu ziliao huibian*, ed. Lu Gong and Fu Xihua (Beijing, 1957), pp. 23–119.

9. P. D. Hanan, *The Chinese Short Story* (Cambridge: Harvard University Press, 1973), p. 165.

10. Ma and Lau, eds., *Traditional Chinese Stories*, p. 471.

11. Hanan, *Chinese Short Story*, p. 151.

12. Ma and Lau, eds., *Traditional Chinese Stories*, p. 476.

13. There is no English translation of the play. I have commented elsewhere that an orthographic riddle of this kind could be transposed into English only by some kind of punning device. Instead of knocking off his hat, for example, the two bears could turn back the lapel of the prefect's robe to sniff at the lining, whereupon he would comment that "They don't seem to be interested in the smell of the outer material—only the inner scent—INNOCENT!"

14. See above, note 8.

15. Hou Jian, "Zhu Xining de 'Poxiao shifen,'" *Zhongwai wenxue* 1.9 (February 1973), reprinted in *Zhongguo xiandai zuojia lun*, ed. Ye Weilian (Taipei, 1976), suggests that the wife is only guessing when she files claim to 200 taels, and the yamen runners alter her claim to 500 to match the 480 found in the saddlebag—they will split the surplus 300 between them.

16. Seymour Chatman, *Story and Discourse* (Ithaca: Cornell University Press, 1978). "Story" and "discourse" have come to be the accepted English equivalents for Genette's "histoire" and "récit."

17. Taiwan, 1965. Li Hanxiang produced the film, and Yao Fengpan wrote the screenplay. Participants in the Hawaii workshop owe a debt of gratitude to Dr. Sophie Sa, through whose good offices a showing of the film was made a part of the program.

18. *Zhongguo xiandai zuojia lun*, p. 327.

19. One of Barthes's "cultural codes." See Roland Barthes, *S/Z* (New York: Hill and Wang, 1974).

Translations

BLACK LI AND WHITE LI

Lao She

THOUGH love was not the central theme of the misunderstanding that arose between the two brothers, I must begin my discussion there.

Black Li was five years older than White Li. They were both schoolmates of mine, though Black Li and I graduated from middle school the same year White Li began his studies there. Black Li and I were good friends, and since I visited their home frequently, I also got to know White Li quite well. In this day and age, five years makes a big difference. The two brothers' characters were as different as their nicknames: Black Li was old-fashioned; White Li was very modern. They didn't argue about this specifically, though their points of view differed radically on every subject under the sun. Black Li wasn't really black. He was called Black Li on account of a big black mole over his left eyebrow. His younger brother had no such mark, so he became White Li. Their classmates in middle school, who had given them these names, thought this was quite logical. Actually, both brothers' complexions were rather pale, and they looked very much alike.

They were both chasing the same woman—pardon me for not mentioning her name. She herself couldn't decide which of the brothers she loved more, though at the same time she wouldn't admit that she didn't love either of them. We were all very worried about them on account of this. Though we knew that neither of them was looking for a fight, we also knew that the game of love wasn't always played according to the rules of friendship.

Finally, Black Li surrendered.

I recall what happened very clearly. On a drizzly night in early summer, I went to have a chat with him in his home. He was sitting

---

Translated by Don J. Cohn (Beijing: Panda Books, 1985), published by *Chinese Literature*.

alone in his room with four fine porcelain tea bowls decorated with red fish standing on the table before him. We were very informal whenever we got together. I sat down and lit a cigarette while he played with his tea bowls. He turned them around, one by one, until the fish designs painted on them were all facing him. Once they were arranged in this manner he leaned back, examining them like a painter who had just completed a section of a new painting. Next he rearranged them so that the fish on the other side of the bowls were all lined up neatly in front of him. Once again, he leaned back to get a better look, and then turned and smiled at me. His smile was as innocent as a child's.

He was fond of playing this sort of game. He had no great talents, yet he dabbled in many areas. He never pretended to be an expert in any field, but he believed that everything he did contributed to molding his temperament. There was no question about his being good-natured. If he had a hobby to pursue, such as repairing an old scroll painting, he could very easily while away an entire day at it.

Calling my name, he smiled and said, "I let Number Four have her." In terms of seniority in their family, White Li was number four, since an uncle on their father's side had two sons. "Brothers shouldn't become estranged on account of a woman."

"That's why they call you old-fashioned," I said with a chuckle.

"You're wrong, you can't teach an old bear new tricks. I couldn't handle a *ménage à trois* anyway. So I said to her, no matter who she loves, I couldn't see her any more. You can't imagine how much better I felt after that."

"First time I've ever heard of a love affair like that."

"The first time? Then perhaps I shouldn't say any more. She can do as she pleases, but at least Number Four and I won't have any more arguments. If this sort of thing happened between us, I certainly hope one of us would give in the same way."

"Then there'd be peace on earth, right?"

We both laughed.

About ten days later, Black Li came to see me. I knew by now that whenever a gray shadow hovered over his forehead, there was something important on his mind. On occasions such as these, we'd always drink half a catty of Lotus brandy. I got the drinks ready quickly, since his forehead was looking unusually dim.

When he was drinking the second cup, his hands began trembling. It was hard for Black Li to conceal his feelings. If something was upsetting him, no matter how hard he tried to remain calm, it always showed on his face. He was such a kind and outgoing person.

"I went and had a talk with her," he said, smiling in a rather silly manner. But this was a genuine smile, since he was getting ready to pour out all his troubles to a close friend. If Black Li had no close friends, he wouldn't have survived for long.

I didn't press him, and there was no need for us to hurry anyway. Our feelings could very easily fill in the little silences that occurred in our conversations. We glanced at each other and grinned. Our facial expressions and intuitive understanding of each other were more important than anything we might say. For this reason White Li always called us "two bumps on a log."

"Number Four got nice and upset with me," he said. I knew exactly what he meant by "nice": First, he didn't want to admit that they had an argument; and second, he didn't want to put all the blame on his younger brother, even though it was White Li who was in the wrong. The word "nice" was a complex expression of his unwillingness to say what was really on his mind. "It was all because of her. It's my fault, I don't know anything about feminine psychology. Remember the other day I told you that I had surrendered? I had no qualms about that whatsoever, but she took it very differently. She thought I was trying to humiliate her. You're right when you say I'm old-fashioned. For me, love is a matter of doing what's right. Little did I know that our lady friend's out to get the whole world chasing after her. Now she hates me. So what does she do to get her revenge? I rejected her, so she stops seeing Number Four. Number Four blew up in front of me. So today I went to apologize to her. If she had just cursed me and let off some steam, maybe she and Number Four could get back together again. Anyway, that's what I was hoping. But you know what? She didn't curse me at all. She said she wanted Number Four and I to be her friends. Of course that's impossible for me, though I didn't tell that to her directly. I came over here to talk to you about it. Problem is, if I don't do as she says, she'll ignore Number Four, and he'll start up with me all over again."

"A very difficult situation." I tacked this on for his benefit. A few moments passed. Then I said, "Why don't I go explain everything to Number Four?"

"That would be fine," he said, holding up his wine-cup, "but it might not do any good. Anyway, I'm finished with her. If Number

Four wants to make an issue of it with me, I just won't say anything, that's all there is to it."

We shifted the topic of our conversation onto some other subjects. He told me he'd been reading about religion the last few days. I knew that his studying religion was purely a whim; Black Li wasn't the type to take up religion out of pessimism, or because he was undergoing some spiritual crisis.

Shortly after Black Li left, White Li came in. He rarely came to visit me, so I guessed that something important had happened. Though still a college student, White Li looked much more astute than his older brother. He gave you the immediate impression that he was capable of being a great leader. The things he said would either lead you down the very path he wanted you to follow or strap you to the guillotine. His manner was extremely direct, the very opposite of his brother. I was also quite direct with him, lest he call me a "bump on a log."

"Number Two came to see you of course." Black Li was the second oldest in their extended family. "And of course he's been telling you all about what's going on." Naturally, there was no need for me to reply in a hurry, since he said "of course" twice. But before I even had a chance to open my mouth, he went on, "You know, I just did it to make a point."

I told him I didn't know that.

"You think I'm really after that woman?" He smiled at me with Black Li's smile, except that Black Li's smiles were never so disdainful. "The only reason I got involved with her at all was to cause trouble for Number Two; otherwise, why would I want to waste my time with her? Aren't all relations between men and women based purely on animal desire? What do I need her for then? Number Two believes that animal desire is sacred, so he went out of his way to kowtow to her. Now that she's rejected him, he thinks it's my turn to kowtow to her. I'm sorry, that's not my style." He laughed loudly.

I didn't smile, nor did I dare interrupt him. I listened carefully to what he had to say and paid even closer attention to his facial expression. Black Li and White Li's faces were similar in every respect, except for the fact that Black Li's demeanor was so totally different from his brother's. For this reason, one moment I felt I was talking to a very close friend, and the next as if I were sitting across from a complete stranger. This was quite discomfiting; the face before me was familiar, but I was unable to find its familiar expression.

"You see, I didn't even kowtow to her once. At the proper moment, I kissed her. She really liked that, a whole lot more than all that kowtowing. But that's not the main point. What I mean is, do you think Number Two and I ought to go on living together?"

I couldn't answer this question immediately.

He smiled—probably he was thinking to himself how I was just a "bump on a log." "I've got my own life to live, my own plans; the same is true for him. The best thing would be for both of us to go our own ways, don't you think?"

"Yes. What are your plans then?" It was no easy task coming up with this question; I already felt extremely awkward.

"This is no time to talk about my plans. Once we divide our family property and start living apart, you'll find out what my plans are."

"You started an argument with Number Two just because you want to move out? Is that the point you're getting to?" Now I was being clever.

He nodded with a smile but said nothing, knowing I probably had more to say. I continued, "Why didn't you discuss it with him peacefully instead of having an argument?"

"Do you think he's capable of understanding me? You may be able to hold a reasonable dialogue with him, but not me. As soon as I mention living apart to him, he starts crying. Then it's the same old thing—'What did Mother say before she died? Didn't she tell us we should always be good to each other?' He brings that up every time, as if the dead were supposed to run the lives of the living. Not only that, if I mention dividing up the estate, he'll disagree, I swear to you, and tell me how he wants to sign everything over to me. But I don't want to take advantage of him like that. He always treats me like a little brother. He thinks he can control other people's behavior. He pretends to understand me, but actually he's just a big anachronism. The present belongs to me; why do I need him to tell me what to do?" His expression suddenly became very serious.

Looking at his face, I gradually began to see things in a different light. White Li was a proud young man who looked down on us two "bumps on a log." All he really wanted was to stand on his own two feet. I also realized that if the two of them tried to talk over their differences, they'd get carried away for hours discussing the whole range of fraternal obligations. If White Li didn't bring this up, Black Li certainly would. A quick argument was preferable to all of this, lest their conflict drag out indefinitely. White Li wanted a clean break, after which each of them could go their own way. Furthermore, if they held a proper discussion on the matter, Black Li would never respond in a straightforward manner. If White Li kicked up a storm first and Black Li offered a lot of resistance, Black Li would appear to be trying to appropriate White Li's share of the estate. At this point I suddenly felt enlightened.

"So you want me to go and talk to Number Two about it, right?"

"That's right. This way we can avoid a big argument." He smiled again. "Of course you shouldn't put him on the spot. We're still brothers." It seemed he felt very uncomfortable with the word "brothers."

I agreed to do as he said.

"The more insistent you are the better. I propose that he and I have nothing to do with each other for the next twenty years." He paused for a moment, forcing a grin. "You can tell him that if he wants to forget about me, he should get married and have a nice fat baby as soon as possible. In twenty years, I'll be old-fashioned myself. If I'm still alive then, I'll come home and play uncle. Make sure you tell him that when he's courting his future wife, he should kiss more and kowtow less; he should spend his energy chasing her rather than kneeling down before her." He stood up, paused for a moment, and then said, "Thank you." It was evident that these last two words were intended for me, but also that he really didn't want to bear the responsibility for having said them.

I discussed this matter nearly every day with Black Li. Every time I went to visit him he had the Lotus wine ready. We'd eat, drink, and talk a lot together, but never came up with any conclusions. This went on for at least two weeks. He understood and appreciated everything I said and even expressed the hope that his younger brother would go out in the world and make a name for himself. But his last words always were: "How can I get along without him?"

"What could Number Four's plans possibly be?" He asked himself this question pacing back and forth in his room. His black mole sunk into the creases on his forehead and seemed to have shrunk somewhat. "What are his plans? Why don't you ask him. If you could find out, I could stop worrying so much."

"He won't tell me." I must have told him that at least fifty times.

"That's dangerous though. He's my only brother. Let him come and argue it out with me; there's nothing wrong with two brothers having an argument. He was never this way with me before. We only started disagreeing with each other very recently. It must be on account of that woman. He wants me to get married? I didn't get married, and look what happened. I'll get married then! What could his plans possibly be? Really! He wants to divide up the family property? Let him take whatever he wants. I probably offended him in some way. Though I never wanted to start a fight with him, I know I have my own opinions on things. So what are his plans then? He can do as he pleases. Why do we have to divide up the estate?"

Once he started on this topic, you could be sure he would drone on for more than an hour. His hobbies increased in number day by day: divination by tossing coins or using the Eight Trigrams, analyzing Chinese characters, reading about religion . . . But none of these hobbies helped him to figure out what Number Four's plans were; on the contrary, they only increased his anxiety. This is not to say that he appeared any more nervous than usual. Actually, he was his usual maudlin self. It seemed as if his actions could never keep up with his emotions. No matter how agitated he was inside, he always moved slowly; he seemed to be playing with his life as if it were a toy.

I told him that Number Four's plans involved his future career and had nothing to do with the present. But he only shook his head.

In this manner, more than a month went by.

"You know," I said, appealing to reason, "Number Four isn't pressing me, so it must be that he has some long range plans. He's not about to run off and do anything big right now."

He just shook his head again.

As time passed, the number of stories about him increased. One Sunday morning I happened to see him entering a church, where I assumed he was looking for a friend. I waited for him outside, but he didn't come out. I had to go somewhere, and as I walked away I thought about how the recent events in his life must have been upsetting for him—his broken love affair; his falling out with his brother; and perhaps there were more things I didn't know about. But two things alone seemed to be too much for him to bear. His actions revealed that life was just a game for him, but this was because he was so preoccupied with the most trivial matters. It made him uncomfortable if the patterns on tea bowls were out of line. Similarly, he arranged things neatly in his mind to soothe his conscience. Perhaps by going to church and praying he could put his mind at rest. While his conscience had been provided to him by the wise sages of yore, at the same time he didn't reject all modern things and modern thinking. As a result, his own "way of thinking" was never quite as coherent as "the way things really were," making it difficult for him to know how to act properly. He was probably in love with her, but he had to reject her for his brother's sake; he certainly never mentioned falling out of love with her to me. He often said, "Let's take a ride in an airplane." Then he'd laugh, but it wasn't really him laughing, it was "the flesh and bones he'd inherited from his parents" that were laughing.

One afternoon I went to see him. It was our custom to begin talking about Number Four immediately—at least this had been the pattern over the last month or so. But that day he looked like an entirely different person. His eyes were bright and he had an expression of great contentment on his face. It was as if he'd just purchased a fine edition of a rare book.

I began the conversation. "What's the good news?"

He nodded, smiling. "Very interesting!" He always said this after experiencing something for the first time. If someone told him an old ghost story, you could be sure he would respond with "Very interesting!" He wouldn't argue with you about whether ghosts existed or not since he believed in the supernatural. "Who knows, there must be stranger things in the world than that," he would say. In his mind, anything was possible. Thus he accepted new things quite readily, but without understanding them very thoroughly. It wasn't that he lacked the desire to understand things, but when he should have used his brain, he used his emotions.

"The principle is the same," he said, "people should make sacrifices for others."

"Didn't you sacrifice your girlfriend for him already?" I was trying to remain rational.

"That doesn't count. That was a passive separation; I wasn't giving up anything that belonged to me. I've spent the last two weeks reading the Four Gospels, and I've made up my mind. I ought to support Number Four; it's wrong for me to try to stop him from moving out. Think about it for a moment. If it's only a matter of dividing up our estate, why can't he just come and talk to me about it?"

"He's afraid you'll disagree with him," I said.

"No. The last few days, I've been thinking about it. He must have something specific in mind, probably something very dangerous, but he wants to make a clean break with me so that I won't get implicated if he gets in trouble. You think he's just young and impulsive? He acts that way just to fool us. He's actually going out of his way for my benefit, since he doesn't want me to suffer unjustly on account of anything he does. He wants to make sure I'm safe first, so he can do whatever he wants on his own with a clear conscience. I'm sure that's it. But I can't let him go now; I've got to make sacrifices for him too. Right before Mother died, she . . . " He stopped there, knowing I'd heard it all before.

I never thought he would take it so far, and I still didn't believe everything he said. Perhaps under the influence of religion he was giving vent to some previously hidden emotions.

I decided to speak to White Li about it on the very slim chance that Black Li was right. Though I didn't believe that what he said was true, I couldn't afford to take any chances.

I looked everywhere for White Li, but he was nowhere to be found. There was no trace of him on the campus, in the dormitories, in the library, on the tennis courts or in any of the little restaurants he frequented. No one I asked had seen him for days. White Li was like that. If Black Li went away for a few days, he would have notified all of his friends. But White Li would disappear like a puff of smoke. I came up with a possible solution: I asked "her" if she knew anything about his whereabouts.

Since I spent so much time with Black Li, she already knew who I was. But she hadn't seen White Li for a long time either. She seemed to be quite disappointed in both of them, especially Black Li. When I asked her specifically about White Li, she directed the conversation back to Black Li. I could see that she cared a lot about—or perhaps even loved—Black Li. She seemed to want to capture Black Li and preserve him like a specimen. If she could find someone better than him, she would let Black Li go; in the event she failed, she'd probably marry him after all. Since I was only guessing, I chose not to play matchmaker for the two of them. On principle I should have done that, but I was much too fond of Black Li and believed that he deserved to marry nothing less than an angel.

By the time I left her place, my heart was pounding. Where was

White Li? I couldn't tell Black Li about it, since as soon as he found out he'd put a notice in the newspaper and stay up all night divining with his coins and poring over his characters. But if I didn't tell him, I wouldn't be able to think about anything else. Why couldn't I just forget about the whole thing? No, that wouldn't work either.

From outside his study, I could hear Black Li humming. He only hummed when he was very happy about something. He hummed on a more or less regular basis when he recited poetry or sang those famous lines, "deep in the boudoir, there lies a piece of flawless jade," though this was not what he was humming now. Listening carefully, I discovered he was reciting the Psalms over and over. He didn't have a very musical ear, so all music sounded the same to him. Likewise, everything he sang came out sounding the same. In any case, I could tell that he was extremely happy now. What brought this about?

The moment I walked in, he put down his book of Psalms. He looked ecstatic. "You're here at just the right time. I was just about to go and see you. Number Four just left. He asked me to give him a thousand dollars. He didn't mention dividing the estate, not even once."

It was evident that he hadn't asked his brother why he needed the money, otherwise he wouldn't have been in such a good mood. He probably had begged his brother to keep living with him, and promised him not to meddle in his affairs. It seemed now that even if White Li had a dangerous mission to accomplish, as long as they didn't split up the family estate, Black Li would have nothing to be afraid about. I could see this quite clearly.

"Praying really works," he said quite seriously. "I've been praying for the last few days, and it turned out that Number Four didn't bring up that old business. Even if he throws away the money I gave him, at least I still have a brother."

I suggested we drink our customary pot of Lotus wine, but he smiled and shook his head. "Go ahead, I'll have something to eat instead. I'm giving up drinking."

I didn't drink either, nor did I tell him how I'd searched everywhere for White Li. Now that White Li was back, why bring it up again? I mentioned "her" to him, but he didn't say a word, and only smiled.

We have very little to say about White Li's relationship with "her," so he told me some Bible stories. While listening to him, I thought there was something a little strange about the way Black Li behaved towards his brother and his girlfriend, though I couldn't put my finger on it. I felt very uneasy about this and continued to feel this way when I got home.

Four or five days passed, but this matter remained on my mind. One evening, Wang Five came to see me. Wang, the Li's rickshaw puller, had been working for them for four years.

Wang Five was as straightforward and reliable as they come. A man in his early thirties, he had a prominent scar on his head. It was said that this was the result of a donkey bite when he was a child. Wang's only weakness was that he enjoyed a drink once in a while.

He'd drunk a bit too much on the night he visited me, which made the scar on his head appear somewhat redder than usual.

"Wang Five, what brings you here this evening?" I was on good terms with him; whenever I left the Li's home late at night, they always got him to take me home, and I always gave him a little money to buy drinks with.

"I've come to see you," he said, taking a seat.

I knew he'd come to tell me something. "I just made a pot of tea. Would you like some?"

"That would be very nice. I'll pour it myself. I'm really thirsty."

I offered him a cigarette and started off the conversation by asking him, "What's on your mind?"

"Ah. . . . I just finished off two pots of wine, but there's something I can't get off my mind. It's something I really shouldn't be talking about at all." He took a long drag on his cigarette.

"If it's anything to do with the Li's, it's perfectly all right for you to tell me."

"That's what I was thinking too." He paused for a moment, but due to the effects of the wine could not remain silent for long. "I've been working for the Li's for a total of four years and thirty-five days. I'm in a very difficult position now. Second Master treats me very kindly and all, but Fourth Master, well, he's my friend. So it's hard for me to know what to do. I can't tell Second Master what Fourth Master's been up to, but Second Master's such a nice guy. If I told Second Master, I would be unworthy of Fourth Master's trust—he's my friend. But when I try not to think about it I get all confused inside. In principle, you know, I ought to be on Fourth Master's side. Second Master's a nice guy, there's no doubt about it. But in the end he's a master. No matter how good a master he is, he's still a master. There's no way we can treat each other as brothers. He's good to me. For instance, on really hot days, when I'm pulling Second Master around, he'll always find some place along the way to stop for a little while to buy a box of matches or take a look at a book stall. Why does he do that? So I can rest and catch my breath. That's what I mean when I say he's a good boss. And since he's good to me, I've got to treat him with respect too. Like they say, one good turn deserves another. You learn that when you pull a rickshaw for a few years."

I offered him another bowl of tea as a way of demonstrating I wasn't ignorant of the proper etiquette. When he finished his tea, he pointed to his chest with his cigarette. "Here, it's right here where I feel for Fourth Master. Why is that? Because Fourth Master is young and doesn't treat me like a rickshaw puller. Those two guys—I mean their personalities—are very different. On hot days, Second Master always gives me time to rest, but that would never occur to Fourth Master. No matter how hot it is he's always telling me to run like the wind. But when Fourth Master and I sit around talking, he'll say, 'Who says that some people have to be rickshaw pullers?' He's talking about how unfair things are for us—I mean all the rickshaw pullers in the world. Second Master treats me well, but he doesn't give a damn about the rest of us rickshaw men. You see what I mean? Second Master is narrow-minded while Fourth Master looks at the bigger picture. Fourth Master doesn't give a damn about my legs, but he cares about my heart. Second Master cares about the little things, he takes pity on my legs—but he doesn't give a damn about this here." He pointed to his heart again.

I knew he had more to say, but I was really afraid that the tongue-loosening effects of the wine he drank would be diluted by the strong tea, so I encouraged him a little, "Go on, Wang. Tell me everything. I'm not an old lady who's going to give all your secrets away."

He rubbed his scar and lowered his head for a few moments of contemplation. Then he pulled his chair up close to mine and lowered his voice. "Have you heard they've almost finished installing the new streetcar line? When that starts operating, we rickshaw pullers are done for. I'm not worried about myself; I'm talking about everybody." He looked up at me.

I nodded to him.

"Fourth Master knows all about it; we're close friends, right? He said to me, 'Wang, you've got to find a way out.' I said, 'Fourth Master, I've got an idea. We'll destroy them!' He said, 'Wang, that's the right idea, we'll destroy them!' So we worked it all out then and there. I can't tell you the details. This is what I came here to tell you." He lowered his voice again. "There's someone following Fourth Master around. It doesn't necessarily have anything to do with the streetcar business, but it's bad having someone tailing you all the time. The worst thing is, if I tell Second Master, how can I face Fourth Master? But if I don't tell him, he might get dragged in for no reason at all. I don't know what to do."

After seeing Wang Five out, I thought it all over carefully.

Black Li surmised correctly that White Li was involved in something dangerous. Beyond wrecking trolley cars, he probably had something even more formidable in mind. Thus his desire to move away from his brother was to avoid implicating him. White Li was not afraid of sacrificing his own life, or the lives of others, but he was unwilling to sacrifice his brother unless there were a good reason for it—such an act would come to no avail. And with the action against the streetcar company about to take place, he had no time to worry about Black Li anyway.

Where was I to turn? Warning Black Li would only stir up a wave of warm feelings in him for his brother. Speaking to White Li was not only useless; it would incriminate Wang Five as well.

The situation grew tenser day by day. The streetcar company announced the opening of the new line. I couldn't wait any longer. I had to go and tell Black Li.

He wasn't home, but Wang Five was still there.

"Where's Number Two?"

"He went out."

"You didn't take him?"

"He hasn't taken the rickshaw for a long time."

From the expression on his face, I knew the answer to my question: "Wang, did you tell him?"

Wang Five's scar turned a bright purple. "I drank too much. I couldn't help it."

"What did he say?"

"He started crying."

"What did he say?"

"He asked me one question: 'Wang, what are you going to do?' I said, 'I'll do whatever Fourth Master says.' All he said was, 'O.K.' He goes out every day now, but he never rides in the rickshaw."

I waited there for three hours. After sunset, he finally came back.

"What's up?" These two words summed up everything I wanted to know.

He smiled. "Not much." I never expected him to answer me this way. There was no need for me to ask him any more questions, since I knew his mind was already made up. I felt I needed a drink, but it's no fun drinking alone. I decided to go. Before leaving, I said to him, "Why don't the two of us go away for a couple of days."

"Let's discuss that in a few days, shall we?" That was all he said.

Passionate men are capable of acting with great indifference. I never imagined him treating me this way.

The night before the opening of the trolley line, I went to his house again, but he wasn't in. I waited until midnight, but he didn't come back. He was probably trying to avoid me.

Wang Five came in and smiled at me. "Tomorrow's the big day!"

"Where's Number Two?"

"I haven't seen him. After you left the other day, he used some strange chemical and burned off the black mole over his eyebrow. Then he just sat there staring at himself in the mirror."

It was all over now. Without his black mole, there was no more Black Li. I didn't have to wait for him any longer. When I walked out, Wang Five called to me, "If anything happens to me tomorrow," he said, scratching his scar, "take care of my mother for me."

About five o'clock the next afternoon Wang Five rushed into my room. His pants were soaked through with sweat. "We smashed all the trolley cars to bits." After that he said nothing and just sat there panting for several minutes. When he recovered his breath, he picked up the teapot and took a long drink directly from the spout.

"We destroyed everything! No one left till they brought in the cavalry troops. They took Little Ma Six away, I saw it with my own eyes. If only we had guns! But all we had was bricks. Little Ma Six is done for."

"What about Number Four?"

"I didn't see him at all." He bit his lower lip and thought for a moment. "There was a hell of a lot of excitement there. If they caught anyone else, I guess Fourth Master would have to be among them. He was one of the people in charge. Don't forget though, Fourth Master's no fool, even though he's very young. Little Ma Six is done for, but I'm not so sure about Fourth Master."

"You didn't see Number Two?"

"He didn't come home last night." He thought for a moment. "I'm going to lay low here for a couple of days."

"That's fine."

The next day, the papers carried the following news:

> The ringleader of a bunch of violent hooligans who destroyed the trolley cars, a Mr. Li, was arrested on the spot. A student and five rickshaw pullers were taken into custody as well.

Wang Five could only recognize one word in the headline: the surname Li. "Fourth Master is done for! Fourth Master is done for!" He lowered his head and pretended to be scratching his scar, while his tears dropped onto the newspaper.

The news spread quickly through the city—Li and Little Ma Six were going to be paraded through the streets and shot.

The cruel sun beat down on the cobblestone streets, heating them to the point where you could feel the heat through your shoes, yet the streets were lined with huge crowds of spectators. The two men were seated in a large open wagon with their hands tied behind their backs. They were guarded on either side by policemen in khaki uniforms and soldiers dressed in gray. As the wagon drew near, the two blades of their bayonets reflected the sunlight with a chilling brilliance. The wooden placards announcing their crimes could be seen swaying back and forth above their heads. The man seated in front had his eyes closed, his forehead was dotted with beads of sweat and his lips were moving as if he were mouthing a prayer. The wagon was very close, and I watched him sway past me. I broke down and cried, stopping only after he had gone past. I followed the wagon all the way to the execution ground. Not once did he raise his head.

His eyebrows were knitted; his mouth hung open. The blood spurted forth from his chest, as if he were praying the moment he died. I took his body away.

Two months later, I ran into White Li in Shanghai. If I hadn't called to him, he probably would have walked right past me. "Number Four!" I called out to him.

"Huh?" He appeared startled. "Hey, is that you? Sounded just like Number Two."

Maybe the way I called to him reminded him of Black Li's voice, but this was totally unintentional on my part. Or maybe it was Black Li himself, alive somewhere inside me, who called out on my behalf.

White Li seemed to have aged, and looked more like his older brother than ever. We said very little to each other. He didn't have much to say to me anyway.

I remember two things he did say though:

"Number Two must have gone to heaven; that's a perfect place for him. But I'm still here smashing the gates of hell."

ALGAE

Mao Dun

I

THE NORTHWEST wind had been blowing hard for two days, and in the tiny village you could hardly hear a dog bark. The sky was a boundless leaden color, except where at the eastern horizon a pale yellow patch, weakly, yet stubbornly, appeared to be trying slowly to melt away that leaden-colored cover of a sky.

Scattered here and there were seven or eight low huts, crouching on the ground, beetle-like. Stacks of fresh rice stalks looked like withered wild fungi; nearby, on the riverbanks and farther down, tallow trees stripped of their leaves reared their newly snapped branches, nobly combating the northwest wind. Those tallow trees were kindly mothers to the peasants; generally they required no special tending, but in winter when their black seed capsules burst into white tips, they sacrificed their slender fingers, endured thousands of knife wounds, and offered their tallow-rich capsules to supplement the peasants' livelihood.

The river meandered westward like a black python, creeping past rice fields criss-crossed with dikes and irregularly shaped mulberry groves, widening as it went farther west, until it merged with the horizon. When summer turned into fall, this cheerful, good-natured little river would be decorated all over with penny-like duckweeds and threads of waterweeds, but now all had been swept clean by the north-

Translated by Yi-tsi Mei Feuerwerker. Algae is an inclusive term that covers any of various primitive, aquatic one-celled or multicellular plants including kelp or other types of waterweed. My translation of Mao Dun's story was prepared for the 1982 workshop, but in revising it I have benefited from consulting the more recent translation of Simon Johnstone. See "A Ballad of Algae," *Chinese Literature* (Winter 1986): 14–27. Despite his title, Johnstone translates the plant as hornwort within the text. I would also like to express my profound thanks to Robert Hegel—who prefers the term waterweed—for his detailed and helpful suggestions as I revised my translation.

west wind, and in the bitter cold the naked body of the river wrinkled into fish-scale waves, its color turned into an angry black.

Caixi, a big tall fellow approaching forty, came out from one of the low huts. He strode to the east end of the threshing ground, raised his face to the sky, and looked all around. That pale yellow patch at the eastern horizon was covered now; the sky had become an enormous lead cover, without even a tiny chink. Caixi looked for a while, then sniffed to test the humidity of the air.

"Damn it! It's going to snow," he muttered to himself and went back into the hut. A gust of northwest wind whistling scurried out from the mulberry groves across the river, lifting the lower edge of his tattered cotton jacket. A mangy yellow dog had just come out from the house, but immediately tucked in his head and arched his back, his tangled fur apparently bristling.

"Eh, you beast, so you don't like the cold either!" Caixi grasped it by the scruff of the neck, then as if needing an object to let off all that energy of his, he lifted the dog and casually pitched it toward the threshing ground.

The dog rolled into a somersault as it landed, then without a yelp, it ran back into the house, its tail between its legs. "Ha, ha, ha!" Caixi laughed as he went inside.

"Xiusheng! The weather's changing. Let's go for the algae today!" Caixi's strong voice at once invigorated the atmosphere inside the house.

There was a dark black object squirming in the corner; this was Xiusheng. He was the "head" of this household, yet he was also Caixi's nephew, about ten years younger, but looking much older. This tiller of the land had suffered from jaundice since childhood. At the moment he was putting five *dou* of rice into two gunny-sacks, checking to see if their weight was even. He straightened up and replied, "Get algae today!? But I've got to go to town to sell the rice."

"You can go to town tomorrow! What'll you do if we get a heavy snow? And what about the money from the tallow last time? Not all gone is it?"

"Gone ages ago. It was all your idea that we redeem our winter clothes. Today we've no oil, we're out of salt, and yesterday the village head came dunning us for the interest owed Master Chen, one yuan fifty. When we sold the tallow didn't I say we should pay back the interest first and wait a bit on the clothes, but you . . . "

"Hm! But if we miss out on today, there won't be any algae left for us!" Caixi shouted irritably, as he went to the back of the house.

Xiusheng cast a hesitant look at the sky outside. He was worried too that it might snow. Besides, the northwest wind had been blowing for two days now, and the algae was probably all piled up in the narrow bends of the river. If they waited a day, snow or no snow, others would get to the algae before them; still he couldn't get out of his mind the village head's words yesterday, "No money tomorrow? All right, then we'll take the rice as security!" Once the rice got into his hands, three yuan worth of rice would go down to one fifty.

"The rice must be sold, but the algae also has to be got in," Xiusheng thought as he took up the carrying pole and tried lifting the two gunny-sacks. Then he put it down and decided to ask if any of their neighbors might be going to town and could sell the rice for them.

II

Caixi went to the back of the house and entered the goat shed—his bedroom. He grabbed a blue cotton sash from the bed planks and tied it tightly around his waist. That made him feel much warmer. No goats had been kept there for two years now—Xiusheng did not have the extra cash to buy kids, but that smell peculiar to goats still lingered. As Caixi loved cleanliness, he frequently put the planks on which he slept out to sun. The dirt floor underneath where the goats used to sleep was also swept spotlessly clean. He did this not because of the goat smell lingering there—in fact he rather liked that faint goat smell—but because of the moldy putrid odor that came from the dank earth.

Caixi was thinking that before the snowfall he would add a couple of sheaves of new rice stalks to his bed. He was just leaving the shed and on his way towards the haystack when he heard a moaning noise coming from that direction. A pail full of water was set on the ground next to the haystack. Then he caught a whiff of a familiar faint goat smell. Right away he knew who it was and bounding over, saw that indeed there was Xiusheng's wife squatting by the haystack and moaning.

"What is it?" Caixi grabbed hold of the sturdy young woman to lift her up. But when he saw that she had both her hands under her distended belly, he let go and asked anxiously, "Does your belly hurt? Is the baby on its way?"

The woman nodded, then shook her head and said with great effort: "No, I don't think so—it's still too early! Maybe there's something wrong with the fetus, just now I went to draw a pail of water and when I got here, my belly—it started to hurt awfully."

Caixi turned to look at the pail of water, at a loss over what to do. "He picked a fight with me again last night," she was trying to get to her feet. "He cursed for a while and kicked me in the stomach. Could be he hurt the fetus. It hurt for a while then and got better, but just now . . ."

The woman heaved a sigh, then squatted down again by the haystack.

But Caixi was shouting angrily, "What, and you didn't cry out? You just let him hit you? Just who does he think he is that he dare hit you? What was he cursing about?"

"He said, the kid in my belly wasn't his, and he didn't want it!"

"Huh, he has a lot of nerve to say that! He's a man, but he doesn't have it in himself to plant his own seed!"

"He said that one of these days for sure, it'll be a white knife going in, a red knife coming out—I'm afraid of him, he might really . . ."

But Caixi laughed, "He wouldn't dare, he doesn't have the guts." Xiusheng's bloodless and somewhat puffy face, his dry twig-like arms flashed before Caixi's eyes; such a contrast to this woman before him, a woman overflowing with youthful vitality, whose flesh strongly emanated a goat-like smell. Caixi was convinced that they were a mismatched couple, convinced that there was no reason why such a strong woman, a woman who could work better than a man her size, should endure the beating and cursing of her sick ghost of a husband.

Yet Caixi also understood why this woman put up with the insults from her husband; she admitted that she had treated him badly in one respect, so she tried to make up for the injury he suffered by working hard and submitting. But was this a good way? Here Caixi felt confused. Maybe all they could do was to go on muddling along. After all it was not Xiusheng's own fault that he was so sickly.

Caixi sighed.

"Still I can't let him beat you and kick you just as he feels like it. What would happen if he harmed the fetus? Whether the child is his or mine, it all comes down to the same thing, it will crawl out of your belly and in any case be a seed of our family!—Hey, it doesn't hurt now, does it?"

The woman nodded, and tried to stand. But like carrying a big drum, that huge belly made it awkward to move. Caixi took hold of her arm to pull her up; at this moment the strong arousing scent of the woman's body assailed his nostrils and he couldn't refrain from hugging her tight.

Caixi carried the pail of water and went ahead into the house.

III

Algae is collected for use as fertilizer the following spring. In the Jiangnan area fertilizer is applied once each spring to the paddy fields when the seedlings are transplanted, and again in July and August when the rice reaches waist high. In Xiusheng's village the old way was to stress the importance of the second application and to use soybean cakes. But one year there had been a so-called incident in the region that produced bean cakes, so the price of bean cakes went up year by year. Peasants could not afford to buy them, and the soybean cake companies went bankrupt.

Thus the poor peasants could only apply fertilizer once. This first application was called "*touyong*" (first spreading), and the best material for it was said to be the algae in the river, what was called "*wencao*" in Xiusheng's village.

Algae could only be collected in the winter when the northwest wind had been blowing; the wind piled the algae together in one place, making it easy to scoop up. But the bitter cold in the open country was really hard to endure.

Deprived of bean cakes, the peasants could do nothing but stake their lives on this struggle for life.

Caixi and Xiusheng went west, propelling a dilapidated "bareback" (flat) boat. They knew from experience that the most algae could be found in a branch stream over twenty *li* from the village; but they also knew that two boats from their village had set out ahead of them. Therefore they had to double their speed to go west a dozen *li* and then turn south another dozen *li* so as to arrive at their destination before the others. All this was Caixi's idea.

They went with the stream but against the northwest wind, which was still blowing strong; Caixi punting with the pole and Xiusheng at the scull.

The northwest wind played with the free end of Caixi's blue cotton sash, again and again entangling it round the bamboo punt pole. Caixi offhandedly took told of the sash and wiped the sweat off his face, then with a loud swash, the pole hit the frozen earth of the river bank, the rim of the boat splashing up a jet of silver white spray. Oo-ah! A powerful cry came from Caixi's thick chest, as fast as flying the pole was deftly turned round, striking the water on the other side of the boat. With both hands Caixi pressed down on the top of the pole, gave a push and then with a pull whirled the dripping four-meter-long pole once again over his head.

He seemed to have found a target to vent his anger and wielded the pole with greater and greater energy, while all over him trickled the hot sweat of victory.

After a dozen *li* so, the river began to broaden. Boundless expanses of newly harvested paddy fields stretched before their eyes. Branching streams like shining ribbons meandered in and out of the vast chess-board of farmlands. The roof coverings of the water wheels looked like thumbtacks, studded here and there along the "ribbons." Spread out in scattered grey clusters were little villages, above which white smoke was dimly rising.

And far and near across the bare fields stood the lofty dark green cemeteries of the rich.

Some water birds fluttered up from clumps of withered reeds, dispersed suddenly like many small black dots falling away into a distance, then disappeared.

Caixi stood at the bow of the boat, holding his pole sideways. The scene before his eyes, familiar as it was, suddenly looked refreshingly new. It was as if nature was telling him something in a silent language. He felt there was also something in him that wanted to get out.

"Oo-ah!" he emitted a long cry to the melancholy fields.

The northwest wind carried his cry away. Slowly Caixi put down his pole. The reeds along the shore moaned softly. From the stern of the boat the sound of the scull came crisp and clear, but it was slow and listless.

Caixi walked back and helped Xiusheng with the sculling. The water groaned as if in retreat.

Before long, they arrived at their destination.

"Let's get on with it! In a while they'll be here and with everybody grabbing, it will be hard on good feelings."

Caixi said this to Xiusheng, then he picked up the biggest and heaviest of the tongs used for collecting algae. They stood one at either side of the bow, thrusting their open tongs into the thick clumps of algae, then closed the tongs, and vigorously twisting, tugged, lifted, and threw algae and mud together down into the bottom of the boat.

The mud and weeds in the stream seemed to have grown into one piece, resisting efforts to tug them apart. River mud and scraps of ice added further to the weight. With chin firmly set, Caixi tugged and twisted furiously. Each time he lifted a load, he burst forth with a cry of triumph. His thick bamboo tongs bent like a bow, making a creaking sound.

"Harder, Xiusheng, come on, hurry!" Caixi spat in his palms, rubbed his hands together, and with redoubled vigor raised his tongs again.

Sweat was oozing even from Xiusheng's rather puffy face. But his movements were only half as quick as Caixi's and each time with his tongs he picked up only half as much algae. Still, his arms were sore, his heart throbbed and fluttered in his chest, and every now and then he whimpered softly.

Mixed with mud and ice, the pile of algae gradually grew high. The boat was also drafting deeper; each time Caixi lifted a full load and pushed down with his feet, the boat listed sideways; ice cold water flowed into the boat, soaking his straw-sandaled feet. He had already taken off his torn padded jacket, leaving only a single layer of clothing, but the blue sash remained tightly tied: from head to waist, he was like a food steamer giving off hot steam.

IV

Sounds of creaking sculls and people's voices were gradually borne closer by the wind. The top of a felt hat flashed in the mound of dry reeds not far ahead. A small boat made its way out with difficulty, then another one.

"Aha, you people here too?" said Caixi merrily. He stamped vigorously and threw all the algae his tongs would hold into the boat, then with a cunning smile, he lifted his tongs and aimed them where he had already noticed that the algae was thickest, opening them up as wide as possible and stirring as hard as he could.

"Eh! How odd! How did you people get here? How come we didn't bump into you on the way?" shouted the men in the newly arrived boat as it likewise drove into the algae.

"Oh, us? We . . ." Xiusheng put down his tongs and began to pant. But Caixi's hearty voice quickly cut him off.

"We flew here through the sky! Ha, ha!"

As he spoke he thrust again and again into the thick algae. "Don't brag! Everyone knows you're an old hand at poking around in the mud!" Laughing, the men on the newly arrived boat started clumsily to twitch their crude bamboo tongs.

Caixi did not answer but hurriedly moved his tongs once more into the places where there was a lot of algae. Then he turned his tongs sideways, looked into his boat and at the stream which appeared as if it had been littered with rags. His practiced eye told him that all that was left now was a surface layer mostly made up of duckweed and fine mosses.

Putting down his tongs, he lifted his sash to wipe the sweat off his face and walked nimbly to the bow of the boat.

The mud that had splashed onto deck seemed to have frozen. Caixi's torn jacket was stuck to the planks; he pried it up and draped it over his back, then squatted down.

"We're quitting," he said, "What's here in the stream is all yours."

"Sure, that's nice talk, now that you've taken all the good stuff," the new people retorted as they got down to work.

In no time the quiet stream was bustling with activity.

Xiusheng lifted a plank and took out the buns they had brought. They were frozen hard as rocks. He gnawed bravely. Caixi ate too but he was also looking up at the sky and thinking; he was trying to figure out whether there might be any branch streams nearby with a lot of algae.

The sky was covered with dark clouds, but the northwest wind had dropped somewhat. From far away sounded a steam whistle, it was from the regular passenger ship passing through the outer port.

"Eh, how come it's noon already? Isn't that the steamboat?"

The algae gatherers were talking noisily, looking up at the sky.

"Xiusheng, we'd better get back," Caixi stood up and took hold of the scull.

This time Xiusheng manned the pole. When the boat had left the branch stream, Caixi gave a wild laugh. "Turn north, let's turn north! There's bound to be some by the shore at the backwater."

Xiusheng was startled. "To the backwater? We'll be spending the night on the boat."

"Why do you say that? Don't you see the weather is about to change? We'll get a boatload today, then we shan't have to worry!" Caixi answered resolutely, pulling on the scull a few times and steering the boat into a side stream.

Xiusheng walked silently to the stern and helped with the sculling. But he had actually used up all his strength; rather than sculling, it would be truer to say that the scull, which had become a live dragon in Caixi's hand, was pulling on him.

The water splashed and splattered loudly. Now and then a few unidentified waterbirds, startled from among the withered white reeds, flew upward, making wailful calls.

Caixi's two iron arms moved rhythmically like levers; his face oily with sweat, his eyes joyful. He broke into a song often sung in the village:

There's a girl eighteen or nineteen
With big tits that quiver and shake
Large buttocks that wiggle and swing
At dawn carrying vegetables she goes to town
Her own hubby hung on one end of the pole.
Fifty li and she turns around.
In a hurry, she runs into her other man—
At the goat shed door
They snuggle up and tumble over.[1]

Xiusheng felt that every line in this song was directed against himself. His rather puffy face turned more pallid, his legs began to shake. Suddenly his waist went limp, his hands lost hold of the live dragon-like scull, his body crumpled backward, and he squatted down on the boat planks.

"What's the matter, Xiusheng?" Caixi stopped singing and asked in surprise without stopping the movement of his hands.

Xiusheng hung his head but did not answer.

"Useless fellow," Caixi said with sympathy, "better rest a bit."

[1]This is a satire on the rich peasants' unreasonable system of child-brides. Rich peasants would arrange marriages for their sons with much older child-brides, in order to utilize their labor, but these pubescent girls often had lovers on the sly.

Then Caixi seemed to remember something and gazed at the water and sky in the distance. In a moment the song rolled out of his throat again.

"Cai . . . xi." Suddenly Xiusheng stood up, "Do you have to go on with that singing?—I'm good for nothing, sick, I can't work, but as long as I have a breath left in me I'd rather starve to death than be a turtle [cuckold] with my eyes open!"

Such direct and resolute talk had never come from him before. For the moment Caixi was at a loss over what to do. He looked at Xiusheng's face livid with anger, and remorse welled up within him; it was true, although the simple song had been around a long time, it was much too like the peculiar relationship among the three of them; no wonder it grated on Xiusheng's ears. Caixi felt that he should not have sung so merrily right in front of Xiusheng; it looked as if he was intentionally mocking and taunting him. But then didn't Xiusheng say he would "rather starve to death"? Actually Caixi had put out untold effort while living under Xiusheng's roof. Now, however, it seemed as if Xiusheng, as "head" of the household, was asking him to get out. At the thought of this, Caixi turned angry.

"All right, so I'll go then!" said Caixi coldly, unconsciously slowing down on his sculling.

Xiusheng seemed not to have expected such a reaction, and at a loss how to answer, dispiritedly squatted down again.

"But," continued Caixi coldly and sternly, "you're not allowed to beat your wife anymore. A woman like that, and still you're not satisfied? There's a child in her belly, a shoot off our family . . . "

"It's none of your business!" Xiusheng jumped up in a wild frenzy, his voice so shrill that it died away. "She's my wife, if I kill her I'll pay for it!"

"You dare, dare you?" Caixi suddenly turned around, his fists tightly clenched, his eyes threatening Xiusheng's face.

Xiusheng was shaking all over. "I dare, of course I dare, I'm tired of living. From one year's end to the next they're after me for grain, for taxes, for debts, hounding me to death! If I eat today, there'll be nothing tomorrow, I pawn my summer clothes, but can't get my winter ones back, I'm sick all over . . . I'm tired of living! Living is nothing but misery!"

Slowly Caixi's head went down, his fists became unclenched; grief and anger filled his heart; it felt like it was on fire. With no one in charge of the pole, the boat swung sideways; instinctively Caixi took hold of the pole and gave it a push, but without taking his eyes away from his pitiful nephew.

"Ah, Xiusheng! It's no use just blaming your fate. And another thing: it's not your wife who's making things hard for you; she puts up with all kinds of hardships to help you cope. She never talks back when you scold, never returns your blows when you hit her. When you were sick this summer, she took care of you and didn't sleep for several nights."

Xiusheng listened dejectedly, his eyes gradually filled with tears. He looked as if he might be melting, squatting weak and limp on the planks, his head hanging down. After a moment, he mournfully muttered to himself:

"I'll die, then everything will be over with. I don't have close kin anyway. If I'm dead, you'll all be happy."

"Xiusheng! Aren't you ashamed to be talking this way? Don't be so suspicious, no one is waiting for you to die. We'll all live together, or we'll die together!"

"Huh, no one is waiting for me to die? They might not say it, but that's what they're thinking."

"Who are you talking about?" Caixi turned around, his hands stopped sculling.

"If not one right in front of me, then one at home."

"Aiya, you're wronging a good person. In dealing with you she has a clear conscience."

"Conscience? A woman makes her husband wear a green kerchief [horns], and she has a conscience?" Xiusheng raised his voice again, not in anger, but rather with a coldness that rose from sorrow and a lack of self-confidence.

"Ah!" Caixi emitted this sound and then fell silent. At times he did feel remorse for his relationship with Xiusheng's wife, but he really could not agree with Xiusheng's view of the matter. To his way of thinking, for a wife with a sick and maimed husband to go with other men had nothing whatsoever to do with whether or not she had a conscience. Apart from having slept with another man, Xiusheng's wife had not changed in any respect, she was still Xiusheng's wife, she did everything she was supposed to do and did it well.

Although these were Caixi's thoughts, he lacked the ability to put them into words; but seeing Xiusheng so depressed, so mistaken about that "good woman," he felt it was necessary to speak to make things clear.

Under pressure from both sides, Caixi became irritable, he pulled vigorously at the scull as if venting his anger—sculling with all his might, oblivious of what direction he was going. "Aiya! Damn it, it's snowing!" Caixi raised his face, flushed with vexation, and cried out instinctively.

"Ah!" Xiusheng raised his head as if in response.

The wind was rising, swirling snowflakes around near and far, making one's eyes dizzy. The small temples, wayside pavilions, cemeteries, stone bridges, even the ancient trees, the things that one depended on for direction in the vast expanse of fields crisscrossed with waterways, all became blurred in the swirling snow.

"Xiusheng! We must get back quick!" Caixi shouted and ran to the bow, and grabbing the pole, thrusting and pushing to left and right, he quickly steered the boat into a small stream. Then round another bend to the broader river. He thought he saw two boats through the snow ahead; those must have been the algae-gathering boats from their own village.

Caixi leaped to the stern, where Xiusheng, blue-faced and gritting his teeth, was trying on his own to pull the big scull. Caixi rushed up and told Xiusheng to "draw tight."[2]

"Oh-ah!" Caixi gathered together all the vigor in his chest and gave a long cry; the scull was like an angry dragon in his hands, splashing waves onto the boat.

But even "drawing tight" was more than Xiusheng could manage.

"Go rest a minute, I can do it myself!" said Caixi.

Like the rapid and regular prancing of a fine horse, Caixi's two iron arms vigorously and evenly sculled the boat. The wind had dropped some, but the snow flakes were getting bigger.

Caixi manned the scull with one hand and took off his torn padded jacket with the other. Looking around he saw that Xiusheng was huddled in a heap, all covered with snow, so he took his torn padded jacket and covered him.

"How pitiful he is, sick, poor, and miserable!" Caixi thought. He felt he had truly treated his nephew badly. Since he had come a year ago to live with Xiusheng, he had with the best of intentions done his utmost to help with the work, but then some devil had manipulated him into

[2]To "draw tight" is to push and pull on the thick rope around the scull, a relatively less strenuous job.

having that kind of thing with Xiusheng's wife, making it seem as if there had been another motive behind his utmost efforts. Xiusheng's depression, his abuse of his wife, all stemmed from that.

The thought seemed like ice water trickling down his back.

"Had I better not go then?" he asked himself. But he immediately reconsidered and answered himself: No! Once he left, would Xiusheng be able to do the work in the fields all by himself? His wife was strong but she wouldn't be able to manage either! Besides she was with child.

"The child is a flower! Xiusheng and Xiusheng's wife all must go on and live! What the hell would I be leaving for?" he cried out in his heart. He gave his chin a vigorous thrust; his eyes were shining.

He rowed fiercely, as if there was a ball of fire burning in his heart; in a minute he had caught up with the two boats in front, in another, he had left them far, far behind.

V

It stopped snowing at dusk. The tiny village had been transformed into a silver white world. Snow covered the tiles of the low huts; where proper repairs had not been done, finger-like icicles hung down; people shivered under these roofs, as though placed inside iceboxes. Waking up from the cold at midnight, they could hear the old north wind howling over their heads.

Next morning the golden rays of the sun graciously shone on this bitterly cold little village. A couple of dogs were rolling over and over on the threshing ground. At the river a couple of women were chopping ice to get water; three boats filled with algae pressed so closely together that they looked as if they had frozen into one. There were those who wanted to take on the cold and move the algae to the prepared field reservoirs, but the mixture of water and mud had frozen it harder than iron. After a few hacks with the iron-toothed rake, they rubbed their hands and said,

"Damn it, this knocks your hands numb. Except for Caixi, who can pry the stuff loose?"

But Caixi's powerful figure did not appear on the threshing ground.

When the sun had risen to the height of a bamboo pole, Caixi returned from town. He had gone to get medicine. There were small herbal pharmacies in town who did what they could for the poor. You described to the pharmacy's one and only clerk the condition of the patient, and for two or three hundred coppers he would sell you some herbs that neither cured nor killed. Caixi said that Xiusheng had a fever and was given some medicine for bringing down fever, including some plaster.

At this moment something was disturbing the villagers.

Caixi was startled from some way off to see that several villagers were poking their heads about Xiusheng's doorway, "Could Xiusheng have taken a turn for the worse?"—He quickened his steps and began to run.

He heard Xiusheng's wife scream for help and his heart beat fast. Because he had suddenly rushed into the house from the bright sunlight, Caixi's eyes lost their use, and it was only through his ears that he sensed that in the corner, where their bed was, a scuffle was going on.

Xiusheng was sitting in bed; his wife, half kneeling and half crouching, was trying with all her might to keep down his two hands and his lower body.

Seeing what was going on, Caixi relaxed a bit, but then he felt muddled.

"What is it? Are you beating her again?" He was trying to suppress his anger.

Xiusheng's wife let go, stood up, and touched her tousled hair. Her answer sounded frightened and confused:

"He insists on going to work on the road! He says he's tired of living, he doesn't have any money, so he's going to risk his life! Just think, yesterday he came home with a fever and moaned all night—how can he go and work on any road? I tried to get him to wait until you got back to talk it over, but the village head won't allow us and he won't agree. I wouldn't let him get up, then he went crazy, saying we might as well all die and get it over with. He grabbed me by the throat, and started beating me up."

Only then did Caixi notice see that there was another person in the room, the village head that Xiusheng's wife had mentioned. The visitation of this "big shot" was the reason why everyone was so upset. The problem was road construction corvée, for three days; no one could get out of it.

A couple of people who had been watching outside the door now came in and gathered round Caixi, all trying to get a word in. With one hand Caixi pushed Xiusheng down under the covers, and said, "What are you getting so worked up about? Your wife means well!''

"I don't want to live anymore. I don't have any money, but life—I do have one!"

Xiusheng was still being stubborn, but his voice sounded weak.

Caixi turned to the village head. ''Xiusheng's really sick. Early this morning I went to get medicine (dangling the packet of medicine before the village head's face). You can't conscript sick people for labor.''

"That won't do!" The village head's face was livid, ''if you're sick, find a substitute or pay cash. No substitute, then one yuan a day. If everyone tried to get out of public work by claiming to be sick, who would do it?''

"Last time when there was labor service, how come the son of Ward Headman Chen didn't go, and didn't pay either? The kid didn't even report sick. Wasn't this all under you?"

"Don't talk nonsense! Tell me quickly, do I put down his name, or are you paying up?—three days is three yuan!"

Xiusheng started yelling again, ''Caixi, I'll go! I don't have any money, but I do have a life! If I die on the road, they'll at least have to give me a coffin to lie in!''

Like a wounded animal, Xiusheng threw off the covers, and shakily jumped to his feet.

''We don't have a cent for you!'' Caixi threw down the packet of medicine, and his arms, like a pair of steel tongs, grabbed hold of the village head's chest, ''Get out, you dog!''

By now Xiusheng's wife and two neighbors were holding on to Xiusheng. Outside the door, the village head let loose a torrent of abuse, threatening to report to the ''bureau.'' Caixi went up to Xiusheng and, like picking up a small child, put him back on the bed.

"Oh, Caixi, what'll we do when he reports to the bureau and they come to get you?"

Xiusheng was gasping as he spoke, his face as hot as if it were on fire.

"Let them. The sky can fall; Caixi will be here." It was a calm and resolute answer.

Xiusheng's wife opened the packet of medicine and placed four or five kinds of herbs into the clay pot. At the end she picked up the plaster, gave it a few pinches with her fingers, as if unable to decide what to do, but finally added it to the pot also.

VI

The sun's rays were coming straight down, bringing warmth to this little village.

Some unmelted snow remained on the threshing ground, looking like a huge network of lard patches. People were moving the algae off the small boats.

One of the people was Caixi. Clad in only a thin jacket, the blue sash still tied tightly around his waist, sleeves rolled up high, he was wielding a big iron-toothed rake, like the "Five heroes cutting into the mountain," loosening the half-frozen mud and algae mixture, and putting it into wooden buckets. The mixture would be put into the prepared reservoirs, then interlayed with already collected "garbage."[3]

"Damn it, is the rake stuck too!—Hey, Caixi!" called someone from the neighbor's boat. From another boat someone said, "Oh, Caixi! Can you take this load of ours with you? It's right on your way."

Caixi, his face covered with sweat, jumped across to offer a helping hand.

The sun caused the earth to steam and human bodies to sweat. Some sparrows were chirping in the tallow trees.

People stepped up their efforts, hoping to get all the algae in place before sundown, and hoping also that tomorrow would be another fine day, so that they could take their boats even farther to where there might be more.

They were laughing, shouting, working, and improvising meaningless ditties, and in the midst of all these voices, Caixi's long cry kept soaring up into the air, tragic and powerful. It seemed at once to be appeal and defiant protest.

---

[3]Garbage—a mixture of straw ash and rotten food leftovers. Peasants go into town to collect this.

A KISS

Shi Tuo

IT WAS 1913 or 14 or 15, I do not know in complete detail. Try to imagine those good times in Orchard City, when life was simple and easy, before the revolution of 1911 had stirred up the populace. But in the space of one night, people said they were free, that they had become the masters of big, old China, that the emperor who had ruled over them for several thousand years was toppled from this time on. It was the time when the city god would go out "on tours of inspection" on his birthday; it was the time when operas were sung everywhere at Lantern Festival, when Aoshan lanterns were hung everywhere and when fireworks were set off everywhere; it was a time when those to be put to death were taken by horsecart to the execution ground; a time when spending money was manifestly spending money: for someone to buy his wife jewelry, he had to heft a couple of strings of copper cash. Matches were still called "foreign fire" then, cloth woven by machine was called "foreign cloth," and mothers still terrified their children by saying that the foreign devils would kidnap them and render them into engine oil. It was the time when there was a snack stall at the intersection across from the tinsmith that sold peanuts, melon seeds, sesame candy, pear cake, dried dates and hill-haws. A girl ran the stand, a handsome one, good at needlework; she was called Sister Liu, or maybe it was Sister Liou. Sister Liu's mother, Mother Liu, was the widow of a yamen runner and had "trod the doorsteps of a hundred families"—do you know the meaning of this phrase? She was the same type as Madam Wang of *The Water Margin* and *The Golden Lotus*—she had been to all the great households and had undertaken as well as arranged all sorts of affairs both legal and illegal; she did this for a living.

Translated by Theodore Huters.

But we must repeat once more: what a time it was! How many wonderful sounds there were at the intersection! At that time the center of the region was not the three or four peculiar buildings at the railroad station, but was this city redolent of dust. The noise from the tavern was deafening: the clamor of waiters running and answering customers and from the drinking games that went on all day merged into a sheet of sound; country people threaded their way through the streets bearing heavy bundles on their backs; the mortar sounded in the druggist's shop, a sound both happy and innocent that would be difficult to describe: it was as if it were saying: "medicine in, sickness out; medicine in, sickness out." Isn't this just what it said? The tinsmith across the way used a wooden mallet to hammer out sheets of pewter—Bang! Bang! Bang! Bang!—then they were cut and fashioned into tea kettles, tea trays, vases, candlesticks. A little farther off his old foe the coppersmith worked with a hammer—Tang, Tang, Tang! Tang, Tang, Tang!—spreading out the sheets of copper. Donkeys for hire to take people out of the city moved restlessly; they were tethered to a wall with iron rings fixed in it and the bells on their necks rang, Huanglang. A carter waiting for customers lay in the shade, facing the sky; he suddenly opened his mouth and sang out: "The able king sits in the golden palace, using his eyes to observe . . . "—let him look all he wants, but he earns a hundred copper cash a day and is an emperor without care or woe; let him look at the clouds in the sky. A yamen runner came by; in front of him was a small landlord who had probably just been issued a summons. "Would you bestow a little something?" the yamen runner muttered solicitously. And when the money had dropped into the hand hidden in his long sleeve, he said joyfully and in large voice that the landlord's case would certainly win. But then one of the carrier donkeys decided suddenly to drown him out and shook the whole area with a tremendous bray; at the same time, all the other donkeys tethered at the intersection began to bray in response. Truly a noise that cannot be captured in the telling. Sister Liu had thus from age twelve minded the stand for her mother in the midst of this bustle, tending to her needlework and listening to the chatter of the carters and drivers. All around were acquaintances who bought her peanuts and teased her when they felt like it; she grew up in this atmosphere until age seventeen.

Age seventeen is when youth begins to reveal its news; people take pride in this and it is a time when they have faith that they will become independent. A naughty young boy had secretly fallen for her some time before, an apprentice at the tinsmith's by the name of Tigerfish. The two of them had dawdled together from the time they were children, but she, of course, always knew what she was about. While she sat beside the stand across the street, he was always up to no good, whether it was sometimes hammering his own fingers or poking holes through the pewter sheeting or breaking a lathe, for which he was harshly scolded by his master.

One day opportunity came at last for the good Tigerfish. His master was not in the shop, having gone to one of the gentry households to negotiate for some business, so Tigerfish decided to let out the feelings, the adoration that he had always been unable to express. But what a method he dreamt up, this little scoundrel! He had already gotten a bunch of pig bristles from the butcher and cut them to a length of about two inches. When he saw Sister Liu with her head bent into her needlework, he sidled over and put the bristles down her collar and then immediately ran off. Sister Liu gave chase, picked up the mallet used to roll pewter and followed him into the tinsmith's shop. We don't know how the mallet avoided injuring Tigerfish, but the two of them began to grapple and were grasping at each other, scolding, laughing, when Tigerfish suddenly embraced her and gave her a kiss.

"Beautiful! Let's have an even better one, you little mother, you!" hollered the errand boy from behind the counter at the drug shop. The waiters, the carters, the drivers all chimed in.

Sister Liu turned bright red with embarrassment and immediately fled to a corner to hide. She thought that she should treat it as a joke and not take it much to heart but she could not know that this little incident would more or less determine the rest of her life. In the evening when she went home she was met head-on by a nasty rebuke from her mother.

"My young mistress, could you please try to consider your mother's position more carefully: I went to a lot of trouble to raise you and if you happen to be spoiled by that little bastard, who will I be able to depend on in my old age?" Seeing that the effect of all her harsh words and rebukes was the opposite of what she intended and that she had, in fact, only scolded her fine daughter into resentment, the yamen runner's widow finally yielded to tears.

She understood Sister Liu, perhaps, or perhaps we should say that she understood herself, for she was terrified that the daughter had the mother's blood flowing in her veins. After all, she and the yamen runner were not originally from this vicinity and had never been formally married, but had simply been unwilling to submit to their fates: they had turned their backs on their parents and eloped. She had sowed her wild oats, but, having sowed them, she had eventually tasted their bitter, medicinal flavor. But more than that, with the yamen runner dead, Sister Liu had become her last property and, like a hunter trying to catch game, she had spread her nets in the sole expectation of an old wastrel who would be rich and lecherous and willing to replenish her lost capital in exchange for the daughter.

Sister Liu did in fact have her mother's blood flowing in her veins: as we said, she was handsome, good at needlework and, after all, who has ever seen someone of talent and appeal who was not both proud and of full temper?

"Mother, don't say any more," Sister Liu adamantly screwed up her brows, "I won't go out of doors for the rest of my life!"

When Sister Liu spoke she meant what she said and after that she no longer went to the intersection to run her stand. Half a year later she married someone and satisfied her mother's wishes, becoming the concubine of the private assistant of the local magistrate. Then they left this small city, the magistrate having been transferred, and her mother accompanied them, now dressed as a real dowager. It never occurred to anyone to consider whether Sister Liu had been willing or not and she, for her part, accepted whatever was arranged for her. Whenever she came out dressed to the nines, whether to pay a call on the local gentry or to attend the theater, her old acquaintances—the carters, the drivers, the waiters, and errand boys—would begin to discuss her and her mother and to exclaim about their good fortune behind their backs.

Time then passed by. From the time when Sister Liu had left, Orchard City had undergone a change: as usual, no one had paid any attention to when it had started, but the center of the region had gradually shifted to the train station. What had once been a wilderness with a few odd buildings in it now had so many more even stranger and much larger buildings erected upon it that there came to be a great clutter of streets. As a natural consequence, people from the country no longer went to the city for a half catty of sugar; when they bought provisions they went to the train station, for printed cloth they went to the station, and they went to the station to widen their horizons and to watch the excitement; all sorts of shops, services and theaters had been opened there just for them.

Fate can often play with people; Tigerfish had planned to learn to be a tinsmith, but he wound up pulling a rickshaw (the tinsmith's had closed down because it could not afford to buy raw materials). He had become middle-aged, taken a wife and had been presented with a number of children by her. In order to supply them all with food and clothing, he went everyday from the city to the station and from the station to the city, running all day without cease. As for the girl who had run the stand at the intersection—the one he had once fallen in love with—he naturally had long since forgotten her; or if he had not forgotten, he did not have the leisure to remember her.

One day he got an unexpectedly good fare. A lady who had long since lost the freshness of youth came in from the station. It could even be said that she was far from the aura of youth even at the times when she was being bashful; she was all flesh and gold: earrings and bracelets dazzled the eye. Tigerfish had a red face with short whiskers, strong shoulders and legs; he picked up this dignified customer and started to move forward.

"You're going to the city, ma'am?" For prudence's sake he asked this only after he had pulled her out of the station and onto the street.

He had guessed correctly, the lady did want to go to the city.

"Look, the old pagoda still hasn't collapsed—that is the same old pagoda, isn't it?" She asked when they were still far away, and began to stir delightedly in the rickshaw.

"That's still it, ma'am," Tigerfish replied. The first thing anyone who has been to this small city thinks of is "it." People are so familiar with "it" that when they are speaking, they treat "it" as if it were a thing with a soul; they take "it" as an old friend—to the point that they remove the name "pagoda" and simply and familiarly call it "it." Moreover, "it" is so important that, according to local wits, without "it" people would not be able to recognize Orchard City: those who went abroad to seek their livelihoods would not know their way home and would have to ask where they were even if they were to be walking upon the streets of Orchard City itself.

"That old pagoda really is sturdy; how old it must be!" The lady could not help sighing.

Tigerfish misunderstood her and could not resist taking the opportunity to add: "It's ancient, ma'am; if you have the time you really should go up to see it."

"In the past people said that a fox-spirit lived at the top; is it still there or not?"

"The fox-spirit moved away a long time ago; it bothered Orchard City long enough and now it's moved away."

Then she asked about Master Kui—the local gentleman who had controlled Orchard City from behind the scenes for some fifteen years. It had been real mischance: Master Kui had long since toppled. He no longer made a tour of the streets of Orchard City every morning, enjoying the greetings of the populace, exhibiting his fine visage. Another group of people was now occupying his old place. He preferred to be alone, locked up year after year in his stately abode. His only hope now was to await death.

"How about Twelfth Beauty. Is she still alive?" She asked next.

Below Master Kui, Twelfth Beauty was one of the ranking personages in this small city. The old bitch had been Mother Liu's deadly enemy, that is, the Mother Liu already spoken of; they plied the same trade. She had gained the submission of the whole city with her sweeping harangues, but most importantly, she knew the confidences of countless great families. As for herself, she had no secrets whatsoever; it was as if she were willing to open her whole person to the public.

"Is she still well?" She asked again.

"She's still well, ma'am, people say she's going to live until she turns into an old witch."

"Do you know how old she is now?"

"I think she's probably about seventy."

"I remember that she had a terrible temper and used to abuse people all the time."

"You're right, ma'am. It's a fault she never changed." Tigerfish pulled the rickshaw ahead, panting. But to speak the truth, even this "fault" of Twelfth Beauty was very different from what it had been. Her teeth had fallen out and only a few white strands of hair remained on her crown; age had finally subdued her and, even if she still had the nerve to castigate everyone in the city, her old legs would no longer acquiesce to her orders. She now sat every day on a large black rock at the city gate, leaning on her cane and continuously muttering to herself. When the occasional cart would come in from the country with its load of firewood, she, like the old heroes who set ambushes beneath their mountain lairs, would block the road with her cane, get up, and snatch off a bundle; this was considered her "toll."

Next, the lady asked after the manager of the drug shop. The new manager was his nephew, who happened to be the errand boy behind the counter at the shop who had cheered when Tigerfish had kissed Sister Liu many years before.

"How about that young carter," she asked with disappointment: "the tall one who was always lying in the shade, singing at the top of his voice—what was his name?"

"You mean 'the able king.' " "The able king" had also died. Like the emperor of almost three hundred years ago, when he had suffered enough hard days and had finished singing the good operas—finally he found a piece of rope for himself, climbed the gate tower and hanged himself.

She sighed deeply over this—to tell the truth it really is worth sighing over: people give no concern to fighting, shouting, crying, laughing, and are full of mechanical calculation; but then they suddenly open their eyes and discover that, when confronted with iron-faced and impersonal time, they are so insignificant, hollow, pitiful, and that they are so powerless!

The rickshaw swayed its way into the city; they did not see Twelfth Beauty. On the black rock where Twelfth Beauty normally sat, an old man was sitting mending his fishing net.

"The tinsmith, is he dead too?" She finally asked timidly.

Tigerfish was running ahead the whole time, pulling the rickshaw.

"You're talking about my master, ma'am; I was apprenticed to him." He stopped awhile to reply.

"How is he, is he still alive?"

"He's still alive. He hasn't suffered enough, so the King of Hell won't take him in yet."

"So he's been down on his luck recently?"

' Worse than that, ma'am, he's blind in both eyes."

"Is he still running his tinsmith shop?"

"The shop failed almost ten years ago."

"That sounds very strange; how did he go blind?"

"It was just his bad luck. He wasn't being careful, so one day he rubbed his eyes and got lead poisoning."

As they were speaking they reached the intersection.

"Look," he pursed his lips and said, "There he is, ma'am, there's the tinsmith."

A beggar squatted on the corner at the intersection. He was old and dirty, his body filthy and reeking of the stench of rot; on the ground in front of him was placed a broken alms bowl. This was the one Tigerfish was referring to, the one who took chunks of pewter and all sorts of useless old pewter implements, put them in his smelter, melted them into liquid, and poured it into magical forms. He was the smith who created all the utensils that added luster to the parlors of new houses as well as to shrines. Hearing someone walk by, he made a loud kowtow, bumping his forehead on the ground and crying out with a mournful voice that is hard to describe.

"Sir or madam of good will, be good to me, take pity on this poor person and store up some merit for your little grandchild."

Tigerfish was of a mind to help him and had stopped the rickshaw and greeted him even before he had finished his wail:

"Teacher, there is a lady here who is asking after you."

"There's a lady?" He suddenly straightened up his body in surprise. His two eyes—long dead and without light, eyes like two gray glass balls that terrified with their dim whiteness, stared into space without blinking; then he smiled.

"Ma'am, take pity on this man with no eyes," he said. "I remember you, I can never forget you. . . . I'll pray for your little grandsons all day long, to protect them from illness, to bless them in their studies, so they'll become officials and get rich—when I had my shop you often came to patronize it. Once you came personally and ordered a pair of candlesticks and also a small teapot—your youngest grandson used it at school, so I put a particular amount of work into it and made a lion on the cover."

If someone knew that these words of flattery were all lies, what would he think? She mournfully, perhaps it should be said hopelessly, stared at this old beggar and then looked away and appraised the intersection. But how different it was from what it had been back then! The age of the carters, drivers, the donkeys for hire, the bundles, the copper cash was past, extinguished along with all the other fine sounds of that time. Where the tinsmith's had been, someone had now opened a cotton-fluffing shop; the tavern where previously the noise from the day-long drinking games had merged into a sheet of sound had become an eating house deserted but for swarming flies. Perhaps it was only the old drug shop that had not changed, but even it looked far humbler than it had before. She dejectedly looked at all of this: the sunlight shining bleakly on the wall, the cotton-fluffing machine making a din;

several local residents—a waiter in the eating-house, a peddler, a man and a woman who had brought cotton to be fluffed—all halted momentarily and stared at her in blank surprise, because it was rare to see a stranger come from afar, especially a woman dressed so elegantly.

"Ma'am," said Tigerfish, "where shall we head now?"

She awoke from her daze.

"Go back," she pondered and then gave a wave of her hand—"go back to the station."

Tigerfish pulled the rickshaw back the way he had come. This was very strange, but the world was full of peculiar people, rich people with nothing to do, and Tigerfish did not give it a second thought. He set the rickshaw down at the station and pulled out his hand-towel to wipe the sweat off. He was then astonished to discover that his other hand was full of money, full of bills and coins; and the lady was blushing and smiling at him from the far-off entrance to the station.

This was she, the daughter of the yamen runner's widow, the Sister Liu who had run the stand at the intersection. A train whistle blew; the train from the other direction was about to enter the station. As she turned her clothes pulled tight over her round back; her earrings flashed brightly and her bracelets hung heavily on her wrists as she went in. But why had she been in such a rush to come here? After having left this small city for ten, fifteen, or even close to twenty years, with Mother Liu probably long since dead, her husband possibly dead even before her mother, she herself entering middle-age, what could this little city have that she could not forget? No one would be willing to explain this riddle. But if she had a son and a daughter—if you will allow the person who wrote this piece a word—she would want them only to grow up, have good fortune, and not copy their mother's example.

LILIES

Ru Zhijuan

THE DAY of the Mid-Autumn Festival, 1946.

This was the date set for our troops to stage a night offensive on the coast. On orders from the regimental commander, several of us comrades in the writer's section of the cultural work corps were sent to various regiments engaged in combat to lend a hand. The commander scratched his head over me for half a day—probably all because I was a woman—before he finally called in a signal corpsman to see me to a first-aid station at the front.

If it has to be a first-aid station, then it'll be a first-aid station—just as long as they don't lock me up in some strongbox! I threw my knapsack on my back and set out with the signalman.

There had been a light rain that morning. Even though it had cleared up now, the road was still very slick. The fall crops in the fields along both sides of the road had been washed by the rain to an emerald hue, a wet green with the glow of pearls and the sparkle of gems. The air was filled with their fresh, moist fragrance. If it weren't for the chilling intermittent artillery fire from the enemy blasting away blindly, I really could have thought we were on our way to a fair!

The signalman took off with long strides and went straight on ahead of me. From the beginning he made a point of keeping ten yards or more between us. My feet were killing me, and with the road being slippery I couldn't catch up with him no matter how hard I tried. I thought of asking him to wait for me, but I was afraid that he'd laugh at me for being timid and scared; yet if I didn't get him to slow up I really was afraid that I'd never locate that first-aid station by myself. I began to get mad at him. Well, strange to tell, it seemed like he had eyes in the back of his head—all by himself he stopped at the side of

Translated by Robert E. Hegel.

the road. But he kept on looking ahead and never even glanced at me. He waited until I had just about trudged up to him and then he galloped off ahead alone. In a flash he'd left me ten or more yards behind again. Since I surely didn't have the strength to catch up with him, I had to be content to struggle along slowly in the rear by myself. It did help that he didn't let me get too far behind, even though he wouldn't let me get any closer; he maintained those few yards of distance between us. If I walked fast, he'd leap forward with great strides; if I walked slowly, he'd dally along ahead of me. Funny thing was, even though I'd never seen him turn around to look at me, I couldn't help getting interested in this signalman myself.

I hadn't paid any attention to him at regimental headquarters and now, from the back, all I could see was that he was tall and thin, not husky at all, but to judge from his strong solid shoulders, he was a sturdy kid. He wore a brown uniform well faded from washing and leggings wrapped up over his knees. He had a couple of sparse twigs stuck into his gun barrel—you could call it camouflage, but it looked a lot more like decoration.

I still hadn't caught up to him and already my feet had swelled up and hurt like they were being burned. I suggested to him that we should rest a while and then sat myself down on a rock that marked a field boundary. He sat down on another rock some distance away, laid the rifle across his legs, with his back turned to me just as if I wasn't even there. To judge from past experience, I knew that this was also just because I was a woman. Whenever women comrades serve with the troops, they always have problems like this. Irritated and ready to put up some resistance, I walked over and sat down facing him. Now I could see his round face, young and innocent. He couldn't have been more than eighteen. Seeing me sit down this close, he immediately began to fidget, just like there was a time bomb buried beside him. He was so ill at ease that to turn his face away would have been wrong, but it wouldn't do *not* to turn away. He wanted to stand up but he was too embarrassed for that, too. Even though it nearly killed me to keep from laughing, I offhandedly asked him where he was from. He didn't say a word, his face flushing as red as a Great Lord Guan on an altar. He mumbled for a while, and then he said that he was from Mount Tianmu.[1] So he was from the same area that I was!

[1] A new Fourth Army Base.

"What'd you do for a living when you were at home?"

"Hauled bamboo for people."

A long look at those broad shoulders of his brought before my eyes a vision of a sea of bamboo like a green mist and in the middle of that sea a narrow stone path, twisting and turning up the mountain. A kid with broad shoulders, using pieces of old blue cloth for padding, was carrying several stalks of green bamboo, their long tips dragging along behind him, scraping the stone steps, as he climbed. . . . This was the life at home that I knew so well! All at once I felt so much closer to this boy from my home area. I questioned him again:

"How old are you?"

"Nineteen."

"How long since you joined the revolution?"

"A year."

"How'd you come to join?" By this time I'd begun to feel that this was no conversation; it was more like an interrogation. But I still couldn't keep myself from asking.

"When the main army withdrew north I went with them."

"Any of your family still at home?"

"Ma, dad, little brother, little sister, and an aunt who lives with us."

"You aren't married yet, are you?"

". . . " He blushed furiously, becoming even more embarrassed; with the fingers of both hands he kept counting the holes in the leather belt around his waist. After a little while he lowered his head, gave a shy smile and shook his head. I also wanted to ask him whether he was engaged, but when I saw the state he was in I could only swallow the words in my mouth.

The two of us sat there at a loss for something to do for a little longer before he raised his head and began looking up at the sky. Then he turned and gave me a glance as if he wanted me to get moving.

As I stood up to leave I noticed him take off his hat on the sly and mop his head with a towel. This must have been my fault—the guy hadn't sweated a drop on the road and here he was scared into a head full of sweat just because I was talking to him. I was to blame for all of it.

It was already two o'clock in the afternoon when we got to the first-aid station, only a mile from the front. It had been set up in an elementary school, six rooms of varying sizes arranged more or less in a triangle. The open-air space in the middle was covered with weeds.

Obviously there had been no classes at the school for some time. By the time we arrived there were already several medics in the station getting gauze and cotton balls ready; everywhere there were doors held up by piles of bricks to serve as cots for the wounded.

Not long after we got there a local cadre came, his eyes bloodshot from fatigue; he had a stiff piece of paper stuck in the front of his battered felt cap pulled low over his eyes to shield them from the sun. He arrived huffing and puffing, his rifle slung over one shoulder and a steelyard hanging over the other; in his left hand he clutched a basket of eggs and in his right he carried a big cooking wok which clattered as he walked along. He put everything down and apologized to us, complaining at the same time, panting and gulping down water all the while. On top of all this, he also fished a rice cake out of his tunic and began to munch on it. I saw him do all these things at great speed, but I didn't catch everything he said. He appeared to be saying something about quilts and that he wanted us to go borrow some. So I asked the medics about it. It turned out that we had to borrow them from the masses because the regiment headquarters hadn't sent any blankets down yet, but after they've lost blood, wounded men get cold very easily. Even if all we could get were a dozen or two wadded cotton quilt linings, that'd still be all right. I had just then been worrying that there'd be nothing for me to do, so I volunteered to undertake this mission. But since I was afraid I wouldn't finish in time, I went ahead and asked that guy from my home area if he'd help me by making requisitions from a few houses before he left. He hesitated for a minute and then came along with me.

First we went to a nearby village. Once there, we split up to requisition separately; he went one way and I went the other. Before long I had written out three receipts and had borrowed two linings and a quilt. My arms were full and I couldn't have been happier about it. I was just about to take them to the station and come back for more when I saw the signalman walking back toward me, empty-handed.

"What's up—didn't you borrow any?" It seemed to me that because of the high level of understanding among the masses here and their political awareness, it was hard to imagine that he couldn't borrow some quilts. I was amazed, and I asked him about it.

"You go borrow them, lady comrade! . . . These masses are dyed-in-the-wool 'feudal'! . . ."

"Which house? I'll go with you." I figured that it must surely be because he didn't say it right that he blew his chance. It didn't matter so much if he didn't get a quilt, but if he made a bad impression on the masses, that was something serious. When I told him to take me there to see about it, he stubbornly hung his head; just like he was nailed down he refused to take a step. I went up close to him and in a low voice I told him all about making a bad impression on the masses. He heard me out, and then he cheerfully took me along.

There wasn't a sound from the main room of the old house when we stepped into the courtyard. A blue cotton door curtain with a red valence hung down over one door and a congratulatory couplet written on fresh sheets of red paper was pasted up on both sides of the door frame. All we could do was stand outside and call "Sister, sister-in-law." I called a couple of times without any answer, but there was some movement inside. After a little while the door curtain raised and there stood a young bride. She was very pretty, with a straight nose, curving eyebrows, and fluffy bangs on her forehead. Her clothes were made of homespun cotton, but every piece was brand new. As soon as I saw that her hair was wound tightly up into a married woman's bun, I apologized as politely as I could, explaining how she oughtn't to take offense at this comrade who just now came by because he doesn't speak very well, and so on. All the while she was listening, she kept turning her face back inside and grinning, biting her lip. I finished talking, but she still didn't make a sound. She kept her head down and bit her lip just as if she were so full of grins that she couldn't hold them all in. I was caught at a loss by this turn of events—what more could I say? I could see the signalman standing off to one side not blinking his eyes as he watched me—just as if he were watching the regiment commander demonstrate some drill. All I could do was thicken my skin and get right down to the matter of borrowing a quilt. So I said my piece about how the troops of the Communist Party were fighting on behalf of the masses. This time she didn't grin, but kept glancing back into the house as she listened. When I got done she looked at me, then looked at the signalman, as if she were weighing carefully what I had just said. After a long time she turned and went inside to get the quilt.

The signalman took this opportunity to say to me in no uncertain terms: "That's what I was just telling her, but she wouldn't lend it to me. Don't you think it's funny. . . ?" I flashed him a glare so that he wouldn't say any more, but I was too late. The young bride was already standing there in the doorway with the quilt in her arms. From the minute she brought it out it was perfectly clear to me just why she'd been reluctant to lend it. It was none other than a fancy quilt with both new lining and new cover; its brocaded cover was made of synthetic satin covered with white "hundred harmonies" lily blossoms on a maroon background. She offered the quilt directly to me as if deliberately trying to aggravate the signalman, saying, "Here, take it."

Since my arms were already piled full of quilts I motioned to him to take it from her. Who'd have thought that he'd turn his head and pretend he hadn't seen it? All I could do was tell him to do it directly. At this, he finally made a face, and with his eyes on the ground went up, got the quilt and, flustered, spun around and left. Unexpectedly, before he got even one step out the gate, there was the sound of a loud "rip." His uniform had caught on the gate hook and a flap of cloth now hung from his shoulder, leaving a considerable hole. With a big grin the bride hurried after needle and thread to sew it up for him, but the signalman was in no way going to let her do it, and he left with the quilt under his arm.

Not far outside her gate somebody told us that the young woman we had been talking to was a bride of only three days and that the quilt was her only dowry. I was sorry to hear this; the signalman, too, frowned and was silent, just looking at the quilt in his hands. I thought that he must be feeling the same way, having heard this tale. That's why he began to mutter to me as we walked along.

"We just didn't understand how things were. It's just not right that we should borrow somebody's wedding quilt. . . ." I couldn't resist teasing him a little so I pretended to be serious and said to him,

"Right. Probably when she was still a girl she got up early and worked late doing extra odd jobs just to save up enough money for this quilt; maybe it is something she lost a lot of sleep over, this brocade quilt. And yet some people have to go and complain that she's 'feudal.' . . ."

He stopped dead in his tracks when he heard this. He stood there struck dumb for a while, and then he said,

"Well . . . then I'll take it back to her!"

"We just now borrowed it from her; if we take it back she'll wonder why." Seeing how sincere and awkward he was, I wanted to laugh, but I really liked him for it. I couldn't tell why, but I had come to love this simple young fellow-countryman of mine from the bottom of my heart.

He listened to what I said, and it seemed to make sense to him. He thought it over a while; then as if coming to a decision he said,

"Well, that's that. If we use it we'll give it a good wash." His mind made up, he grabbed up all the quilts that I was carrying, piled them up one after another on his shoulders and took off with great strides.

After we got back to the first-aid station, I told him he could go back to regiment headquarters. His spirits immediately cheered up; he gave me a salute and ran off. But he thought of something before he'd taken many steps. He fished around in his satchel and came up with two plain steamed buns. He held them up to me and then reached out and put them on a rock beside the road.

"There's dinner for you!" he said and then he left, his feet not even touching the ground. As I walked over to pick up those dry, hard buns, I noticed that he'd stuck a wild chrysanthemum in the barrel of his gun; I don't know when. Along with the twigs it wagged back and forth beside his ear.

Even though he was some distance away, I could still see the flap of cloth hanging down from his shoulder, fluttering in the breeze. I really regretted not having sewn it up for him before he left; now at the very least he'd have a bare shoulder all night long.

There weren't many people available to work at the first-aid station. The local cadre had mobilized a few women to help us boil water, cook, and do other odds and ends. The new bride had come with them, and she was just like before: her lips clamped together in a steady grin. She'd glance at me out of the corner of her eye, but from time to time she craned her neck this way and that just as if she were looking for something. Finally, she asked me, "Where'd that young comrade go?" I told her that he was not assigned here and that now he'd gone off to the front. She smiled with embarrassment and said, "I guess I was kind of hard on him when he tried to borrow the quilt just now." Having said that, she clamped her lips tight and grinned again, but she got to work neatly spreading the dozen or so quilts and wadded cotton liners we'd borrowed over the doors and tables (two of the little school tables pushed together made up a cot). I watched her spread her own new quilt with the white lily blossoms over a door set up as a cot outside under the eaves.

After it got dark, a big full moon rolled up over the horizon. Our general offensive hadn't started yet. Since the enemy were always afraid of the night, they had set big bonfires on the ground and were firing their artillery blindly, shooting up flares one after the other. It was as if they had lighted any number of gas lanterns there in the moonlight to make everything on the ground naked and exposed. It would be even harder for our attack in this "daylight night"—we'd have to pay a big price! I even came to detest that beautiful bright moon.

The local cadre came back again with a reward of several home-made dried vegetable moon cakes for us. Sure enough, today was the Mid-Autumn Festival.

Ah, the Mid-Autumn Festival! In my home area, every family would be setting out a tea table in front of their gate by now, with an offering of incense, candles, and several plates of melon, fruit, and moon cakes on it. The children would be anxiously hoping that the incense would burn down fast so that they could all the sooner divide up the things that had been offered to the moon goddess. They would be jumping around beside the tea table, singing:

When the moon is at its peak,
Beat the gong for sweets to eat . . .

Or they might be singing:

Dear Lady in the moon
Takes a shine to you, a shine to me . . .

Thinking of this made me remember that young fellow from my home area, the kid that hauled bamboo. Maybe a few years ago he had sung this song, too! . . . I took a bite of that wonderful home-made moon cake and thought about how that home-town kid was probably right now lying on his belly in our defense works, or maybe in the regimental command post, or he might even be in those twisting, turning communications trenches! . . .

After a while our artillery opened up and the sky was sliced across by several red signal flares. The attack had begun. Before long the wounded began to be brought in a few at a time and the air in the first-aid station began to get tense.

I took a notebook and went to register their names and units. I'd ask the ones with minor wounds, but for the seriously wounded I'd have to pull open their I.D. or check the insignia on their uniforms. When I pulled out the I.D. of one badly wounded soldier, the words "Signal Corpsman" gave me an unexpected shudder and my heart leaped. Only when I calmed down did I see the name of a certain *battalion* written on his I.D. Ah! No, my home-town boy was a signalman from *regimental* headquarters. But for no clear reason, I wanted to ask somebody whether casualties ever get overlooked on the battlefield. Besides carrying messages in battle, what does a signalman do? I didn't know why I wanted to ask such irrelevant questions.

For half an hour or so after the battle started, everything went smoothly. The wounded men gave us bits of news, all about how we'd broken through the first line of barricades and the second line of barbed wire, had occupied the enemy's front line fortifications, and now were fighting in the streets. But by this time the news stopped coming, and the wounded who came in later wouldn't say more than simply, "We're still fighting," or "We're fighting in the streets and alleys." From the mud all over them, from the look of total weariness on their faces, and from the stretchers that seemed to have been dug up out of the mud, we all knew perfectly well just what kind of a battle was going on in front of us.

There weren't enough stretchers; quite a few of the severely wounded who couldn't just then be sent to a hospital in the rear were left here. I had no way to relieve any of their suffering; all I could do was get the women to wipe their faces and wash their hands, feed the ones who could eat a little, and change clothes on the ones who had a clean uniform in their knapsacks. For some all we could do was open their clothing and wash off some of the filth and blood on them.

Needless to say, this kind of work was nothing to me, but the village women were both embarrassed and afraid. They just couldn't do it. They'd race each other to tend the stove, especially that new bride. I had to speak to her about it for a long time before she agreed to help, blushing. But all she'd consent to do was serve as my aide.

The roar of the artillery in front of us had already died down. It felt like it was nearly daylight, but in fact it was only midnight. Outside the moon was very bright, even higher in the sky than usual. Out in front a seriously wounded soldier had been brought in. All of the cots inside were full, so I had them lay this casualty down on the door outside under the eaves. The stretcher bearers lifted him onto the door, but they stayed crowded around the cot, not wanting to leave. One of the older stretcher bearers must have taken me for a doctor; he grabbed hold of my arm and said, "Doc, no matter what, you've got to think of some way to save this comrade! If you save him, I'll . . . all of us stretcher bearers will give you an inscribed banner! . . ." As he spoke, I discovered that several of the other stretcher bearers were staring at me with wide eyes just as if I could heal the wounded man with a nod of my head. I wanted to explain it to them but just then I noticed the new bride standing beside the cot with a pan of water in her hands. She gasped. I quickly pushed my way through to have a look. I saw there a round face, young and innocent; the skin that had been tanned a dark brown now had turned an ashen gray. His eyes were closed peacefully, and at the shoulder of his uniform was a large hole, a flap of cloth still hanging from it.

"He did it all for us . . . ," the stretcher bearers said, trying to take the blame. "There were ten or so of us crowded into a little alley just getting ready to move forward. This comrade was walking along behind us. Who'd have thought that some bastard reactionary would lob a grenade down on us from a roof somewhere? The grenade was rolling around in between us spitting smoke, and just then this comrade yelled to us to get down fast, and he threw himself on the thing. . . ."

The new bride gasped again. Forcing back my tears, I said a few words to the stretcher bearers and sent them away. When I turned around, I saw that the young woman had quietly moved an oil lamp over and had opened up his uniform. Her shyness and embarrassment of just now had totally disappeared; she was solemnly and reverently washing him clean. That tall, young signalman just lay there not making a sound. . . . With a jerk, I came back to my senses; I jumped up, and clattered off as fast as I could go to find the doctor. When the doctor and I got back with a hypodermic and medicines, the new bride was sitting there by his side leaning over him.

She had her head down and stitch by stitch was mending the hole in the shoulder of his uniform. The doctor listened for the signalman's heartbeat, then quietly stood up and said, "There is no need to sew it up." I went over and touched him; sure enough, his hand was as cold as ice. The young woman seemed to see nothing, to hear nothing of any of this; she just kept on making fine, tight stitches, mending the hole. I really couldn't bear to watch her, and I whispered to her, "Don't sew any more." She gave me a peculiar glance, then put her head down again and went on stitching. I wanted to pull her away; I wanted to push away this oppressive atmosphere; I wanted to see him sit up, see him grin his embarrassed grin. But I unintentionally bumped into something beside me, and when I felt it with my hand, it was the food he had given me, those two hard, dry, steamed buns. . . .

The medic had people bring over a coffin, and they began to fold up the quilt that had been over him before putting him in it. The young bride turned pale and snatched the quilt away from them, glaring at them fiercely. Quickly, she spread half of the quilt evenly and smoothly in the bottom of the coffin and then drew the other half over him. The medic was at a loss and said, "That quilt . . . was borrowed from the masses."

"It's mine—" she yelled, her voice full of anger, and she wrenched her face away. In the moonlight I could see her eyes glisten; I could also see the quilt, its white lilies on a maroon background, those flowers that symbolize purity and devotion, now laid over the face of this ordinary young man who had hauled bamboo.

DAYBREAK

Zhu Xining

"YOU'RE in luck, Young Three," Black Eight said to me. "There's going to be a big court trial the first day you're on the job. Good chance to learn."

"Surely, Squire Eight. I'm all green, and you must teach me."

"Don't mention it. It's just so-so being in the service of the Yamen. Once green, twice weaned." Pulling his pipe out of his hairy lips, Black Eight tapped it against the paddle-like cane resting against my chest. "As soon as you learn how to use this gadget, you'll have found your meal-ticket for a lifetime."

The way he acted and spoke showed he was a born mentor of the young.

"Have patience with me and I'll obey your instructions, sir." Fawning words, and I had been using them over and over again. I smoothed the skirt of my uniform. I was at a loss where to put my hands, as though piling up all that flattery had turned me into an imbecile.

The main hall blazed with light like a shrine where some secret rite was going to be performed. My fellow bailiffs must have been all present in the two galleries. It was really cold. The uniforms bulged over the fur-lined and cotton-padded coats underneath, still the wearers stamped and stamped trying to get some warmth. A passer-by might think they were engaged in some strange drill. Perhaps not even three comforters wrapped tightly around could protect one against the bone-piercing wind coming out of the long, funnel-like corridors. There was nothing to be envied about a man out in such rawness, and Black Eight said it was a meal-ticket for a lifetime!

Dad had spent five stone of wheat to get me this position. The night

---

Translated by Hou Jian. From *An Anthology of Contemporary Chinese Literature* (Taipei: National Institute for Compilation and Translation, 1975), vol. 2.

watch had just sounded midnight when my old man roused the whole family. To give up the warm bed was sheer torture, but it would not do to dally on the first day of a new job. It was cold. Ma said, and my wife echoed: put on more clothes.

The uniform was new, and badly tailored: it should have been made a lot roomier. One single cotton-padded coat under it was no good against the chill, and I was shivering even before I left my room. A fur coat with nothing else under it would be no use either, for it could not keep the warmth in. Ma and my wife calculated, tried this way and that, pulled and shoved, but they just could not get both the fur and the cotton inside the uniform. All that this tugging and squeezing did was to make me sneeze, though it also woke me up. Senior sister-in-law had meantime poached the eggs, three each for Dad and myself. While we were eating, Ma, not willing to admit defeat, kept ransacking through different trunks till she found an unsurfaced sheepskin of my father's that could be coaxed under the uniform. Then Dad and I left home.

I could not say how young a boy Dad took me to be, but he insisted on carrying the lantern and seeing me to Black Eight's. Here and there I could hear some early roosters crowing. The lantern light was too dim to show much of the ground, but the shoes could tell what they were walking on: the crackling sound could come only from ice or hoarfrost.

"This weather!—such stubborn dry cold!"

Dad was speaking from inside his hood and the words were barely intelligible. I could not find the strength to push back my hood and answer him. We just buried our heads deep in the wraps and trudged on in the deserted streets. It was a deep dark night under a heavy black sky. Dad and I, it seemed, had to shoulder it between ourselves. The thought weighed down on my heart.

Dad should have felt easy now that Black Eight was going to take me to the Yamen himself. But no, he had to walk all the way with us to the gates and stood there lingering, each of his hands buried deep in the other sleeve. The lantern, with its handle in one of Dad's sleeves, lit upward, revealing his face—the fat, rotund face of a businessman, streaked yellow and black like the gilded statue of some bodhisattva with the golden foil peeling off. He was gazing at something, absent-mindedly, silhouetted against the light and smoke coming from peddlers selling chili soup, tarts, cakes, and steaming gruel. These trades-people catered to the officers in the Yamen. Their fires, illuminating the street, threw the shadows of the cages[1] against the whitewashed walls on both sides of the Yamen gates, the bars showing up light and dark, like the criss-crossing pattern on pieces of plaid cloth.

"Early shift, Squire Eight?"

The guard, with a musket on his shoulder and steam coming out of his mouth, greeted Black Eight. Shadows cast on his face and body made him look as though he were being hanged in one of the cages.

"A tough job, pal! Isn't it about time for changing guards?" Black Eight puckered his mouth toward the cages, "No business for a long time now."

"Business will be coming soon, though," Black Eight turned to speak to Dad.

But Dad was still gazing absorbedly at something, and there was a tenseness about his stare that seemed desirous of holding fast whatever had come into his vision, fearful that once his attention wandered, he would lose it. If he had been allowed to come inside, he would no doubt be stamping and shuffling his feet in the cold now, right beside his son, to attend on the magistrate.

The winter night was long, so long it felt as if the day would never break.

"Come on here, Young Three." Black Eight beckoned me to an elderly man who looked quite familiar. "Let me present you to Big Zhang, Z-h-a-n-g, Zhang, an old-timer in the West Gallery who has served under seven magistrates. It won't hurt you to listen to him."

I hurried up and bowed obsequiously. "Your servant, Squire Zhang." He was merely a fellow bailiff in my gallery, so that the bow was not exactly called for. As a newcomer, however, I had to be friendly, even deferential, the more so since Black Eight had sought him out for me to meet. In fact considering the difference in our age, a bow would neither degrade me nor do him too much honor.

"Master Young Three of the corn-dealer behind the Temple of the Fire God." Black Eight patted me on the shoulder. "I leave him in your care."

---

[1]Or standing cages. The cage was a device both for tormenting a criminal and exposing him to the public. The top part was like a pillory with a hole in the middle for the criminal's head. It was so high that bricks could be either put in under the criminal's feet to avoid strangulation or removed to hasten it. It was not an officially prescribed form of punishment, but a sort of government lynching. Death resulting from it was therefore always attributed to either accident or the man's bad health.

"O.K., Old Eight. We're old buddies. Need I say more?"

This Old Zhang must have been well over sixty, though the way he looked he was as sprightly as any of the younger men. Of all the people in the galleries, he wore the lightest amount of clothing.

"Winter, early or late, I never wear more. I've not missed a day in my calisthenics for thirty years. You don't think I've kept at it for nothing, do you?"

"Good for you, Old One. The thousand-year turtle and the ten-thousand year tortoise, and you're both of them. Can't get the better of you!"

"Well, if you think I'm boasting, we can get together some time and try a little leg flexing. I'll double your time."

Apparently, they had been used to this kind of banter.

"You mustn't laugh at us, young fella; when we oldsters meet, we do have some meaty morsels to chew."

Under the patronage of these friendly and jolly elders, my job should not be too hard on me. It might even be worth five stone more of Dad's wheat. After all, he owned a foodgrain store.

"I say, young fella, lean that meal-ticket of yours against the wall," Squire Zhang was referring to the cane held close to my chest. "You don't have to hold it so tight. It'll be quite some time before the magistrate ascends to the hall."

I learned then that the magistrate was an old opium addict; as soon as he opened his eyes from sleep, he could not wait for the regular smoke, but had to gulp down a jigger of opiate solution before he settled down for a leisurely hour of the opium pipe.[2] He could not preside over the court otherwise, or hold through even if he could start.

---

[2]The author's knowledge of this differs from the translator's. To the latter, opium solution is toxic, often fatal, and was a fairly common means of suicide, especially for women. Juices extracted from the opium poppy are dried and become dark brown to black in color; they are then boiled to remove the impurities. What is produced is the "opium earth," the most treasured being that from the province of Yunnan, literally "cloud south" (south of the Cloud Ridge), hence the "cloud earth" below. The "earth" is softened with water before use. A dose is taken up with a stylet or tweezer, roasted over the flame of a small paper- or glass-chimneyed lamp burning vegetable oil, and finger-rolled into a ball. The toasting makes the ball bubble, hence "opium bubble." When one smokes, the "bubble" is stuck on the small hole in the "bowl" of the pipe, and maneuvered with the tweezer over the lamp again to ensure that it will burn through. When in a hurry, the bubbles may be taken internally. The burned-out ashes can be either mixed with fresh "earth" for bulk or swallowed for relief of pain. The rich magistrate could undoubtedly afford a handy supply of such bubbles always.

"What's coming up is a whopper, and it'll take a long time to get it over with. His Worship needs at least ten bubbles to weather through."

"You said it."

From under his belt Black Eight fished out his pipe and tobacco pouch and offered a pinch of tobacco to everybody around.

"What grade is it, Squire Eight?"

"Well, I may be below the bottom grade,[3] but the tobacco for my pipe is always Grade One Fragrance—the only thing worth something about me."

One of the bystanders tried to butter up the old gaffer. Puffing and savoring, he said, "I'm sure this is the highest grade at the Phoenix Terrace. Squire Eight's being modest."

A real abstainer, I stood there like having so many extra fingers and toes, more than I knew how to dispose of. I thought I'd draw back stealthily, but Black Eight obviously wanted to impress those present by his patronizing attitude towards me. He took out of his lips the green jade mouth-piece of his pipe on which he had just puffed once; wiping it on the palm of his hand and leveling the stem, he handed it to me in a gesture of friendly invitation.

I waved both my hands in refusal, wondering what I should do in order not to seem rude. At such a time I could not blame Dad for treating me like a child.

"Religious conviction?"

"No . . . I never learned . . ." Under pressure, I managed to at least blurt this out. So saying, I backed out of the crowd. I blew on my fingers to keep warm, but the icy wind from the corridor made me feel as if I had no trousers on.

There was some commotion in the hallway upstairs. Perhaps the magistrate was about to make his appearance. The light cast the shadows of two or three people up there onto the flight of granite steps; the heads of these moving shadows pointed downward, so that they looked like men trussed upside down and swinging to and fro.

Two men who looked like house servants came out carrying a large fire-bowl to the chair behind the tall desk in the very center of the hall. The pungent odor of burning charcoal added to the festive air of a Chinese New Year suggested by the table curtain of golden satin on

---

[3]During the Qing dynasty (1644–1911), toward the end of which this incident supposedly took place, the bureaucracy was divided into nine main grades; but bailiffs, constables, and clerks were outside the pale.

which was embroidered a coiling dragon with four claws.

Those top-graders of the Phoenix Terrace were gossiping about today's case. Black Eight showed himself the most knowledgeable of the lot, for he alone was doing most of the talking.

"Where there's adultery there's murder. Remember that and you cannot go wrong."

"It's said the dead man's number one wife coughed up a big sum to bribe the judge."

"Some news!" interposed Squire Zhang of the thirty-year calisthenics. "Expect to go scot-free and not hand over silver! Who ever heard the like?"

"The number one wife is the plaintiff, so why should she? I wouldn't. It shows there's more than meets the eye."

"Seems to me you've wasted your half dozen years in the Yamen," Black Eight observed, pointing the bowl of his pipe at the younger man. "To go to court, do you win with reason or with lucre? She's brought in the suit. Don't you think she'd want to win? And then there's the two hundred taels of spoil."

"What, not five hundred taels?"

"The plaintiff at first sued for two hundred taels. Even this sum had been an afterthought. Dead men tell no tales, you know."

"Hah, the squad's in for some goodies!"

"The suit that was filed has been corrected to read five hundred taels, and that's three hundred taels more than was originally contended. Every party should certainly be getting something out of that."

I could not quite make out what they were saying. Instead, I felt this was not at all like my idea of a new job; rather, it was more like going to the flea market, where people bargained in secret codes, and I could not understand a thing. I felt slighted, left out, and could not help longing for the warm bed at home, so far, far away. It all seemed to be of another world—the warm bed, the warm home containing it, and the old and young ones contained in it. As the old saw had it,

> "Don't ever in the gov'ment service be,
> Or you barter away your liberty."

Dad must have gone home by now; he could not be hanging around the Yamen gates all this time, staring at the pair of sinister, blood-thirsty cages. A man getting on in years must have lost the youthful vigor needed to withstand the raw night air.

Even when we had reached the Yamen, Dad kept on repeating his advice to me over and over again. "Be on the alert, keep your eyes open: the new job requires a quick mind and ready ears." I could not see it was all that serious. His Worship was lying back there smoking his opium, the lesser brass were shuffling around in the galleries smoking their pipes. When they had smoked to their hearts' content, when they had prated all they could, they would only be going back to their daily routine at the Yamen. For instance, now that Black Eight, Squire Zhang, and the others were dispersing, I knew very well how to follow their example. All I had to do was to lug the stick after me and to go to my assigned place. No more. Perhaps no trade could be mastered without first serving some sort of apprenticeship; the executioner's, for example, in which one started with cleaving melons. This trade, however, seemed to be an exception to the rule. The lining up and attendances at the court were not things that had to be taught, but might be learned by oneself. But I did muse to myself that I might as well sign up Squire Zhang for a master, though not for his calisthenics. Since Black Eight seemed to be too much in demand and so hardly ever around to spare much time for me, I was reduced to learning from Zhang. Zhang and I rubbed shoulders in our positions so I could not go far wrong imitating him. To be sure, I could not say Black Eight had received five stone of wheat for doing nothing; after all, he had introduced me to Squire Zhang.

More and more people were milling around in the upstairs hall. Every time the cotton-padded curtain moved, my heart would throb in anticipation of the magistrate's arrival. Wasn't this like waiting at the theater for the Peking opera to start? All that was wanting were the drum and gongs playing the overture. After the curtain had moved several times, a man with the appearance of a mandarin finally emerged. This must be His Worship now, I thought, this old hump of a man. But Squire Zhang whispered to me that it was only the second mandarin, and I wondered if there might not be a third, or even a fourth.

Down in the yard a band of soldiers trooped in, consisting of a squad of musketeers and a squad of lancers. The lances had red tassels under the heads, and the sheathed sabres they bore constantly knocked against something or other. Were they the supernumeraries on stage, or was their coming like the usual posturing before a military tribunal?

Somehow, I was all this time thinking of the theater. Obviously, one would never know what it was like in the magistrate's Yamen without being in some way associated with it, like being a bailiff.

At long last, His Worship showed up and relieved the tension building up in me. Far from the dignified swagger that I had been led to expect, his was a slouch that spoke of a pain in the loins. The magistrate did not wear his chest patch, the insignia of his office, though a long string of beads like an oversize Buddhist rosary hung down his neck. The hat on his head was not the official one, and the boots, even seen from afar, did not appear to be new. I remember my Grandma telling me during my childhood how, upon assuming his first office, a newly-made mandarin would go to the john with a piece of new cotton spread under his feet in order not to soil his boots, and change them if they were spattered ever so little. Not this magistrate, apparently. His sickly face was sallow and swollen, and he was paunchy in the middle. The old clothes he wore hung loosely on his person, and he seemed a man who would not bother changing his boots even if he should by accident have stepped into a whole puddle of urine. The sense of grandeur betokened by the new piece of cotton underfoot must have long been dissipated over the opium lamp. What could be more glorious than the beady flame inside the glass chimney of that lamp? Both the cotton and the flame could put a man's head in the clouds, the satin boots adorned with pieces of cotton cloud and the "cloud earth." For our magistrate, though, the bricks of "cloud earth" must be much more practical and to the point.

His Worship sat down sidewise, a tobacco pipe several feet long protruding from his mouth. His attendant crouched beside him to fill the bowl with threaded tobacco and then lit it. The man's position left his brazen, verdigris-colored sheath and sword trailing on the tile floor. I could not help wondering how such a flunkey could be much of a swordsman. The weapon obviously should have been a spice pouch or a snuff-bottle.

The magistrate, though sitting to one side, had his face turned toward the documents on the desk. He was also sipping noisily from a small chick-heart red teapot, so noisily he could be heard down in the yard. I suspected he needed several mouths to be able to smoke, sip, and speak all at the same moment.

"Bring in the culprit."

The magistrate appeared to have uttered this command, though so indistinctly that I could not be too sure. The man who had been taking care of the magistrate's pipe stalked to the front of the hall in big, quick strides. With one hand set on the handle of his sword and the other perched on his waist, he chanted in a strange dialect with a shrill tone reminiscent of the cry of a baked-potato hawker:

"Bring in the Culprit Zhou of the House of Xu!" He then waved towards the galleries. I could not see his hand, only the horse-hoof sleeve clawing the air. Then two boys appeared, each with a yard-long piece of hollow bamboo to extinguish the candles in the sconces on the side walls, leaving only the pair of tall ones on the magistrate's desk.

Everything up and down the hall was plunged into darkness with the exception of the magistrate's swollen face. It was as though a magic net had been cast over the scene, with one opening from which light issued, and in its center was framed a cadaverous face, the magistrate's, that never seemed to have seen the sun. He needed but a flowing red beard to look like that of the hellish judge so often seen in a temple.

From far away (was it this world or the next?) could be heard the clanking of metal rubbing against metal. Heavy chains were being pulled laboriously forward like the cable of a boat being towed, inch by inch, up some steep rapids. Slowly, painfully slowly, the sound drew near.

Black Eight had said it was to be a big case, that there was murder where there was adultery, and that two of the cages were in for use. Just listen to the chains. What torture, what horror, and what bitterness were now plodding onward along the ice and frost.

It might be due to the unconscious exaggeration of my sympathy, or it might be due to the oppressive bleakness of the small hours; one way or the other, my teeth were chattering, chattering as though they had the iron chains grinding across them, link by link, iron chains that were even then being dragged over the frozen earth.

"O—O—O—"

A low, deep-throated rumble came from the galleries as though a faint howling whisper had drifted up from some forsaken tomb, or the growl of a feeding tiger warning off some approaching predator. It undulated in such a way that one could not tell whether it was near or far, far away. In some inexplicable nightmares, men have often enough been tortured by haunting sighs such as this.

The delirious low roaring sound went up into the dreary blackness, giving a listener the creeps. Then the culprit, like a puny animal, was dragged into the hall, shackles and all, and there knelt on the granite steps. The kneeling was done so naturally and easily, one might think the culprit quite familiar at court.

Squire Zhang nudged me. The first time I had thought it was inadvertent, but I soon learned that as a bailiff I was not only supposed to beat the culprit but also to emit a whining growl in order to awe him. Since that was how it was, I joined in the chorus, and was myself soon cowed by it. I could well imagine what it did to the culprit, especially in the predawn darkness.

The figure kneeling on the stone steps looked pathetically small, so small one was afraid she might freeze before the day broke and become stiff and brittle enough for a mere touch to shatter her.

The magistrate, comfortably settled in the big armchair covered with bearskin, appeared to have seen nothing, for he went on smoking his pipe as noisily as ever, his rhythmic "puff—puff—" loud enough to be audible in the galleries. He was quite unhurried, as though prepared not to hear the case before daylight. From the din he made, one would imagine that the jade mouthpiece had to be extra thick, extra heavy.

From out his livid, thick lips, a dense cloud of smoke was emitted, encircling the two tall, red candles. The hopes and fears of the culprit must have been rising, falling, and set adrift with the smoke, which was constantly changing shape—as unpredictable as the good will of the magistrate.

His Worship at length saw fit to stretch out his hand, take away the pipe, and yawn luxuriously with his mouth gaping open. He then knocked the pipe against the bronze firebowl—clang, clang—again and again. His servant, looking quite fair-skinned, scurried over and half kneeling, waited on his master. The latter did not permit him to fill the pipe, but whispered something to him in such a low voice that I could not hear anything.

"His Worship commands you, Zhou of the House of Xu, that you explain your grievance if you have a grievance, and admit your guilt if you are guilty," the servant intoned in his shrill, alien accent.

The kneeling black figure pitched forward as though on the point of falling, but she only knocked her head several times against the tone.

"Wronged, Your Sagacious Worship!" Then she slumped over and did not budge for some time.

"If so, Zhou of the House of Xu," the magistrate said, in the same accent as his servant, an accent that sounded naturally resentful; "How long have you been carrying on with Dai, your lover?"

"I'm wronged, Your Sagacious Worship. I never knew the man," the woman prisoner who had been called Zhou of the House of Xu cried hoarsely, tearfully. "Your kindness, Your Sagacious Worship. If Your Worship had not spoken, I would not have known the man's name. Your help to clear me, Your Sagacious Worship!"

The woman sounded young. Black Eight had said she was sold a concubine for five hundred taels of silver, a goodly price to be sure, so that she must have pretty good looks. Only it was too dark to see. All I could dimly discern was a slender waist and loose, unkempt long hair hanging down. She wailed her grievance, but quiet reigned up and down the hall; there was no response. It would seem the great hall, the seat of government authority, might have its spoken echo of heavenly and human justice in plenty—and her plaint did receive a hollow echo from the lofty official edifice. But the cruelty of man to his own species proved the more powerful for all that. The magistrate was to the magistracy born, and born to be an opium smoker to boot. What could one do?

"Confess!" the magistrate sternly exclaimed and continued mumbling through the jade mouthpiece of his pipe which he had returned to his lips. The way he was staring up at the rafters one could swear the woman was not kneeling at the front of the hall, but strung on a beam.

"Your Worship is the sagacious live bodhisattva. . . . My master . . . my master, he died a horrible death . . . " On mentioning her "master," the woman appeared to have fainted. There she lay on the hard steps, not stirring. Such must have been a familiar scene to the people up and down the hall. Nobody went to help her. It was as though nobody took the murder case very seriously, or that a culprit could be left to die then and there for all they cared.

A slight moan, gossamer-like, rose as from the nether world. Was it the resurrection of an aggrieved ghost? But the woman pulled at her chains and straightened, muttering the while more like a talkative old hag than a young girl.

Breathlessly, the woman then gasped out her tale. She related how, born under an ill star, she was sold by her greedy parents for five hundred taels of silver when she was only fifteen years old, sold as a concubine. She had been living in the House of Xu for exactly two years, and the family's fortune steadily went down. People heaped all the blame for this on her shoulders. Nobody, she complained, thought that her mistress might have been more responsible for it. Whether this was because people did not want to offend the number one wife or that they did not know any better, she could not say. It was pitiful, of course, to become a widow at seventeen. My wife married me when she was eighteen, and a very naive girl she had been, too. But here was one who had a lover at such a tender age, and could murder her husband for money to give to another man. Either her mistress had framed her or she must be a real monster. She continued her story.

"On the seventh of the Month of Sacrifice, there was no money at home, or food. The New Year was around the corner, and we did not even have anything for the next day's worship. So my master got up very early that morning, saying he was going to look up some relatives for help. He said he would go to the mistress's first, for they had promised to give him something before the year's end so that he could set up a business in New Year goods."

As it turned out, the foolish husband was out the whole day. It was snowing then, powdery snow that made the day bitter cold. Debts had been piling up at all the neighborhood stores, and she had nowhere to turn for more credit, the year's end being the time to settle old scores. The poor young woman had been left home to bear alone the cold and hunger of an endless winter day.

Steps, deceitful steps, came near and passed on, teasing the distraught woman. Blasts of dry snow battered the paper-paned window. So young and so helplessly buried in ice and hunger. At her age she should be waiting for her father to come back, or her mother; but no, she was waiting for her husband, a husband almost three times her age who had fallen on lean days. Maybe he would bring back some food or, perhaps, some half-enjoyed mistress—to be toyed with, and in return to be fed and clothed, however poorly. And this was the bitter cup of her life, drunk in the silence of resignation.

Now it was not the sound of deceitful, despairing steps, nor was it that of the dry snow thudding against the window. It was the sound of the second watch, and she heard the feet of her man staggering over snow and gravel. Even before she could open the door wide, a strong whiff of his alcoholic breath rushed through the chink—the stench of fermenting chaff for hogs.

The man tottered in, a bulging bag slung on his shoulder. Was it filled with loaves of bread? Potatoes and carrots? She would not allow herself to think of salted meat or other delicacies for the festival ahead. Like a solid heap of rocks it stood on the table. But when the bag was emptied out on the big table, she could hardly make out what the contents were since there was only the feeble light of a small lamp burning with one single rush to see it by. In the will-o'-the-wisp dimness it took her some time to recognize it to be silver ingots of various sizes!

"Five . . . five hundred taels! Open your eyes wide and look!" The man exclaimed indistinctly, his tongue feeling as swollen as the sole on his shoe, either from the cold or from drunkenness. Could it be that so harassed by poverty he had turned robber? Or how else to account for all this silver?

"I . . . I sold you, at cost. No loss . . . no gain either; and I've had you for a plaything all of two years. Quite a bargain, eh?" The man's nose was red, obviously from the cold, for he did not seem at all sad about the transaction. The little woman did not want to believe him. She wanted him only to produce a couple of hot rolls from his pocket.

"You . . . you look unmoved!" The man lurched toward her on unsteady feet, but changed tack in midcourse; he leaned against the table, there to scoop up the palely shimmering white lumps of silver, ogling her the while. "To . . . tomorrow at . . . at dawn they . . . they'll come to fetch you." He stretched out his hand to grab at her. "Come, we . . . we got only . . . this night, my little . . . little darling concubine. . . . We . . . we've loved too."

The inebriate eyes, bleary and bloodshot, made her shrink. Once, she remembered, he had thrown up, and covered her face, breasts, and the pillows with filthy vomit. So she dodged, her eyes averted meanwhile to gaze intently only at the silver on the table. The heap now became a mound to her, a mound that was a grave in which to bury her alive. Well, she thought, if you must sell me, sell me then. Just seventeen, and good for perhaps eight or ten such changes of hand every two years. The grave that was to bury her now would let her come up again, to be transmigrated into still another family in something like two more years. But all this could be just a bad-natured jest. It did not sound real. What was real was the hunger, and the cold.

"Come on, my . . . darling concubine . . . little maid!"

Like a vise his cold hand clutched her slender, delicate wrist. She could have evaded him if she had wanted. But she wavered between doubt and belief. Could she really believe he had done as he said? How else was she to explain the mound of silver? Her mistress's family could not be so open-minded as to lend him five hundred taels all at once.

A young woman's heart was so very easily softened. If, in all his adversity, he had to have his pleasure of her, let him. And the man took out a piece of crunchy layer cake.

"Are you hard-hearted enough to sell me?" Somehow, she had found time to ask, though her stomach was burning with hunger. She started devouring the cake, not in a leisurely manner, layer by layer, but ravenously chewing and cramming. The man on top of her was burning, too, with another kind of flame, and how ferociously he bit and scratched! It was barter pure and simple, each taking what he most needed. Still, the woman was watchful for the vomit, the slimy, sour-odored something that had once covered her face, her breasts, and their pillow. And she ate on, thinking, "So this is the last night. Well, I shouldn't miss much here. I was born to be a cheap woman!"

The young woman never shut her eyes that night. It was a similar grave mound of silver that had buried her two years ago, and she had not been afraid then. But, now, perhaps, the passage of two years in her young life was making her reflect. She thought of her ill fate and curled up in one corner of the *kang*. She wept, brooded, and watched her man sunk so deep in slumber that she felt as if she were keeping watch at a wake.

The blizzard had stopped. The snow must have been heavy, for the window was all alight as on nights of a full moon. She could not see the few bitter bamboos in front of the window—they were probably bent down under the accumulating snow.

What might the new man be like, the man who was willing to pay her husband five hundred taels of silver for her?

The young woman crawled off the *kang*, and stared at the heap of silver on the table, musing the while. The long, cold night had exhausted her, now she had lost her wits, and her tears were frozen. She had no idea what she was doing, but she found herself collecting the silver into the lap of her skirt, and moving it to the far side of the bed on which her present husband lay snoring. She had to make several trips, thinking all the while, "I must put the silver where it is safe. You'll have to return it to the buyer," she silently addressed the sleeper. "I won't be here for him and you'd have to make good the entire amount. I'm going back to mother. If you fail to sell me once, could you be so mean as to sell me again?"

"Stop!" The magistrate gavelled his desk. "How many trips did you make to move the silver?"

"Speak up!" chimed a voice from up there. Was it the second mandarin?

"Can't remember, Your Sagacious Worship! At least . . . at least five or six times . . . can't remember exactly . . . "

"Five hundred taels of silver, and you said you finished moving all that in five or six trips? And only on the skirt of your dress?"

"Can't remember, Your Worship." The young woman had been telling her story, and she seemed quite calm now. "Can't remember," she repeated, in a tone not at all harried, but more like that used at home when some trivial thing was mislaid, and when there was a world of time in which to locate it. "Four or five times perhaps. The skirt of my dress was only so big. I'd have liked to take up more, but couldn't. Your indulgence, Your Worship. I'm not so very strong either."

A snigger could be heard up in the hall—the magistrate's, no doubt, for he alone had the prerogative.

"Listen to her," observed one mandarin on the left of the magistrate. "With a skirt as small as that, how could she move five hundred taels of silver in four, five trips? It's a bold lie, this damned hussy!"

The woman did not argue, but lifted her face sidewise as though looking for something. She did not seem to mind too much the cold stone steps on which she was kneeling. It occurred to me then, why must the culprit kneel while answering questions?

"Gesture, then, to show how high was the pile of silver, and how wide all around, that is."

The young woman tried to show with her hands, narrowing, and then widening again her imaginary measurement until she was satisfied. "About this size," she said. It was approximately the height and circumference of a large bowl, upside down.

"Did you count how many big pieces there were, and how many small ones?"

"No, Your Worship. I wouldn't know the difference even if I did." Her hands remained in the air, measuring. She continued her tale of woe.

After she had finished moving the silver, she opened her trunk. Not that there was much of anything in it, what with all the selling and pawning. But she put on all that could be put on, and wrapped up the rest in a bundle, small and feather-weight. She meant to go to her mother's at the North Xi Tower five miles or so away. She used to cover that distance in less than two hours. But now with snow on the ground, she had no idea how long it would take her, nor indeed how far away yet was the break of day.

Her master was still sleeping like a dead man. "You have been guilty of all the vices, drink, sex, greed, and bad temper," she murmured, again silently. "Wherever I go, you're bound to get me back. But I don't want to go very far. I'll have to come back here somehow, some time; this is my home. You're not selling me this time though. Don't be so mean and try to sell me again. If you love me at all, it is very cold-hearted of you to want to sell me in the first place. Watch well your five hundred taels of silver, so you can return it in the morning." Wiping a tear, she left.

The blizzard had stopped. Opening the door, she almost thought the day was breaking, for before her lay a vast expanse of white snow which blinded her eyes. But luckily it was not so very deep. And the day could not be too far off.

She continued to brood. Poverty is a powerful persuader. He's been reduced to groveling by it. All his store has gone. He's sent his wife to her maiden home. With nothing else to sell, he next thought of selling her. Was she to leave this way? Irresolutely, she looked back at the darkened room once more. Must she go back? What kind of life would it be with him in the future? Wouldn't it be better to let herself be sold? If the buyer could afford to pay five hundred taels of silver for a woman who is not even a virgin, he should be in very comfortable circumstances. Let him come for her then. She thus mused, but this did not deter her steps.

Their store up front had been sold. Under its eaves were hung a row of wind-dry preserved chickens, white like herons; so were the doors and the windows thickly covered with snow. The little woman stopped before the bamboo branches bent under the weight of the snow. She gazed blankly into space. Then she seemed to hear her husband's snore again. Get going. And passing through the long, narrow courtyard, she slipped through the back door.

No wind, nor snow. Yet when she came out of the back door, the blast of cold air greeted her as if it could peel the skin off her face. No footprint could be seen in the little back alley. Then she reached the city gate, which was slightly ajar, with a chain locking the two portals. In one corner of the covered gateway lay a heap of drift snow; there were no guards around to challenge her. She edged herself out sideways. Once she left the city behind her the day began to break. The exertion made her warm. Perhaps her scapegrace of a husband would come for her before evening, but she would not go with him. She must insist on spending the New Year at her father's home. However poor, her parents were still better off than her husband, in whose home there was neither money nor even food. Besides, her husband himself could go to his first wife's home for the festival. Both of them might then have a better time.

Trudging hastily in the morning snow, her bound feet made curious traces. It was blowing quite hard now in the country, and the snow on the ground was not so even. She saw no one until she reached the first village; then a man on a piebald donkey overtook her, both man and beast snorting clouds of steam through their nostrils.

A trail of hoofprints left distinct marks in the snow behind the donkey. The parti-colored beast was equipped with saddle showing embroidered cloud patterns of every color, and had nine large bells of white brass hanging from his neck. It was quite a spectacle, what with the jingling bells and everything; the musical ding-dong made her feel she should be in either broad daylight or a clear and glittering starlight. But the sky was bleak and chilly, while the day was just on the point of breaking, so that she could not quite tell whether it was going to be fine or overcast.

The bells tinkled off and on. She dared not lift her head to see, but, instinctively, she felt the man watching her out of the corner of his eyes, watching the little woman who was stealing away from her man. Then the tinkling stopped altogether, and she knew the man before her had halted. She hesitated, not knowing whether she should go forward and try to follow another path or . . . but then there was no other path.

"Do you think you can walk very far with those little, spiked shoes, miss?" The man had dismounted, and was standing on the side of the road under a withered and frost-bitten willow tree.

The woman still dared not lift her head, but with bent eyes stared at the pair of spiked overshoes over-topping her small, embroidered slippers. They had always been good for rain and snow, but walking a long way in them?

"Let's take turns riding . . . if you don't mind."

She dallied all she could, but as long as she was determined not to turn back, she realized—however slow her pace—it would inevitably bring her abreast with the rider.

"I thank you for your kindness, Squire," she curtsied. "Please go your way."

"This's no time for ceremony, miss. We're both away from home, and then there's all this snow . . ."

The little woman thought to herself: Could this be some evil man out to get me? Keeping her head bowed, she moved forward, saying "I thank you kindly, Squire. A little way yonder's my home." She had not looked at the man long enough to know if she should have addressed him as squire, or that big brother might not have been a more appropriate appellation. She went her way; the man did not mount, but, leading his animal, walked beside her. The bells continued jingling though at a more leisurely pace—ding, dong. The way he spoke, one would think he was an honest, kindly man.

"So early and quiet in the morning, with not a soul in sight. How could your family allow you to be out at such an hour? They should have sent someone to meet you."

"Not quite, squire. I've been on this road often enough; it would be a lot worse to walk on when the sun comes out and melts the snow." She lied, but the man's words made her see how foolhardy it was for a young woman to walk five miles in the snow and so early in the morning. She should have realized this before.

"How far away, your village?"

"Only . . . the one ahead . . . Quite close by. Please go on."

"No need for haste. A mere six miles or so. However slow I go, I should be home in time for lunch. It's you I'm worried about, though, you and your shoes. Do they pinch?"

The little woman still refused to look at the man. "Not badly, Squire," she said. She examined her small spiked overshoes, the fur-lined galoshes encasing his feet, and the front hooves of the donkey. They all plodded forward on the snow as yet undefiled.

"Your village doesn't seem as close by as you'd have it. It may take you hours to reach? I say, don't stand on so much ceremony when we're both away from home. This donkey's been castrated and is quite tame. You don't have to be afraid of him."

They had covered another third of a mile or so while they were talking. It seemed the man would walk with her the whole way if she demurred further. Reluctantly, she accepted the offer, and climbed on to the saddle. He never tried to assist her, only holding the bridle firmly, and the little gesture assured her what an honest man he must be.[4]

"I'm much obliged to you, Squire. But now you'll have to . . ."

"Don't mention it. A little walking'll do me good. It's warmer this way, at least."

Must be about eight o'clock now, she thought. Here and there, a few people were abroad. There were stirrings in the cottages round about. Suddenly, there was the neighing of a horse. It sounded far away, but before the blink of an eye, the thumping of hooves was heard approaching.

"It must be the mounted police," he observed.

The man pulled the bridle, and sidled the donkey to the shoulder of the road to make way. They turned to see a team of three horses galloping toward them, kicking up a cloud of snow dust. Before they knew it, the trio was beside them.

"Halt. This is it!"

A black horse in the group pirouetted and halted before the pair. The donkey, frightened, jerked forward and back, unsure whether to crouch down or run away.

"You sure of the identity, wardman?" asked the constable on a red horse, reins in hand.

"Burn her to ashes and I'll still recognize her. But just ask her if she knows me!"

"Are you from the House of Xu?" the rider of the red horse asked.

"My husband's name is Xu. Mine is Zhou."

The constables acted fast. Before the poor wretches knew what had happened, the man was handcuffed, and two hemp ropes like serpents had wound around her, binding her fast to the donkey's back. Under the saddle, the constables found four hundred and eighty taels of silver in ingots of various size. The culprits were caught red-handed.

The wardman congratulated the policemen: "What luck, sirs! breaking a case in less than an hour. You'll be promoted for this."

"When merits are rewarded, don't think you're going to be left

[4]The idea is that, except in special circumstances, a man does not touch a woman other than his mother, wife, sisters, or daughters.

out!" teased the overjoyed officers who felt they could now afford to be affable too.

The culprits were taken to the scene of the crime. There, her husband lay on the *kang* in a pool of blood, and the silver was gone. The woman fainted right away.

Now in the presence of the magistrate, she insisted that was all she knew about the matter, and that she told between sobs and tears.

"Your Worship, you august living bodhisattva! My husband died a horrible and grievous death. If Your Worship can redress the outrage done to my husband for my mistress and me and avenge our wrongs, then, even if I can't repay you in this life, I'll be Your Worship's slave, . . . your horse . . . or other beast of burden in the next one . . ."

A hum rose even before the little woman had concluded her account. I thought to myself, the young woman has stated her case, fair and square. Her story caught everybody by surprise, and hence the subdued though audible muttering up and down the hall.

All of a sudden, a squad of soldiers darted forth from the shadows on all sides, shouting at I knew not whom, but several of them leveled their muskets and ran toward the little woman, as though intent on hitting her. I was dumbfounded.

"Every word the truth, every word the truth, you august living bodhisattva!" She screamed, lifting her elbows to ward off the butts of muskets raining down on her, though quite a few hard blows must have found their mark at the same time. "Every word true, every, O!" I could hear the cry of anguish, the heart-rending cry of a little child. The chains clanged on the granite like the cracking of ice on the Da Kai River . . . a cracking that is heard far away in the city in the dead of night when the thaw sets in during early spring. Could the ice that the chains formed on her person also have its spring thaw?

"Bring in the tortures!"

This was proclaimed as casually as "Bring in the dishes!" The magistrate bestirred himself ever so slightly, and spat in a most dignified manner.

Two each at the head of the files of bailiffs in the galleries were called out. The first pair forced the young woman to lie prone on the ground and arranged the chains. The other two put their bamboo poles in position on her buttocks.

Somehow, I felt it was not the woman who was going to be thrashed, but myself. I shivered and trembled in the dark as though suffering from ague. I was quite sure the woman could not be shaking more. What were they up to—those four big hulking men so roughly handling such a defenseless woman? This "something" spread out and pressed down so flat on the ground—could it be a human being? Or was it just a piece of cowhide laid out to dry in the tannery?

The bamboo poles rose and fell rhythmically on—was it a lump of clay? The powerful whacking of bamboo against flesh was a dull thud one did not often hear, not to mention the cruel chanting of the forty strokes! Surreptitiously, I closed my eyes and stopped my ears at the first blow.

"I'll tell, I'll tell!" The young woman shrieked every time a blow hit her, almost like an echo—or was that the way things should be, a blow followed by some such shriek as "I'll tell, I'll tell"? The flat little heap writhed under the weight of the two guards. "I'll tell, I'll tell," the shrieking repeated, like an excuse, an attempt at respite. As in my school days when I was called on to recite and could only repeat, "My men, my mount, my team; my troop . . ."[5] The more I stared at the cane held in the teacher's hand, the more apprehensive I grew of its welt-producing power, and the more my mind turned into an absolute blank.

"Tell about the adultery."

It must have been the second mandarin pronouncing peevishly and importantly. The command was heavily nasal—did he have a bad cold? Squire Zhang turned to a man on his left and whispered, "It seems to me, the second mandarin didn't get enough kicks from his opium pipe this morning."

"I'm wronged, Your Worship! What adultery?" The woman was sobbing so piteously and low she might, for all I knew, have passed out again. For a long time she made no noise at all.

"Ready the tortures." Again the heavy nasal tone, in an alien accent different from the magistrate's.

A commotion went up in the galleries once more: sticks were striking the ground. I did not quite know if and how I should handle the cane held to my chest, the instrument that was to be my lifetime meal-ticket. It was hard and cold to the touch, and it seemed my fingers could freeze on it.

---

[5]From the *Shijing* or *Book of Songs,* which children were required to memorize as a fundamental part of their education.

"I'll own up, I will . . . Your Worship, let me tell . . . "

Could the culprit go on with her recital beyond "my man, my mount" this time? She appeared shrewd enough, and cunning, for when she saw that the four guards were none too hurried about their business, she hedged.

"Your Sagacious Worship, what other confession do you want me to make? Every word true, Your Worship, every word true."

A thick cedar pole was then placed horizontally across the woman's thighs. I had no idea how it was to be used. The woman writhed a little, and her voice was barely audible. The wriggling lump of something sprawled out at the entrance of the hall seemed gagged, barely capable of producing anything beyond a weak whine—where was the human being? Convulsions like a strong wave again engulfed me, and I shook. The brass buttons on my uniform rattled against my cane. Tick, tock, tick, tock—like a tit, tat, tit, tat, on went the clock. I was abashed.

The woman did not look to me like a brazen slut or glib-tongued shrew. Could she possibly endure the forty strokes and still not speak out with the truth? If the flogging did not do it, there was perhaps no other confession to be wrestled from her. Why not stop the torturing then?

Things did not turn out as I speculated. The cedar pole now rolled down to the calves of her legs, and the two guards each placed one foot on one end of the pole. They did not seem to have put their weight on it, yet the woman squealed as though she were being strangled: "I'll tell, I'll tell!" But to no avail. The two strong guards had now stepped up with both feet and were standing with their full weight on the pole now. They must have weighed four hundred pounds between them.

What a shriek pierced the still night air! It was sharp enough to bring the moonless night into broad day. When my wife was delivering her first child, it took her from the first watch to morning, and she screamed, ah, how she screamed! Across the big courtyard I heard her, and I could not believe a person could make such sounds. But this woman, why, her howl was not only inhuman, but I couldn't think of any beast or bird capable of producing such a blood-curdling, bone-chilling cry. It reminded one of the smash of a whole shelf of porcelain falling over; or the piercing screech of the rotating blade on the lathe in a cabinet-maker's shop that, slipping, strikes the axis accidentally with force enough to drill a hole in a man's head: or the squeak of the braking pin protesting against the rim of a wheel when the oxcart rolls recklessly downhill: or the gritting of the dentist's file when it moves back and forth across the teeth. All these are terrible noises; but frightful as they are, the woman's wail surpassed them all.

I began to doubt my aptitude for this new trade. To have a trade is to earn a living, but this kind of trade was more death-dealing than life-sustaining. How could people be so ruthless? Even if this woman had murdered my father, mother, wife and children, I could not possibly harden myself to torment her this way, not with that kind of wail in my ears. But the piteous cry did not seem to have any effect on the other mandarins and officers. As for the magistrate, he could not seem to enjoy himself enough, puffing contentedly at his infernal pipe. And the bunch of lesser officers beneath him—did each of them really have a heart of stone, totally inured against any human feelings? And look at the two men balancing on the cedar pole; see how they relished their circus display of pole walking, sure of their hard-earned skill on the rolling pole.

The woman tore her hair in large handfuls. "Let me die, let me die!" She writhed, wriggled, and convulsed like an earthworm cut in two. From time to time, she half turned to clutch vainly at the cedar pole that, rolling-pin–fashion, was kneading her legs like dough. When the pole came down to her calves, she would try to raise herself, but when the pole rolled up to her thighs, she went down again. And so the procedure repeated itself as though a machine had been there to force her to rise and fall, rise and fall, until the magistrate brought his gavel down on the desk.

Gaveling and clearing his throat, he counseled her: "According to the law of His Imperial Majesty's court, being guilty of murdering your husband for money, you cannot escape death. So why should you go through all this torture for nothing, seeing you're a smart woman?"

"Let me die . . . Let me die . . . O my dead husband, come and get me . . . O my God . . ."

She sprawled on all fours, moaning and groaning in so soft a voice that one suspected she was communicating with someone underground. Abruptly, she straightened out above the knee, lifted her head, and shrieked: "O you who have died, why don't you come to redress the wrongs done to me? Why don't you redress your own wrongs? Who murdered you? Who robbed you of your silver? Speak! . . ." Madly, she swung her head to and fro, her hair flying.

The magistrate did not interfere. He was waiting for his servant to pour him another cup of tea and to trim the candles, whose wicks had burned long and black.

Noisily sipping his tea, the magistrate gave an order to his servant with perfect composure: "Get the needles, and prick her perfidious lips!"

"No need for that!" The woman pulled herself together and appeared strangely calm. Hoarsely she went on: "Just Your Worship instruct me how I should confess." She gasped for breath. "My father's family have no money for Your Worship. Even if they had, they would not want to spend it on me. Or they would not have sold me as a concubine for five hundred taels!"

She sank down. It was as though the bitter rancor she felt had so far sustained her, and now that she had vented it, she simply collapsed.

"Listen to that slick tongue, and you'd know she is a slut not above committing any sort of crime!" observed the second mandarin with a cold sneer.

From now on, the trial went fast. The little woman would boldly affirm any leading question that the court put to her, and the interrogation was completed in no time at all. When she was ordered to sign her confession, she just crouched there, resignedly stretching out her hand to take the pen which a guard gave to her, and with the man holding her unsteady hand, drew on the document spread out before her—was it a cross or a circle?

One rooster crowed, and it was taken up by others far and near. They were trying to call the day in. But the day would not come.

For every day there's a tomorrow of course, but what sort of a tomorrow would it be? She was taken out, her head bowed to her chest, her hands dangling loosely at her sides, and her hair hung unkempt and lifeless. For an instant, her form blocked the light: then she was engulfed by the darkness. But one could still hear her, hear the heavy chains on her cramped legs as they dragged across the granite courtyard covered with ice and snow.

"She can't escape flaying," whispered Squire Zhang to the man on his left, at the same time blowing on his hands.

"But she still has more than half a year to live."

"Of course the execution will have to wait for the Judiciary Department's report to the throne for approval. That means she'll get her just deserts next fall."

"Not necessarily," cut in the man next to the one on Squire

Zhang's left. "If the case should be judged a robbery, then not even the prefecture need be bothered. The magistrate can use his own discretion and simply put her in the cage."

"A woman culprit in the cage? Well, I've lived quite a few years, but never seen that yet."

The shape of the cages rose up before me. It was said to be put into them was like being strangled, though I had never seen them in operation. As to flaying—I could not even bring myself to think of it.

The sound of the iron chains scraping along gradually disappeared. But it again grew louder and nearer. It was more regularly rhythmic this time, one clang to each step. The one they brought in was a tall man.

Once more, the deep-throated growl rose in the galleries, calling attention to the power of the Yamen, the kind of growl emitted when a cat has a mouse in its clutches. I had better join the chant, so that Squire Zhang did not have to nudge me again. Yet I was ashamed of doing so just to intimidate someone. I was shuddering, and could hear my teeth chatter. I was not at all sure I succeeded in making the proper kind of growl.

This must be the adulterer who robbed and killed, I thought to myself. He lay prostrate there: did someone push him, or was he tripped by his leg irons? They let him struggle alone with his entangling chains, falling clumsily in doing so, but struggling on nonetheless, till at long last he managed to disentangle himself and knelt straight.

"Your humble subject Dai . . . kneels . . ." I could not quite make out what he said his name was. Fortunately, the magistrate was so intent upon his sipping and smoking that he did not seem to care who was brought in

The man seemed to be panting. Against the bright candles up the hall, one could see jets of white steam gushing forth far and thick. The way it looked, he and the magistrate seemed to make a pair, puffing away together, except that as a criminal, he was a bit out of place.

The magistrate still had himself turned to one side. It must have been on account of his long pipe that he sat in such a ludicrous, undignified posture. So accustomed was he to opium and tobacco fumes that his eyes, naturally slanting downward, squinted all the time to make them look like phoenix eyes. He took up the sheaf of documents in front of him and, the back of his head leaning toward the candles, began to leaf through them, now and then licking his forefinger to more easily turn the pages. His queue was so close to the flame, I was afraid it would surely catch fire sooner or later.

After deliberating with the documents for a long while, the magistrate turned at last to face the culprit. Nonchalantly, he asked the man's name, legal domicile, birthdate, and other such inconsequentia.

"How many years have you been the lover of Zhou of the House of Xu?"

"Please, Your Sagacious Worship! Your humble subject has no idea why he has been arrested and thrown into jail. What is the charge against him?"

From the man's tone one could gather he was no longer young, perhaps over forty.

"So you don't know the charge, eh? Well, we'll give you one hundred strokes and you'll have a better memory," answered the magistrate, pointing his long pipe at the man. He did not seem at all angered by the culprit; rather, it looked like the facetious banter of an elder brother joking with another.

"I'm telling the truth, Your Worship. If there is the least bit of falsehood in what I say to Your Worship, may thunder strike me, and Your Worship behead me."

"That would be a lot of trouble. We'd have to go through the three judiciary departments and the imperial court itself. Far better for all concerned if you're kept whole."

Now and again the magistrate had a propensity to clear his throat and then force out a loud spit. He must have hit the ashes in the firebowl, for I did not hear it strike the floor tiles. But wouldn't there be some sizzling if he had hit the burning charcoal?

"With Your Worship's mirror hanging high . . ."

"The five hundred taels of silver, where and how did you get them?"

"It's what your humble subject collected in the East Country from accounts on cattle for the year-end settlement. I had received close to five hundred taels, but purchases for the New Year in town had reduced the total . . . "

"All right, all right, don't fabricate!" said the magistrate in the intonation of the Mandarin dialect, and quite impressively, too. Then he struck the desk with his gavel, ponderously swept the galleries with his eyes, in a manner reminiscent of the professional raconteur about to begin a new chapter in his tale. He was on the point of saying something, when a bold, loud, and luxurious yawn interrupted him. It was some time before he raised the thumb and forefinger of his right hand into a sign signifying "eight" and issued the command: "Give him a good thrashing." The tone was ceremonious and tentative.

"Hold on, Your Worship! You can't use torture to force my confession!"

The man protested, but nobody listened to him. The magistrate called one of the servants to him, whispered something behind his fingers which tapered into inch-long nails. The galleries became agitated again.

"You should go up and have a try at it, Young Three," Squire Zhang whispered to me. "Eighty strokes, and I guarantee you'll sweat. It'll warm you up faster than burning cotton stalks."

"I . . . I'm not cold!"

I did not really know what I had said. I only felt that it was worse to be called on to flog somebody than to be called on to receive the flogging. A timid man like me—how could I beat anybody? What was more, should other humble citizens like myself who took no bribes and abused no laws be walloped just because the magistrate said so?

Squire Zhang craned his neck to our team and said something. I was assigned to be one of the ministers of torture. Black Eight came over behind me, placed a bamboo stick in my hand, and asked me to put away the what-d'you-call-it I was holding against my chest. I acquiesced in whatever he asked me to do, though I still had no presentiment that I was going to beat anybody. Gingerly, I took up the bamboo stick which seemed to weigh one thousand catties.

"You know how to count?"

"Aha . . . " I answered vaguely.

"Count aloud, partner, as loudly as you can. It's like the hawker's trade: cry what you sell." Black Eight followed me to give the advice: "Since the magistrate has not specified, you can use as much strength as you want. Only remember one thing: pull the man's genitals free, and place them between his thighs."

"Pull free?" What a filthy idea!

"Don't let the genitals be under the man's belly, or there'll be shock, and the devil to pay!"

It was still dark and the ground was strange to me. I had misgivings that I might miss the steps and stumble and make a laughingstock of myself. So I simply shuffled my feet on the ground and wormed forward.

The culprit was pushed down prostrate on the ground with only his neck straining up. One hardly thought a man could have such a long neck.

"Come on," the man opposite me raised high his bamboo stick, waiting for me to start.

The prostrate culprit bellowed lustily, but I was in no mind to listen. I was in a daze, and no longer conscious of what I was doing. Yet Black Eight's injunction remained in my brains and I bent over to grope in the man's groin, though without knowing what I was doing.

"Never mind that," the man holding the criminal's feet said impatiently. "That's taken care of."

The first stroke down and my wrists became like rubber. I even forgot the count. What was the stick hitting? The hem of the man's coat had been rolled up to his waist, and his cotton-padded trousers pulled down to his ankles. The bulging flesh thus revealed gave me a sensation that I had experienced only with my wife. Was this kind of flesh to be beaten? I was no wife-beater, though of course in the privacy of our chamber we used to play certain jokes. No, I could not touch him. Yet, mechanically I was hitting the piece of flesh, and counting with my partner. In counting I seemed to have found a measure of composure, as though my shouts could somehow make me forget my action, and become oblivious to the culprit's loud curses and cries for mercy.

Even so, I was aware that my stick was constantly striking my partner's and the collision hurt the webs between the thumbs and forefingers of my cold-benumbed hands. It was so excruciating, I wanted desperately to stop. My thoughts, however, served only to intermit the rhythm of the flailing, making me painfully aware of my incompetency. I became more and more confused, and the two bamboo poles, mine and the other man's, began to engage in a war of their own in mid-air. This business was not as easy as I thought.

Black Eight must have been watching my discomfiture. And the "partners" in the galleries and the mandarins up in the hall? When the beating was over, I dragged the bamboo after me like a defeated man and, dark as it was, I had not the nerve to lift my face. I was perspiring all over. What with the clack, clack of the pole bumping along the granite and all, I felt desperate. I'm no good—so what? I don't really depend on this job. To go on with it is enough to drive a man crazy anyway. I've nothing to lose except the five stone of wheat. And I can easily make good on that: I can hire myself out and earn the wheat to pay my father. Let Black Eight keep his grain; he's welcome to sell the job to someone else and pocket my five stone!

Getting back somehow to my old stand in the gallery, I began to talk. I was good and mad, but with whom or what I had no idea.

Though Black Eight did not come over to me, nor did Squire Zhang complain, anger still raged as though I had been made a fool of. The perspiration in my undershirt got cold and stuck to my spine like ice. It was more than flesh and blood could stand.

The culprit persevered in his old statement. He insisted that on the night in question he had put up at the Welcome Inn close by the West Gate. Furthermore, of the four hundred odd taels of silver he had collected, so much came from this village east of the river, and so much from that, some of which he had spent on candles, incense, sacrificial vessels, and piece goods at the chandler's and draper's in town. In short, he could account for every single item on his person and had witnesses to bear him out.

His ledger had been taken from him by the constables, he asserted, but witnesses both in and out the town could be summoned at a moment's notice.

"Bring in the keeper of the Welcome Inn," the magistrate readily ordered.

I muttered to myself, "Whoever you might bring in, please don't get me to do the beating this time." In all my twenty odd years of existence, from the dawn of memory to the present day, I've never really shown ill will towards anyone, let alone ruthlessly beat a person with my own hands. I had no rancor against this man, and worse, he could not even hit back! Besides, I hardly had the heart to treat a beast roughly, not to mention a human being. The way things were going I'd run berserk sooner or later. And Black Eight called this "a meal-ticket for a lifetime." I could not stand it for one day. Obviously, this was not my line of work.

When the magistrate saw that the keeper of the Welcome Inn had not been brought in immediately, he demanded of the head bailiff why such an important witness had not been subpoenaed right away. The head bailiff answered that the man had been taken in, but that he was lying so sick in the detention area, he would have to be roused and allowed time to get dressed before he could be presented in court.

Although it was still quite dark in the galleries, there was light enough now to see people moving around. Black Eight came down; a squat shadow set off by the light behind showed that it could not be anybody else.

He approached the end of my file, grabbed me and said, "Put down that thing, Young Three, and follow me." We turned to the moon gate not far to the left and went outside. He was quite familiar with the terrain, but I could not see the rises and depressions along the way. I stumbled after him in the dark, wondering what urgent business made him hasten thus. I had no time to inquire, however.

Black Eight took me to a side room in the west courtyard. In the kitchen opposite I could see a tall mound of steaming baskets wrapped in white vapor. Enough of its light shone over into the room I was in to enable me to see dimly the shapes of the furniture.

"No time for explanation. Hurry and take off your uniform."

"Take off the uniform?" It suddenly dawned on me that he was perhaps dismissing me. To bring me staggering all the way in the dark and for this reason! I turned cold: so the job bought with five stone of wheat is lost, and lost in such a casual manner? To be sure, I loathed the job, but that was my business. Black Eight, how could you be so inhumanly cruel? Could anybody else, new on the job and with no practice, have used the bamboo pole better without making any mistakes? Even if he wanted to kick me out of the Yamen, this ordering me to strip was hard to stomach. After all, the uniform was bought with my own money. Did he think I would keep it to pass myself off for an officer and go around swindling somebody? That was an insult indeed, that implication. No, I would not permit it without a reckoning. Five stone of wheat down the drain and not even a murmur! . . .

All this was of course mere bravado. I had no way of proving he had received the grain. I might as well give up. Just chalk it up to Dad's bad luck.

While all this was going on in my mind, my hands had not been idle. Without consciously adverting to the fact, I had taken off my black belt, and was now busy undoing the brass buttons on my tunic.

"How come you have an unsurfaced fur on? This'll be troublesome."

Before I could say anything, however, Black Eight was running toward the kitchen, where steamed bread was being removed from the baskets. He rushed over as though to a fire.

The way he acted, I could see that it was possible Black Eight was not going to dismiss me; perhaps, he was being solicitous enough to want to get some outer garment for me to cover the bare fur.

One way or another, I was so much in a daze I left my clothes unbuttoned, forgetting completely about the cold. The black belt still hung down my neck, and I waited vaguely for I know not what. The vapors in the kitchen enveloped everything: in the thick steam one could see only some indistinct figures moving about.

If the scene at the court could be likened to the Audience Hall of Yama, king of the nether world, then this must be Hell's torture chamber, complete with a mountain of swords and cauldrons of boiling oil. In the baleful haze the baleful ghosts were lifting their tridents to remove loaves of bread, white and plump, from the steaming baskets.

Black Eight rushed back as though running from a fire out of control. He was holding a floating something against his chest.

"Hurry, take off your tunic, and put this on." It was a long gown.

"The vice squad has been negligent in its preparations. We've got to help each other out. You'll impersonate the innkeeper now. We're much obliged to you, really."

Black Eight said this breathlessly while helping me off with my coat.

"I . . . I . . . "

"Please agree to do it, my little brother. There's a great deal more than meets the eye in this matter; I'll explain afterwards, when we'll have time for a couple of drinks. Now we simply have to hurry."

Black Eight kept me in tow. We did not go the old way through the moon gate, but turned left and made for the front courtyard. All along the way he whispered instructions: "You've seen and heard how things operate at the hall. When you go up there now, you don't have to make up any story at all. Just say firmly you don't know the guy, that it snowed so terribly the night of the seventh that not a soul came to you for lodging. That'll be all there is to it."

"Those up the hall may recognize me," I desperately fumbled for excuses.

"Not if you stand back far enough. It'll take a man of extraordinary eyesight to recognize you. You're chosen for the role because yours is a strange face here. You don't know, of course, but there's a hell of a lot to the case. For one thing, the vice squad has never been sent on a case since His Worship, Magistrate Feng, assumed office. You see, he brought his own band of select soldiers from the capital. Naturally, they got all the credit.''

I was only paying half attention to what he was saying. Instead, I was deliberating with myself: how can I do this? Good-for-nothing as I am, I've never cheated anybody. And what I am asked to do now requires that I deny my own conscience. But going there involved the risk of a thrashing. Although I'm not a man who enjoys flogging people, even less inviting is the prospect of being flogged.

But flogging was the least of my worries. Wouldn't I now be involved in an act that was sure to send the man to the cage? Life is a thing determined by Providence—was I to betray a life for Black Eight's couple of drinks?

Black Eight interrupted my reverie: ''This has been the first case handled by the vice squad since Magistrate Feng's arrival. A quick and neat job it's been; let these soldiers see for themselves that the squad isn't made up of just parasites. For one thing, all the constables in the squad are our fellow-townspeople. If we don't support our own, we ourselves'll be in for disgrace. Isn't that right, Young Three, eh?''

''But wouldn't I be framing somebody, and getting him in trouble?''

We were then passing through a pitch dark passage. Even Black Eight had to slow down his gait a bit.

''Whether the man'll be really framed is the business of the magistrate. How could little people like us be responsible?''

''Still, our part in this man's condemnation would make it a case of willful and premeditated . . . ''

''O.K., O.K., Young Three, you don't have to throw your old saws at me. I don't blame you for your scruples, of course. This is only your first case on the job. But you'll learn in time, too.''

The strange thing was, to be sure, that it never occurred to me to refuse being involved in it altogether; rather, as if in a trance, I just stumbled after Black Eight, earnestly arguing the while as though convinced I could dissuade him from his plans.

''At least''—I was breathing hard, not from exertion, but because the strain was telling on me—''At least, Black Eight, this is a violation of justice.''

''What's justice, anyway? Not relevant. Here we're engaged in law, and the law says he who kills must repay with his own life. Are you so sure the keeper of the Welcome Inn hasn't been bribed beforehand by the defendant to bear false witness? You're still green at the gills, Young Three. What do you think those cages are there for?''

While we were talking and trotting along, two men who looked like underlings of the vice squad met us. They each grasped one of my hands, saying ''Hurry. It's lucky the magistrate hasn't lost his temper yet.''

What did the fools mean? Whomever the magistrate might be angry with, it could not be with me. How strange the mandarin should get angry so easily. The Yamen had less justice than a brothel. Anyway, I was brought in at my wit's end, kidnap-fashion, to the entrance of the hall, and there forced to kneel. Inwardly, I was sizzling. Had my Dad spent five stone of wheat for this? I'd settle the score with my Dad when all this was over and I got home.

The granite steps were hard and cold like ice. The cold seemed to penetrate through the hem of my gown and the cotton-padded trousers to the very marrow of my bones. Looking up at the magistrate at such close quarters, I got quite a shock. The face resembled that of a corpse, recovered days after the drowning—a bloated, wax-yellow face steeped in smoke, on which the eyes had swollen to slits. The flames of the candles flickered, and the face became now light, now dark, giving one a feeling of unfathomable evil.

I seemed to have forgotten what I was kneeling there for, or what I was expected to do, as I just waited for those up the hall to give me my cue. Meantime, I was shivering so violently I almost felt my bones falling apart. I glanced at the man kneeling beside me, rattling in all his chains. But I didn't have the heart to look him square in the face.

''Are you dumb?'' A voice exclaimed over my head, though not from the magistrate. This must have meant me, but what was I to say? I was not dumb, but should I shout or cry mercy or what? I lifted my eyes only as far as the edge of the decorative cloth hanging over the magistrate's desk, and there stopped. In a daze I could still hear the magistrate drawing on his pipe—puff, puff—and was quite horrified at the idea that the bowl might descend on my head any time. The fear untied my tongue.

''If it pleases Your Worship, the Wel . . . Welcome Inn's . . . '' I did not know how to proceed.

''Wrong, Your Worship, all wrong. This man's not the proprietor of the Welcome Inn.'' The shout quite upset me. Involuntarily, I turned to glance at the man whom I had beaten just a moment ago.

The candlelight gave the man a fierce look. His beard grew close to his swollen eyes; but unlike the magistrate's mere slits, his were as wide open as saucers. His appearance should be enough to convict him. Luckily, we were in a court of law; he looked so fierce, I knew he could easily drag me over and crush me. Was I to oppose such a man? I averted my eyes quickly.

''Take a good look at him,'' the magistrate said, his pipe between his lips. ''Did he stay at your inn the night before the Congee Festival?''

''Please Your Worship, no.''

''Ah,'' the magistrate leaned back and rested his eyes; whether his eyes were closed or open, it made little enough difference in his face.

''Something wrong, Your Worship. I've been a frequent customer at the Welcome Inn, and I don't know this man.''

His second denial disconcerted me still further. I was at a loss how to go on, for the situation was getting more and more perplexing. Should I be exposed, I was sure I would be given at least some scores of strokes, even if by sheer luck I should escape the cage. Black Eight had really got me in hot water! What he had asked me to do was no joking matter. And why should I have been so docile as to run such a risk? All right, I thought to myself, if worst comes to worst, I'd hit back first.

''What's the matter?'' The magistrate still kept his eyes closed. One wondered to whom he had addressed the remark.

''Impersonator, Your Worship. He isn't the . . .'' The man, still kneeling, inched toward me wildly. If he succeeded in reaching me, there's no telling what might happen, court or no court. Fortunately, one of the soldiers stopped him.

''What's the matter?''

''Please Your Worship, if I'm not the keeper of the Welcome Inn, could it be this lunatic?'' In the interest of self-preservation, I had to treat the affair as more than a joke now. The lie, unaccustomed and outrageous, made me tremble, but since the mandarins had been informed of my illness, perhaps they would think it natural.

''Has anyone paid you money to make you say what you just said?''

''No, Your Worship! Every word true . . . '' I just remembered the young woman's appropriate plea, and used it.

"Is that the truth?"

"Every word true," and I was praying that the ordeal would be over soon. If they did not take me away quickly, I would not be able to stand it much longer.

"Come!"

That was from the magistrate. I lifted my face in time to receive a great shock, and cold sweat oozed all over me: he had stretched out five fingers in a most ominous manner. I protested I was being wronged. Indeed I was. A flogging was the last thing I had bargained for. It was a disaster falling straight out of the blue!

I might have saved my breath. A group of men came over, sent me sprawling on the hard, ice-cold steps. While I was pinned down, a hand groped between my thighs. If I should blurt out the truth now, and tell on Black Eight, might I not spare myself the fifty strokes? But I had only begun to think on this when the bamboo sticks started raining down on me. I struggled and howled, like a man delirious. But there was something wrong: I did not feel hurt at all. Rather, my tormentors seemed intent on dusting my clothes. The thump, thump, thump sounds near the hem of my gown were loud and genuine, but the bamboo poles weren't even coming close to a single strand of my hair.

Then it dawned on me. This was true art, art that marked my colleagues as real pros. I couldn't help admiring these old-timers. The fifty strokes over, I was held up to face the poker-faced magistrate's closed lids.

The fifty strokes were admittedly nothing. Still, what offense had I committed that I should be punished in this way? Was being the proprietor of an inn crime enough to warrant the thrashing? This was utter nonsense.

"Is what you said really nothing but the truth?" The magistrate seemed to have dozed off, and was speaking in his sleep.

"Every word true, every word true, please Your Worship!"

Like a poet groping for the exact expression, the magistrate slowly rocked his head. What could he be thinking? Not even bothering to open his eyes, he finally waved his horse-hoof sleeve to signify my release.

I signed my statement, and put my fingerprint on it, but had neither the time nor the inclination to read what was written. It was only when I bent my head for the signing that, for the first time I sensed the stale oily smell on the collars of the stranger's gown I had been given. It was a smell that one never detects on his own clothing. I wondered how it could have escaped me. Then I found I was not shivering any more. My mind, too, was as clear as it had ever been.

Yet I was greatly bewildered. I did not think about, nor understand, what I had been made to do. My only desire was to get away from this place, to take off the smelly gown, without a moment's delay.

The winter night was endless. The roosters crowed and crowed, ushering in the long-awaited dawn, still hesitant, still dubious. Running around in the maze of halls and passageways, one did not see much of the sky. But the ground was well covered with a thick layer of snow-white frost, and that was enough for my purpose.

"You're real good, Young Three! You're now sure of a great career in our trade." Black Eight hastened over from a distance and grasped my hand. The way he came over, it was as if I was a toddler just learning to walk and he was afraid I might fall.

"Thank you kindly, Black Eight. I'm afraid I'm not made for this job."

But what I said signified nothing more than a pat reply. I was still confused. I could be certain of no reason either for staying or leaving. This is only the beginning, I thought to myself, why not wait and see? One can't be sure what the future holds in store. For the time being, I felt terribly tired, and could hardly keep my eyes open. Also, I was cold. My nose was freezing to the point of dropping off.

But the day was breaking at last. The sun would rise each and every day. We both yawned, and the white vapor from our breath filled the chill morning air. Who cares? Such overwhelming exhaustion! And my hands and feet were frozen stiff!

As Black Eight said, "It's just so-so being in the Yamen's service. Once green, twice weaned."

It was quite possible I was half way between greenness and ripeness, just like this hour, this sky, this dawn, which was neither night nor day. Even though it was a moment that would not last long, it would still take quite a while before the sun would rise. So I mused.

Index